STRATEGY AS PRACTICE

SAGE STRATEGY SERIES

The objective of the *SAGE Strategy Series* is to publish significant contributions in the field of management in general, and strategy in particular. The books aim to make a scholarly and provocative contribution to the field of strategy, and are of a high intellectual standard, containing new contributions to the literature. We are especially interested in books which provide new insights into existing ideas, as well as those which challenge conventional thinking by linking together levels of analysis which were traditionally distinct.

A special feature of the series is that there is an active advisory board of strategy scholars from leading international business schools in Europe, USA and the Far East who endorse the series. We believe that the combination of the SAGE brand name and that of an active and strong board is a unique selling point for book buyers and other academics. The board is led by Professor Charles Baden-Fuller of City University Business School and the Rotterdam School of Management, and Richard Whittington of the Said Business School, University of Oxford.

Editors

Professor Charles Baden-Fuller, *City University Business School, London and Erasmus University, NL*
Professor Richard Whittington, *Said Business School, University of Oxford*

Editorial Board

Professor Frans van den Bosch, *Rotterdam School of Management, Erasmus University, NL*
Professor Roland Calori, *EM Lyon, France*
Professor Robert Grant, *Georgetown University, USA*
Professor Tadao Kagono, *Japan Advanced Institute of Science and Technology*
Professor Gianni Lorenzoni, *University of Bologna, Italy*
Professor Leif Melin, *Jönköping International Business School, Sweden*
Professor Hans Pennings, *The Wharton School, University of Pennsylvania, USA*
Dr Martyn Pitt, *School of Business and Management, Brunel University, UK*
Professor Alan Rugman, *Kelly School of Business, Indiana University, USA*
Professor Joachim Schwalbach, *Humboldt-Universität zu Berlin, Germany*
Professor Jörg Sydow, *Freie Universität Berlin, Germany*

STRATEGY AS PRACTICE

An Activity-Based Approach

Paula Jarzabkowski

SAGE Publications

London ● Thousand Oaks ● New Delhi

SAGE Publications
1 Oliver's Yard
55 City Road
London EC1Y 1SP

SAGE Publications Inc.
2455 Teller Road
Thousand Oaks, California 91320

SAGE Publications India Pvt Ltd
B-42, Panchsheel Enclave
Post Box 4109
New Delhi 110 017

British Library Cataloguing in Publication data

A catalogue record for this book is available from
the British Library

ISBN 0-7619-4437-0
ISBN 0-7619-4438-9 (pbk)

Library of Congress Control Number: 2005901610

Typeset by M Rules
Printed and bound in Great Britain by Athenaeum Press, Gateshead
Printed on paper from sustainable resources

For Robbie

CONTENTS

FIGURES AND TABLES

FIGURES

TABLES

QUICK REFERENCE GUIDES

EXHIBITS

ACKNOWLEDGEMENTS

There are many people to acknowledge for the help they gave me in overcoming the trials and tribulations of this, my first book. First, the editors of the *SAGE Strategy Series*, Charles Baden-Fuller and Richard Whittington, who saw enough merit in the initial proposal to provide advice on how to develop it into a book. Then many thanks are due to those colleagues who so generously read and offered advice on drafts: Frank Blackler, Arne Lindseth Bygdås, Stewart Clegg, Leif Melin, Suzanne Regan, Richard Whittington and David Wilson. In particular, David provided wise counsel on the process of writing a book, while Richard really helped with polishing the finer points of the final version. Thanks are also in order for Julia Balogun, Liz Blackford, Jim Love and Sue Rudd, who were supportive and tolerant during those periods of stress when I thought it might never come together. Intellectually, I am indebted to the Strategy as Practice community (www.strategy-as-practice.org), with whom so many interesting discussions were held that have fuelled the thinking behind this book. In terms of the research base, I am grateful to the three universities that provided such generous access to their strategizing practices and the research participants who gave freely of their time.

During the writing process I was fortunate to have three wonderful writing breaks at Birchope Byre in Shropshire, where I had the peace and beauty of John and Alison Hazell's cottage and the surrounding countryside to inspire me. In the final stint of writing, I was also welcomed to the University of Auckland by Peter Boxall and Peter Smith and given fabulous support and help with all the last-minute crises, such as the death of my laptop.

Other people gave equally valuable support by providing me with understanding respite from writing, such as Jo and Dave, with whom many convivial meals and bottles of wine were enjoyed, and Pat and Philippa, who always welcomed me with warm friendship over home-made cake and cups of tea. I am also grateful to Korky and his friends, Polly and Charlie, who always made me laugh. However, the main thanks are certainly due to my husband, Robbie, who gave me so much wonderful, generous, unstinting support in every way during the process and helped me celebrate its ending in such fine style.

INTRODUCTION

Strategy as Practice: A New Perspective

Key points

- Strategy as practice in relation to other fields of strategy research
- Broad themes of the strategy as practice research agenda
- The activity-based view
- Guide to reading this book

Strategy is not just something a firm has – a position. It is also something that a firm and its multiple actors do. The problem of doing strategy, how it is done, who does it and what they use to do it, is important for both practitioners and strategy theorists. On the one hand, managers at all levels of the firm want better answers to these questions so that they might become more skilled practitioners of strategy. On the other hand, academics face the perplexing problem of a gap between their theories of what strategy is and its actual practice. This is because much strategy research has remained remote from the study of that myriad of activities and practices involved in doing strategy. This book explains a new research perspective, strategy as practice, which addresses the problem of doing strategy research that is closer to strategy practice.

As strategy as practice is a new perspective, this book both sets out some theoretical foundations for the field and provides a body of empirical work, which can contribute to its empirical and theoretical development. Broadly, the book addresses the question: How do the strategizing practices of managers shape strategy as an organizational activity? This introductory chapter serves four purposes:

- locates strategy as practice in the broader field of strategic management;
- introduces the broad aims of the strategy as practice research agenda;
- explains the activity-based view of strategy as practice used in this book; and
- provides readers with a guide to the features of this book.

STRATEGY AS PRACTICE IN RELATION TO OTHER FIELDS OF STRATEGY RESEARCH

Strategy as practice is part of a broader practice turn in contemporary social theory and the management sciences over the past 20 years.[1] It has been imported into such diverse management fields as technology, knowledge management, organizational learning and accounting.[2] More recently, the practice turn has entered the strategy field, recommending that we focus on the actual work of strategists and strategizing.[3] This practice turn in strategy may be attributed to two main influences, in strategic management specifically and the management sciences more generally.

First, there is an increasing frustration with the normative models of science that dominate strategic management research. Much strategy theory is generated from large-scale studies in the micro-economics tradition, which reduce the complexities of doing strategy to a few causally related variables. Such studies focus on firm and industry levels of analysis, with scant attention to human action. With their implicit assumptions of rational choice, they reduce actors to, at best, simplistic figures represented by a few demographic variables that may be questionably linked to firm performance. The dominance of economic assumptions in strategic management research is a straitjacket that has made strategy theory increasingly remote and out of touch with the complexities of strategy in practice (Bettis, 1991; Ghoshal and Moran, 1996; Lowendahl and Revang, 1998; Prahalad and Hamel, 1994). Indeed, despite some 40 years of strategic management research, we still lack a valid theory of how strategies are created (Hamel, 2001).

Second, building upon Weick's (1979) influential suggestion that we make better use of verbs and gerunds, such as organize and organizing, instead of static and reified concepts such as organization, the broader field of management research has been seeking more 'humanized' theories that bring actors and action back into the research frame (Whittington, 2002). The growing shift from static, parsimonious and generalized forms of theorizing to dynamic and complex explanations that reflect action (Langley, 1999; Mohr, 1982; Weick, 1979) may be partially attributable to an 'after modern' or 'post-industrial' phase in the management sciences. Organizations in a knowledge-based, post-industrial society are increasingly individualistic, fragmented, localized, pluralistic and contested, as opposed to standardized and collective entities (Cummings, 2002; Lowendahl and Revang, 2004; Whittington, 2004). These changing conditions, in which organization may not be considered a coherent whole, pose challenges to practitioners and researchers. Meaningful relationships between theory and practice will be better assisted by dynamic, locally-contextualized theories that can reflect the complexities of practice in an after modern world (Pettigrew, 2001).

The strategy as practice research agenda is situated in the context of these after modern developments in the management sciences and a growing disenchantment with the theoretical contributions, empirical conduct and practical relevance of much strategic management research. Practice research aims to understand the messy realities of doing strategy as lived experience;[4] to go inside the world of strategy practitioners as they struggle with competing priorities, multiple stakeholders and excessive but incomplete information in an attempt to shape some coherent 'thing' that may be perceived as a strategy by markets, financial institutions and consumers. Strategy as practice is thus concerned with the detailed aspects of strategizing; how strategists think, talk, reflect, act, interact, emote, embellish and politicize, what tools and technologies they use, and the implications of different forms of strategizing for strategy as an organizational activity. Strategy as practice as an agenda thus marks a clear departure from the positivist economic assumptions underpinning much strategy research.

STRATEGY AS PRACTICE AND OTHER AVENUES OF STRATEGY RESEARCH

Strategy as practice is, of course, not the first research agenda to attempt to break through the economics-based dominance over strategy research. Rather, it may be seen as the culmination of broader shifts in strategic management, to which a practice perspective can contribute. Strategy as practice is distinct from, but responds to, challenges and issues raised in strategy process, resource-based view and dynamic capabilities research. These avenues of research and their distinctions and complementarities with strategy as practice are now briefly discussed.

Strategy process

Initially, and perhaps most dominantly, there is the legacy of the strategy process school of research, which made significant departures from content-based theories of strategy by introducing a dynamic view of strategy as a process in which the role of the managerial actor is problematized. While process research made important steps forward in humanizing strategy research and generating more dynamic theories, from a practice perspective it does not go far enough in two ways. First, while process problematizes the role of top managers, it does not carry this through into studying what various managerial actors do. Second, process research is primarily concerned with explanations at the firm level of analysis, necessarily sacrificing more fine-grained analyses of activity construction (Johnson et al., 2003). The contributions of the process school and the ways that a practice perspective builds upon and furthers its agenda are now briefly outlined.

The process school is not a consistent body of theory in itself, comprising various strands, which will be briefly summarized here as the Bower-Burgelman (B-B), action, and change process veins of research. Beginning with Bower's (1970) influential study of the way that the resource allocation process shapes strategy, the B-B vein of process research counteracted rational choice theories of strategy-making. Building on Bower's model, Burgelman's (1983, 1991, 1996) studies developed a theory of strategy as an evolutionary process involving multiple managerial actors from the corporate, middle and operational level of the firm. Analysis of the different roles played by these managers has led to an important problematizing of top managers' involvement in strategy creation. Top managers' influence over the way others perform strategy lies in their control over the structural context but, paradoxically, once they embed strategy in an administrative structure, such as resource allocation, they find it hard to alter or shape that strategy. Administrative structures thus contextually bind the strategic actions of top managers, leading to inertia and performance down-turn. By contrast, lower-level managers play the main role in providing initiative and impetus to change strategy. The B-B vein of process theory thus instated multiple levels of managers into the strategy making process, exposed the weakness of rational choice notions and initiated a dynamic theory of strategy as a multi-level process evolving over time.

However, the agency and influence by which different levels of managers shape the evolution of strategy is rather less addressed; that is, how different managers act and interact remains hollow, leaving a somewhat sterile picture of what people actually do (Johnson et al., 2003; Noda and Bower, 1996; Pettigrew, 1992). This branch of strategy process research thus remains very much at the firm level of explanation, rather than the action and activity level, negating fine-grained analysis of the everyday actions and interactions involved in the formation of strategy. This problem is to some extent shaped by a cautious approach to situated concepts of context, since the B-B vein of research remains at the more observable contextual levels of structure and strategy. The omission of situated context is deliberate: 'The problem with situational context, however, is precisely that it is unique to the situation; one can't generalize about it' (Bower, 1970: 71). Hence, Bower sets up a 'separate category', structural context, to isolate and omit the messy situated aspects of context that are of a 'personal and historical nature' and this omission continues to colour the B-B school of research (Noda and Bower, 1996). However, from a practice perspective strategic and structural context cannot be abstracted from situation, as it is the situation that makes both strategy and structures relevant to action. Practice theory aims to understand strategy as a situated activity. Strategy as practice thus extends the B-B theory of process in two important ways, managerial agency and situated activity, in order to better understand how different level actors interact to shape strategy (see, for example, Regnér, 2003).

The action school is largely the province of Mintzberg (1990), whose definition of strategy as 'a pattern in a stream of actions' is pertinent to practice. This definition arises from the concept of strategy as emergent action, as opposed to intended strategy. This school of thought further problematizes the role of the top manager, since top manager intentionality or choice is subject to the intentions arising from other actors and events within the firm. 'To assume that the intentions of the leadership are the intentions of the organization may not be justified, since others can act contrary to these intentions' (Mintzberg and McHugh, 1985: 162). This draws out a theme that is core to a practice perspective; the potential disparity between top managers and other actors. Strategy is not an output of the organization as a coherent, collective whole. However, the action school then focuses upon grass roots strategies that emerge from the organization in a bottom-up fashion. While this shows the emergent nature of activity and provides an effective counterpoint to rational choice assumptions, it negates the actions of top managers in strategy-making. The action school is more concerned with the messy emergence of strategy at the grass roots level than with the complex relationship between intention, and emergence or its implications for top managers (Hendry, 2000). Strategy may indeed be a matter of emergence rather than managerial intention, but its overall outcomes in terms of strategy content and firm performance are a managerial responsibility. Strategy as practice acknowledges this, addressing the thorny problem of top managers' involvement in shaping strategy in the face of emergence.

The change process school focuses upon firm-level change as an outcome of action in context (for example, Johnson, 1987; Pettigrew, 1985; Van de Ven and Poole, 1990). Pettigrew (1973, 1985, 1987, 1990) is perhaps the primary exponent of this method, highlighting the political and cultural aspects of context and how these are implicated in strategic action. The managerial actor is clearly instated within the strategy process as a political entity with interest and intent. However, we also see the constraining and enabling nature of contextual features, such as culture, upon managerial action. This school thus develops contextual explanations that further problematize rational choice theories and invite us to focus upon strategy as situated managerial action.

To this extent, the change process school of strategy is most closely associated with strategy as practice. However, this school's absorbing focus is upon the sequence of events involved in change (Van de Ven, 1992). This school thus deals with the firm as the level of analysis and the sequence of events within a change as the unit of analysis. By contrast, a practice perspective is concerned with activity as the level of analysis and the actions and interactions that comprise activity as the unit of analysis. This analytical distinction enables a more fine-grained understanding of those detailed actions and practices that constitute a strategy process (Brown and Duguid, 2001; Johnson et al., 2003) without the presupposition of change.

Undoubtedly strategy involves change. However, it also involves a good deal of maintenance and reproduction. Such reproduction is not insignificant, since stabilizing strategy is also important to an organization (Chia, 1999; Hendry and Seidl, 2003; Jarzabkowski, 2004a). Strategy as practice shifts the analytic focus to how strategy is constructed rather than how firms change, in order to understand the myriad of interactions through which strategy unfolds over time, each of which contains the scope and potential for either stability or change (Tsoukas and Chia, 2002). Strategy as practice thus privileges the construction of strategic stability alongside strategic change (Wilson and Jarzabkowski, 2004).

These distinctions between strategy process and strategy as practice in terms of managerial agency, situated action, activity rather than firm-level analysis, and the construction of strategic stability are, to be sure, subtle and fine-grained; a matter of nuance, foregrounding, and focus more than a hard delineation (Johnson et al., 2003). Indeed, a clear intellectual debt is owed to the process field, particularly the latter change scholars. Nonetheless, the distinctions are important for developing a theory of practice, as the following chapters will demonstrate. Furthermore, they appear also to be of concern to contemporary process scholars. That is, strategy process seems to be at something of a crossroads, where it is concerned with these problems in the strategy process field. For example, Chakravarthy and White (2002) note that process research needs to attain better theoretical and practical relevance by explaining how strategies are formed and implemented, not only how they are changed. Similarly, Garud and Van de Ven (2002) note the problems of linear analyses of change events and suggest that research must focus upon the emergence, development and obsolescence of change processes. To do so, I maintain that research needs to take a practice perspective on strategy as a socially accomplished, situated activity arising from the actions and interactions of multiple level actors.

Resource-based and dynamic capability theories

Another avenue of strategy research that has developed increasing presence over the last 15 years is the resource-based view (RBV) and its more dynamic 'cousin' dynamic capability theory (Barney, 1991; Helfat, 2000; Lengnick-Hall and Wolff, 1999; Teece et al., 1997). While based primarily in an economic paradigm (Conner, 1991), these theoretical developments in the strategy field aim to address and counteract the typical industry levels of analysis in much strategy research by focusing upon competitive advantage as it arises from heterogeneous firm-level resources and capabilities. From this perspective, competitive advantage might arise not only from tangible assets, but also socially complex assets, such as culture, knowledge, capabilities embodied in specific actors, and the learning routines of an organization. It thus addresses some of the concerns of the practice field by attempting to reinstate actors and unique or situated action into strategy research.

However, this research agenda tends to fall short of its ambitions to explain how heterogeneity within firms is associated with differences in firm performance, resorting to positivistic methods that are too coarse to access deep understandings of how firms differ and, indeed, what difference that makes (Rouse and Daellenbach, 1999). As a result, in the RBV at least, unique features that might well make a difference, such as the situated nature of managerial action, are left within the 'black box', failing to address the very problem that RBV raises (Priem and Butler, 2001). Dynamic capabilities represent something of a development on the RBV, being in the same broad family of theory, but aiming to go beyond the criticisms of RBV as excessively static and commodified (Scarbrough, 1998; Spender, 1996). Rather than conceiving of resources as something a firm has that gives it unique advantage, dynamic capabilities are concerned with the learning processes that a firm does. This is a distinctive contribution from a practice perspective, since it acknowledges more dynamic forms of theorizing. However, despite considerable research, dynamic capabilities still fail to deliver a coherent account of strategy-making:

how capabilities are developed and modified over time and what difference that makes to the strategy of the firm (Cockburn et al., 2000). This may be because capability-building theory has also fallen prey to the dominant positivistic traditions in strategy research and so lacks sufficient fine-grained analysis to furnish a more dynamic theory of dynamic capabilities (Regnér, 2005).

A practice focus can address these short comings in RBV and dynamic capability theory by providing a more micro focus on those activities and actions from which socially complex resources are constituted (Johnson et al., 2003). Most importantly, because it is concerned with situated theories of action, a practice perspective can shed light on the way capabilities emerge, are developed, modified and changed over time, furthering our understanding of the essence of dynamic capabilities. Indeed, early work in the practice vein is beginning to identify the micro-foundations of dynamic capabilities that are fundamental to the competitive advantage of firms such as Alessi (see Salvato, 2003). Strategy as practice research can only add to the RBV and dynamic capability research agenda, helping scholars in these areas to utilize practice methodologies and theoretical concepts to further their ambitions of explaining how and why firms differ and what difference that makes to competitive advantage.

INTRODUCING THE STRATEGY AS PRACTICE RESEARCH AGENDA

The strategy as practice research agenda is concerned with strategy as a situated, socially accomplished activity constructed through the actions and interactions of multiple actors. Broadly, this research agenda has three focal points, each of which provides a different angle from which to examine strategy as practice:

- practice;
- practitioners; and
- practices (Whittington, 2002).

PRACTICE

A focus on practice explicitly aims to take us beyond the false dichotomies that characterize much of the strategic management field (Clegg et al., 2004; Johnson et al., 2003; Wilson and Jarzabkowski, 2004). The strategy literature is populated with polarized categories such as content/process, intended/emergent, thinking/acting, formulation/implementation and foresight/uncertainty. Many of these divides are academic conveniences, based in theoretical traditions that have little relevance in practice. In practice research, the 'practice' under investigation is strategy as a flow of organizational activity that incorporates content and process, intent and emergence, thinking and acting and so on, as reciprocal, intertwined and frequently indistinguishable parts of a whole when they are observed at close range. For example, the content of a firm's strategy is shaped by its process, which feeds back into the content in ongoing mutual construction. Indeed, earlier process theorists have alerted us to the relationship between process and content (Pettigrew and Whipp, 1991) and the false division of formulation and implementation, proposing that strategy is a process of 'formation' (Mintzberg, 1978). A practice perspective goes beyond studying the relationship between such concepts to addressing them as mutually constitutive. It aims to get inside the flow of strategy as a practice in order to understand how dichotomies such as process and content, emergence and intent, and thinking and acting elide in the ongoing shaping of the practice. This, of course, represents something of a challenge, since the academic language that we have for conceptualizing and analyzing strategy is characterized by these dichotomies (Chia, 2004). Nonetheless, a practice agenda attempts to take strategy research beyond some of these inadequacies in the academic construction of strategy by examining strategy as a practice.

PRACTITIONERS

The next focal point of the strategy as practice agenda is practitioners; it aims to reinstate the actor in strategy research. Much of the frustration with the positivist traditions in strategy research is because they marginalize the actor (Lowendahl and Revang, 1998; 2004). They ignore the fact that people do strategy. Strategy as a practice arises from the interactions between people, lots of people – top managers, middle managers, employees, consultants, accountants, investors, regulators, consumers. While all these people might not be designated formally as 'strategists', their actions and interactions contribute to the strategy of an organization (Mantere, 2005). Therefore, a practice agenda addresses the issue of multiple actors as skilled and knowledgeable practitioners of strategy, examining how their skill is constituted in doing different aspects of the work of strategy (Whittington, 2003). Practitioners are seen as social individuals, interacting with the social circumstances involved in doing strategy. The focus is thus upon how practitioners act, what work they do, with whom they interact, and what practical reasoning they apply in their own localized experience of strategy (Chia, 2004; Ezzammel and Willmott, 2004). The aim of the practice agenda is to see strategy through the eyes of the practitioner.

PRACTICES

Strategy as practice is also concerned with practices: those tools and artefacts that people use in doing strategy work (Jarzabkowski, 2004a; Whittington, 2002, 2003). These practices take many forms, and their use and influence in the practice of strategy is still poorly understood. They might be broadly categorized in three ways. First, there are the 'rational' administrative practices that typically serve the purpose of organizing and coordinating strategy, such as planning mechanisms, budgets, forecasts, control systems, performance indicators and targets. Strategy as a practice is littered with such rational practices. However, following Bower and Burgelman's process research on the way administrative practices shape strategy and Mintzberg's (1990; 1994) exposure of the false rationality implied in strategic planning and design, we know the purpose of these practices is not necessarily rational. Therefore, they have, with some exceptions (for example, Grant, 2003; Jarzabkowski, 2003), largely disappeared off the research agenda. However, for managers, rational practices continue to be relevant (Hendry, 2000). Regardless of how rational they are in use, they are part of the everyday work of doing strategy. Practice research, thus, remains interested in and addresses these practices as mediating mechanisms by which skilled actors interact in pursuit of their own strategic ends.

Second, there are those 'discursive' practices that provide linguistic, cognitive and symbolic resources for interacting about strategy. This is a broad umbrella to cover a range of practices, of which two main types of interrelated practices stand out: the discourse of strategy and the strategy tools and techniques that provide an everyday language for this discourse (Barry and Elmes, 1997; Hardy et al., 2000; Jarzabkowski, 2004a, b). Increasingly, research shows that strategy is mediated by the language that strategists use, with this language in part created by the academic concepts, tools and techniques that populate strategy classes, textbooks and popular media. While the use of such practices to inform strategy making is still largely under-explored, the limited body of empirical research shows that they have consequential effects for the practice of strategy (for example, Hodgkinson and Wright, 2002).

Finally, there are those practices that create opportunities for and organize the interaction between practitioners in doing strategy, such as meetings, workshops and away days. While these are clearly consequential for the practice of strategy, there has been little empirical investigation into the way they influence and mediate that practice (Hendry and Seidl, 2003; Schwartz, 2004). Such practices are referred to as 'episodes' that serve as micro variation and selection mechanisms, provoking change or reinforcing stability in strategy. Individually any single episode may be more or less consequential, but as typical occurrences within the organization they have powerful effects in the stabilizing and change of organizational activity.

In studying these three types of practices – administrative, discursive and episodic practices – the practice research agenda is not focused specifically on practices per se. Rather, it is interested in practices-in-use, practices as mediators of the interaction between practitioners in shaping the practice of strategy (Orlikowski, 1992, 2000). Practices are referred to as mediators because consequential actions and interactions in shaping strategy are frequently indirect. They are mediated through a range of the above practices such as meetings, conversations, budget mechanisms and PowerPoint presentations. For example, the strategy director of a telecommunications company discusses the uses of the value chain, a typical strategy framework, in the following way:

> It's linear and really what we are dealing with isn't like that. It's more of, more of a square or something, many more connections to take account of and not linear like that. But value chain's handy. People recognize that. You know, you put up the five or six boxes in an arrow and it makes sense . . . It's a communication thing. It lets you communicate.[5]

In this statement, it is not the value chain per se that is of interest, but how it has been used to communicate with others about strategy (Jarzabkowski, 2004b). This is the focus of practice research: to study practices-in-use as mediators of action, examining their consequences for the strategy, the actors who use them, and the interactions that are conducted.

The strategy as practice research agenda is broad ranging, drawing together a multitude of issues under the broad themes of practice, practitioners and practices. As a new field, it is still ill-defined and open in its language, concepts and terminology. This represents something of a challenge for its empirical study, not least methodologically (Balogun et al., 2003). This book contributes to the research agenda by developing a set of theoretically and empirically robust concepts and a methodological framework that also provide a basis for further study in the field.

THE ACTIVITY-BASED VIEW OF STRATEGY AS PRACTICE

The strategy as practice research agenda is still largely theoretical. The empirical focus and the choice of analytic units for operationalizing practice remain open. This book builds on early developments in the field by locating within an activity-based view. The activity-based view is specifically concerned with the empirical study of 'practice' as a flow of activity (Johnson et al., 2003; Whittington et al., 2004). It therefore focuses upon the practice of strategy through this activity, as opposed to through practitioners, or practices. With reference to Figure I.1, this is not a clear demarcation so much as an entry point into the study of interrelated phenomena, as the study of activity will, inevitably, bring in practitioners and their practices. The activity-based view addresses 'the detailed processes and practices which constitute the day-to-day activities of organizational life and which relate to strategic outcomes' (Johnson et al., 2003: 3).

In order to further the empirical study of strategy as an organizational activity, there are two key issues to address:

- What is activity?
- How should we study it?

In some senses these are deep philosophical questions that are well beyond the scope of this book. They are also important questions in the social theory of practice. Indeed, one aim of this book is to examine some of the practice-based theoretical underpinnings to these questions. However, let us first examine how they are addressed in the activity-based view of strategy as practice.

Figure I.1: Activity as the focus of this book[6]

WHAT IS ACTIVITY?

A broad definition of activity is: 'Activities . . . are the day to day stuff of management. It is what managers do and what they manage. It is also what organizational actors engage in more widely' (Johnson et al., 2003: 15). An activity-based view is thus concerned with strategy as a broad organizational activity. It is both something that managers do and also a phenomenon involving a wide distribution of organizational actors. Here the activity-based view engages with the agenda to understand strategy as a practice involving a large number of people at all levels of the organization. However, if activity involves everyone, what makes it strategic? For example, is all activity strategic? This is difficult to define. Consider Exhibit I.1, the story of Fred, a track supervisor on the London Tube. While Fred's actions are consequential for the strategy of the Tube, is his activity the activity that strategy as practice scholars should be studying?

To some extent, an analysis of strategy can be conducted at any level of the organization, including the 'Freds' whose work contributes to strategy. In particular, if we wish to go beyond false dichotomies, such as strategic and operational, then denying Fred's work because it is operational is also false. However, it also seems that some common sense needs to be applied to a definition of what type of activity we wish to study as strategically important. The activity-based view suggests that such activity will relate to strategic outcomes (Johnson et al., 2003). This leads to the second question posed.

Exhibit I.1: Doing strategy? Greasing the rail head on the London Tube[7]

Fred and the London Tube

Once upon a time there was a track supervisor on the London Tube called 'Fred'. Fred worked the Victoria Line. Over the years, he noticed an increase in rail wear on his section of the line and increased the rail lubrication to compensate. Rail lubrication is grease applied to the inside edge of the rail head, which helps the wheels pass without binding against the rails (that squealing noise you sometimes hear).

When Fred retired, the new supervisor, who knew nothing about the problem and who was alarmed at the grease consumption levels, reset all the rail greasers to the standard levels. The wear on the train wheel flanges suddenly went up to the extent that the depot technician responsible for checking wheel condition was forced to cancel 13 trains for the evening rush hour. The London Tube was in chaos! It took six months of investigation to 'track down' the problem. Eventually, it was discovered that Fred's operational activity of maintaining the rails on his section of track had been vital to the Tube's strategy of running a timely and efficient commuter service.

- Was Fred a strategist? Hardly!
- Was Fred's activity strategic? It would be hard to justify that definition.
- Was Fred's contribution important to the strategy of the London Tube? Undoubtedly!

HOW SHOULD WE STUDY STRATEGY AS ACTIVITY?

In order to study strategy as an activity that relates to strategic outcomes, some notion of intentionality is implied. While Fred's tale is an anecdote and we should not make too much of it, it is doubtful that Fred's intentions were focused on strategic outcomes at the organizational level. 'Intentionality' means that this activity is intended to have an outcome that will be consequential for the organization as a whole – its profitability or survival. This is not implying that intentions will be met. Simply that if we wish to study something in real time that is consequential and that is expected to have strategic outcomes, we will enter the field a priori to knowing those outcomes. Therefore it is helpful to allow the research participants to help us define what activity is strategic and why. This can be done at a number of levels, since many actors do participate in shaping the strategy of an organization (Balogun and Johnson, 2004;

Mantere, 2005; Rouleau, 2005). However, an activity-based view draws attention to top managers.

> It does not presuppose the primacy of managerial agency but rather encourages the exploration of the centrality of management within the complexity of the processes that go to make up and influence organizations. An activity-based view of strategy allows for, but does not commit to, managerial agency. (Johnson et al., 2003: 15)

In framing what activity is strategic, it seems appropriate to let the managers who are at the centre of that activity define both the activity and the hoped for strategic outcomes that orient it. This provides an empirical entry point, a particular flow of activity to examine as strategic. From this starting point it is possible to examine who contributes to the activity, how it is constructed, what dynamics of influence shape the activity, and with what consequences. This book adopts this approach, allowing top managers to define, prior to the start of data collection, what activity is strategic. However, keeping in mind the widespread organizational engagement in activity, this research problematizes managerial agency. On the one hand they may define those activities that are intended to have strategic outcomes but, on the other hand, they cannot ensure that those outcomes will be realized through strategy as an organizational activity. In addressing these questions and issues, this book will contribute to the empirical interpretation of the activity-based view, and so to its theoretical development.

AIMS OF THIS BOOK

Taking into account the issues raised by both the broader strategy as practice agenda and the more specific challenges raised by the activity-based view of strategy as practice, this book has three aims:

- to explain how strategizing, what managers do, shapes strategy as an organizational activity;
- to contribute to the empirical interpretation and the theoretical development of an activity-based view; and
- to generate a set of themes, definitions and concepts that can further the development of the strategy as practice field.

HOW TO READ THIS BOOK

Reading a book is a big undertaking in our busy lives! This overview is designed to help readers select the most relevant chapters for their purposes. Additionally, the book has particular features that will enable readers to negotiate their way through material that might at times be quite new or complex. The overall book is in three parts.

STRUCTURE AND CONTENT OF THE BOOK

Part I deals with the theoretical and analytical foundations of the book. Chapter 1 sets out the social theory of practice themes that underpin the concept of strategy as an activity. Chapter 2 undertakes a review of the relevant strategy literature, developing three research questions that guide the empirical study. This chapter also identifies the unit of analysis, strategizing and the level of analysis, strategy as an activity, providing definitions for these terms that orient the remainder of the book.

Part II is the empirical heart of the book. It is based on a study of strategy as practice in three UK universities over a seven-year period. Chapter 3 introduces the cases and explains the particular features of universities that make them critical contexts for strategy research. Chapters 4 to 6 address the three research questions. They present the core themes and concepts derived from the empirical study, drawing upon the data for illustrative extracts, exhibits and practical examples of the issues under discussion. Chapter 4 explains two types of strategizing, procedural and interactive strategizing, and the influences they have in shaping strategy. Chapter 5 builds on these concepts by developing a typology of four strategizing types that each shape phases of strategy in different ways. Chapter 6 deals with the complex problem of multiple strategies, examining the implications of pursuing several potentially contradictory strategies at the same time.

Part III draws the book together. Chapter 7 presents the components of a strategizing framework that has been developed from the empirical material. It shows how this framework addresses the main aim of the book, to explain how strategizing – what managers do – shapes strategy as an activity. Chapter 8 revisits the themes that have arisen throughout the book, showing how this book has met its two broader aims: first, to contribute to the empirical interpretation and theoretical development of an activity-based view; and second, to provide a set of core concepts, themes and definitions that contribute to the wider strategy as practice agenda.

SPECIAL FEATURES

To enhance readability, the following features are incorporated into the book.

1 Each chapter may be read as a stand-alone chapter, although the empirical chapters have a logical progression and do cross-reference Exhibits.
2 Every chapter begins with a summary box of the key points in the chapter.
3 The main points in each section of each chapter are pulled together into Quick Reference Guides. Through these Quick Reference Guides readers can access the main points of a piece of text, refresh their memory on a topic already covered, and scan a chapter for particular items of interest.

4 Each chapter concludes with the key points to take forward. These points emphasize the main contributions the chapter has made to our understanding and explains how they lead into the following chapters.

WHAT TO READ: CHAPTERS FOR DIFFERENT AUDIENCES

This book has three audiences:

- researchers in the area of strategy and organization;
- students taking courses on strategy as practice, related areas such as strategy implementation and strategy in action, and the wider field of strategic management generally; and
- reflexive practitioners, particularly those working in contexts with similar issues to universities, such as professional service firms and public sector and not-for-profit organizations.

These audiences have different interests and purposes in reading such a book. While the book comprises a whole argument, chapters that might have more relevance for each of these audiences can be identified:

- Strategy and organization scholars will be primarily interested in the theoretical contributions of the book and are thus best directed to read Chapters 1, 2, 6, 7 and 8. These chapters set out the theoretical framework and argue for the contributions of the empirical data, with Chapter 6 providing a glimpse into the evidence upon which the argument is built.
- Students will find that Chapter 2 provides them with an overview of the strategy literature that is relevant to understanding strategy as practice concepts, while Chapters 4, 5 and 6 bring these concepts to life with empirical explanations, which might best be tied into a theoretical understanding by reading Chapter 7.
- Reflexive practitioners, on the other hand, are keen to know what lessons they can gain from this book that will add to their own practice. Here I suggest Chapters 2, 3, 4, 5 and 6 as the most pertinent chapters for setting out the issues of strategy as practice and its key practical contributions. Chapter 2 sets out the concepts for the research study. The empirical chapters then ground these concepts in comparisons of actual practice.

For all readers, this book is a research monograph that has a dual purpose: to introduce the field of strategy as practice as a new perspective and to develop an argument based on empirical data that contributes a body of evidence to this new field.

NOTES

1 Evidence of the practice turn in contemporary social theory may be found in Ortner, 1984; Reckwitz, 2002; Schatzki et al., 2001; Turner, 1994.
2 See the following authors for examples of the practice turn in management: technology (Ciborra and Lanzara, 1990; Orlikowski, 1992, 2000), knowing in action (Blackler, 1993, 1995; Boland and Tenkasi, 1995; Cook and Brown, 1999; Gherardi, 2000), communities of practice (Brown and Duguid, 1991, 2001; Wenger, 1998), accounting in practice (Hopwood and Miller, 1994).
3 See the following for evidence of the practice turn in strategy: Chia, 2004; Hendry, 2000; Hendry and Seidl, 2003; Jarzabkowski, 2003, 2004a; Jarzabkowski and Wilson, 2002; Johnson et al., 2003; McKiernan and Carter, 2004; Whittington, 1996, 2002, 2003, 2004; Wilson and Jarzabkowski, 2004. Additionally the website www.strategy-as-practice.org has some 1000 members in its community.
4 The fascination with lived experience indicates the ethnomethodological roots of the practice turn, which stands in stark contrast to positivist science (see, for example, Garfinkel, 1967).
5 This extract is from a series of interviews I have conducted with strategy directors about their strategizing practices.
6 I am grateful to Richard Whittington for his suggestions on this diagram.
7 This example was initially garnered from Biffa Waste Services, who have named their corporate intranet 'Fred's Head' to highlight that everyone's knowledge and actions are important to the overall firm strategy. Greater detail and verification were then gathered from 'Tubeprune' at www.trainweb.org/tubeprune.

PART I: DEFINING AND THEORETICALLY LOCATING AN ACTIVITY-BASED VIEW

The aim of this section is to locate the concepts of an activity-based view of strategy as practice in the literature. Chapter 1 deals with the social theory of practice. Four core themes from social theory that apply to the study of activity are developed. These themes provide a sensitizing framework for thinking about the empirically-grounded material in the following chapters. An activity system framework for analysing activity, which will be used in the empirical chapters, is also developed. Chapter 2 provides an overview of the strategy literature that applies to an activity-based view. Key terms, such as strategy and strategizing, are defined and the core analytic concepts are grounded in the relevant strategy literature. This literature review derives the three research questions that guide the empirical study in Part II.

1 CORE SOCIAL THEORY THEMES IN STRATEGY AS PRACTICE

Key points

- Strategy is situated activity

- Becoming: situated activity is always under construction

- Situated activity is distributed

- Managerial agency: practical-evaluative wisdom in dealing with situated, distributed activity that is becoming

- An activity system framework

In a university planning meeting, the top team is discussing the static research and commercial income figures for the 5-year forecasts.* This is an issue that has been perplexing them for some time, particularly the research figures, which have been a problem for a couple of years despite various interventions. They agree that static targets are unacceptable. They must set tough goals. Dave emphasizes: 'It's simply not good enough. We must set TOUGH surplus plans of an increase each year and we MUST achieve those targets which we have not been tough on in the past.'

Tim agrees and suggests a way to action their goals by altering the current monitoring and control procedures for handling income generation: 'We need to have two committees; an academic side to handle and sort out academics and research contracts, and an income side to handle the commercial and administrative side.' The Vice-Chancellor likes the suggestion: 'Be tougher with academics to pull in more research income and get the commercial income up as well.' They quickly coalesce around the new goals for the activity and the procedural means for achieving them. Andy points out that 'It's unlikely to be achieved by democratic means.' Dave agrees: 'It's got to be authorized or recommended from the top . . . You want to keep the surplus increasing, which is realistic to ask for.'

Andy reinforces the tough message about income from research, which they have been grappling with for some years. 'It's not enough for research just to be good in itself. It has to have financial benefits as well.' Joe reminds them that the increasingly competitive environment for research funding and for their commercial services means that people are already working very hard to achieve the current figures. Increased financial output is a lot to expect in the current environment. However, he agrees that they need to try.

The team then gets instrumental about who should chair the new committees, the specific commercial and research targets to be agreed with different departments, the incentives and punitive measures that they think might encourage and control the departments, and, based on their personal relationships with individuals, which of them would be best at negotiating the dual targets with each department. Sam raises a point about whether these are contradictory activities: 'Should we clarify these objectives? We want to have maximum research income but also commercial income. It seems we want it all. Maybe these are not compatible objectives?' The Vice-Chancellor silences him quickly: 'We want BOTH.' The dual goals for research agreed, the team goes on with discussing the various practices they have available to construct activity, which they hope will result in increased research and commercial income over the next 5 years.

*While names are disguised to preserve anonymity, this is an extract from a meeting that I observed personally.

This extract, comprising some 20 minutes of a two-hour meeting, captures top managers in a moment of 'strategizing'. In it they are using data, developing goals, articulating targets, appraising the environment, reflecting on past practice, modifying control systems, coping with uncertainty, affirming power structures, considering social relationships with others, and legitimizing action. They do so in a practiced way, arriving at a point of sufficient decision to move on to the next agenda item, secure in the knowledge that they have the necessary practices to progress the 'dual goal' strategy to the next stage. A small strategizing incident in many such incidents.

In this strategizing incident, we can see many of the issues addressed by a practice agenda. The practice turn places the micro practices and processes that constitute the activity of strategizing at the centre of strategy research (Jarzabkowski, 2003, 2004a; Johnson et al., 2003; Whittington, 2002, 2003). Through a myriad of such micro incidents, comprising the ongoing fabric of strategizing, strategists construct parts of a larger flow of strategic activity. They do so with recourse to the situated practices and artefacts that are meaningful within their context, with little concern for the dichotomies that typically characterize strategy research. Polarizations such as content versus process, intended versus emergent, foresight versus uncertainty, and formulation versus implementation dissolve meaninglessly in practice (Clegg et al., 2004; Johnson et al., 2003). In one simple 20-minute incident of strategizing, we can see both the content and process of the research strategy, the intent embodied in the 'decision' for dual goals but also that decision's emergence from an ongoing process, the practical iteration between hoped for futures and current uncertainty, and the formulation of strategy in a tightly iterative cycle with its implementation. The outcome of the single incident is a contribution to ongoing activity that will trigger interactions with a range of other actors and actions over time, contributing to the strategy of the organization. In studying such practical incidents of strategizing at close range, we can begin to understand how strategy is shaped, the implications of the various practices available for shaping it, and some of the consequences of that shaping.

However, before launching into an analysis of the relationship between strategizing and activity, it is important to outline broadly the theoretical basis of the practice turn. In this chapter, four concepts in the social theory of practice that apply to the study of activity are highlighted:

1 Strategy is explained as situated activity.
2 Situated activity is shown to be in a continuous state of construction.
3 Construction of situated activity is distributed amongst multiple participants, which poses particular problems for those whose job is to 'manage' strategy.
4 For managers, strategizing involves practical-evaluative agency in the face of situated, distributed activity that is in a continuous state of construction.

As these four concepts are discussed, their application to an activity-based view of strategy as practice is developed, leading to an activity system framework that guides the empirical study.

STRATEGY IS SITUATED ACTIVITY

'Situated' is a key practice term that populates the literature with little or no definition, as if its essential meaning is understood. However, 'situatedness' is a deeply embedded concept that has multiple layers of meaning, many of which have been sacrificed to the superficial context of interpersonal interactions (Contu and Willmott, 2003). Situated refers to the way that activity both shapes and is shaped by the society within which it occurs. Since all activity is situated activity, actors cannot be considered separately from the context or situation in which they act. Suchman, one of the primary proponents of situated activity, defines the relational nature of actor and situation:

> First, cognitive phenomena have an essential relationship to a publicly available, collaboratively organized world of artifacts and actions, and secondly, that the significance of artifacts and actions, and the methods by which their significance is conveyed, have an essential relationship to their particular concrete circumstances. (1987: 50)

This definition of situatedness captures the fundamental character of practice; individual cognition that both constructs and is constructed by a shared world on an ongoing basis. It also highlights two important aspects of situatedness; that situation provides an interpretative context and that this context imbues artefacts and actions with meaning. First, situation provides an interpretative context for action (Brown and Duguid, 1991; Lave and Wenger, 1991). That is, any particular action derives meaning, 'significance', from the situation in which it is enacted: 'In so far as actions are always situated in particular social and physical circumstances, the situation is crucial to action's interpretation' (Suchman, 1987: 178). The interpretative nature of situation comprises two important elements, social embeddedness and history.

Let us think about these terms in relation to the above extract, top managers in a university considering how to increase income from research and commercial revenue streams. The situation that lends meaning to these goal-directed activities is deeply embedded. Economically and politically, the need to pursue two concurrent but potentially contradictory goals of research income and commercial income is situated in a 20-year historical trend in OECD (Organization for Economic Cooperation and Development) countries of declining state-funding and increased market-based competition in the public sector generally and the higher education sector specifically. This situation provides a set of contextual conditions that generate urgency about strategy for team members. The economic and political situation means that all of their activities must provide revenue within the context of increasing competition for resources. This realization extends to their more localized situation, which is the University's success in generating revenue from various activities. Historically the University has good research rankings, but it has struggled to raise the percentage of revenue from research for three years, despite attention and various modest interventions by the top team. This situated nature of research activity lends particular weight to their decision to 'get tough' on research income. The embedded and historical nature of the situation is inextricably involved in the way the top team wishes to shape research activity strategically.

The embedded nature of situation is explained by broader social phenomena, such as social institutions (DiMaggio and Powell, 1983; Giddens, 1984). The reason that many organizations appear similar, particularly from the outside, is due to their situatedness in social, political and economic contexts that provide broadly similar concepts of what an organization is. However, situatedness also serves to explain the localized nature of activity in which institutional codes of conduct are not uniform. Local situatedness explains why, from the inside, organizations look so different. For example, all three cases in this book have similar concerns about managing the tensions between research and commercial activity, because of the economic and political climate in which they are located. To this extent, situatedness is a broad institutional concept responsible for common forms of social practice in different localities. However, internally the universities pursue similar streams of activity in quite different ways, with different outcomes due to both the different historical connotations of those activities and also the practices available to enact them within their local context. Practice must, therefore, take into account both the broad social situation that provides institutionally embedded codes of conduct and the micro interpretations of that situation in constructing activity within an organization (Jarzabkowski, 2004a). This embedded construction of situated activity is termed 'praxis'. Praxis is a chain of social events 'where operation and action meet, a dialectic synthesis of what is going on in a society and what people are doing' (Sztompka, 1991: 96). Praxis comprises the interaction between macro and micro contexts in which activity is constructed (Whittington, 2002). Macro or wider societal contexts constitute a current of social movement, 'what is going on in a society' (Sztompka, 1991: 96). Micro contexts comprise any given group engaged in their own local construction of practice, 'what people are doing' (1991: 96). Strategy is a situated activity that is located within this praxis; constructed by actors in interplay with broader social, economic and political institutions.

A second consideration arising from Suchman's definition is 'the significance of artefacts and actions', which refers to the situated practices available for action. For example, organizations have a multitude of artefacts, such as planning procedures, resource allocation mechanisms, committees, logos, acronyms, presentations and templates, which have particular significance in that organization. These artefacts have technical purposes, such as allocating and organizing resources, and also social purposes, such as legitimizing activity and signifying power relationships within the organization (Bechky, 2003). Artefacts are thus inherently associated with actions and actors. For example, in his attempts to increase control over revenue from a commercial initiative owned by a department, a senior university manager, in an interview, explained to me the use of committees, auditors and audit statements:

> I had a go on my own and was unable to do it . . . So my next strategy was to use the Resource Committee which has more legitimacy in financial matters than I do but even then we had to use auditors . . . to actually prove that there was a case. They've got the internal audit to suggest that there is a lack of standardization . . . doesn't fit normal good practice in terms of control systems and there's also a lack of effectiveness.

This extract shows power relationships in the use of artefacts and professional roles in order to ascribe legitimacy to an act of resource authorization between top managers and a department, with the broader objective of shaping the commercial income strategy. This is not solely a feature of potentially politicized artefacts, such as audit statements. Other studies have found that even seemingly apolitical and acontextual artefacts, such as whiteboards and Post-it notes, are important social, political and technical mediators of activity in organizations because of the social interactions involved in their use (Blackler et al., 2000; Eden and Ackerman, 1998). The artefacts are not meaningful in isolation but in the way they are used to lend meaning to a situation. Artefacts are thus situated social and technical tools that are inherently entwined with the activity of doing strategy in a particular context. This will hardly be surprising to practitioners, since the skilled use of existing organizational practices as resources for collaborating with, co-opting or coercing others is one way in which they display their competence as strategists; because they know the done thing, they are able to get things done (Whittington, 1996).

Finally, Suchman's definition of the 'essential relationship' of activity and artefacts 'to their particular concrete circumstances' alerts us to a key ontological issue in strategy as practice. The term 'practice' suggests that strategy arises out of daily experiences that assume reality for the people participating in them. That is, 'in practice' is commonly understood as 'in reality', indicating that we need to get inside the lived experience of practitioners as they are doing strategy, understanding the multitude of actions and practices that constitute their 'reality' in doing strategy. The practice turn's obsession with getting inside 'lived experience', 'reality' or 'concrete circumstances' does not indicate an objective reality that we could understand if only we could study it in sufficiently micro-detail. Rather, the practice turn perceives reality as situated activity over time: that activity comprising reality for the people participating in it as it moves over time in context. It is thus largely constructivist in nature, despite its diverse epistemological foci and underpinnings.[1] This ontological perspective is adopted in this book, referring to strategy as socially constructed activity.

An activity-based view conceptualizes strategy as situated activity. The key points of situated activity are drawn together in the Quick Reference Guide at the end of this section. Situated activity arises from the interaction between people and the embedded, historical layers of context, from which they derive codes of conduct and which they imbue with localized meaning. In the construction of strategic activity, people resort to and fashion artefacts that will enable them to draw upon, convey and modify this meaning. Situated activity does not, therefore, assume an objective, stable state with a durable set of meanings, but is an ongoing process that remains under construction. An activity-based view of strategy is concerned with the dynamic and mutable construction of activity, in which 'Mutual intelligibility is achieved on each occasion of interaction with reference to situation particulars rather than being discharged once and for all by a stable body of shared meanings' (Suchman, 1987: 50–51).

Quick Reference Guide 1.1: Key points in situated activity

- Situated activity arises from the interaction between embedded layers of context from institutional to localized level.

- Situated activity is constructed by actors, with recourse to those situated artefacts that lend meaning to activity.

- Situated activity is socially constructed. It constitutes reality for those actors involved in constructing it.

BECOMING: STRATEGIC ACTIVITY IS CONTINUOUSLY UNDER CONSTRUCTION

Suchman's quote highlights the point that strategy as a situated activity is always under construction. If 'mutual intelligibility is achieved on each occasion of interaction', then strategy is never a reified state but is continuously constructed through activity. This continuous construction is known as 'becoming'. Becoming encompasses three important themes about activity – inertial, stabilizing and changing activity – that are at the heart of practice-based theorizing.

Strategy is typically a teleological activity, meaning that it is future oriented. Hence it is imbued with terms such as vision, mission, goals, objectives, directions; all words that conjure a future anticipated state. To this extent, strategic activity is goal-directed activity. However, this does not naively assume that goals are achieved. Rather, strategizing oscillates, as evidenced in the opening extract to this chapter, between some desired future and current activity, in which current activity helps to create the future, while anticipations on the future shape current activity (Sztompka, 1991). Oscillation between these states involves an ongoing feedback process of becoming in which 'the heavy hand of the past is present in the future' (Pettigrew, 1990). Unfortunately, much strategy research has engaged with this process in a dichotomous way, giving primacy to either the future or privileging the heavy hand of the past. In the former, the future is a projective state involving change, while reliance on the past equates with inertia in current activity. Inertial patterns of activity arise from the problem of recursiveness.

> Recursiveness means the socially accomplished reproduction of sequences of activity and action because the actors involved possess a negotiated sense that one template from their repertoire will address a new situation. [While] recursiveness is always improvised . . . equally, there can be a durability about recursiveness that constrains attempts to transform the sequences. (Clark, 2000: 67)

Such recursiveness is a core theme in many social theories of practice (for example, Bourdieu, 1990; Giddens, 1984). It accounts for the stability and long duration of social order that characterizes a social system over time (Lockwood, 1964). However, in strategic management, this recursiveness has largely been associated with inertia and failure. For example, the principles of recursiveness underpin the determinism of strategizing routines, the tendency to competency traps, and the bind of core rigidities (Jarzabkowski, 2004a). Such studies focus on the way past templates lead to present inertias; strategy is a reified state that has 'become' rather than is becoming. Indeed, inertia is a noun not a verb. However, even inertia is a 'socially accomplished' (Clark, 2000: 67) pattern of activity, constructed by actors in interaction with their context. For example, Orlikowski (2000) draws attention to the enactment of inertia as one of the ways that technology is used in practice, showing the reproduction involved in enacting such inertia. Inertia is, therefore, one possible path in the becoming of activity.

Given the problem of recursiveness and its predisposition to inertia, another major direction in strategy research has addressed the problem of how organizations change (see Wilson, 1992). Research that examines strategic change is future oriented, examining how the strategy will become something different. Despite this future orientation, much earlier change research focused on change as a reified state, also. An organization undertook strategic change and, having changed, instituted a new stable order (Tushman and Romanelli, 1985). More recent change literature has adopted a becoming perspective, acknowledging that change is not a reified state but a process of chang*ing*; that is, an ongoing process of becoming that does not involve some 'future perfect' state in which the organization has 'changed' (Orlikowski, 1996; Tsoukas and Chia, 2002). Changing is thus a second possible path in the becoming of activity.

Additionally, a practice perspective is interested in the stabilizing of activity. The polarization between inertia and change in strategy research begs the point that attaining stability – stabiliz*ing* – is also a dynamic, skilled and purposeful activity. Indeed, in a pluralistic world in which activity is fragmented, distributed and pulled by multiple competing demands (Giddens, 1991), we could say that stabilizing activity is problematic (Chia, 2004). Stabilizing does not imply inertia but the ability to construct and reconstruct activity without sliding into inertia or occasioning change. Stabilizing activity is of interest to strategists who are, after all, as concerned with realizing strategy through the exploitation of existing resources, capabilities and actions as they are with changing activity (March, 1991). It therefore behoves us, as strategy as practice scholars, to develop a plausible explanation for stabilizing as a path in the becoming of activity.

If strategy is in a continuous process of becoming, analytic attention is directed towards those practices that are associated with its construction in inertial, stabilizing or changing paths of becoming. Most importantly, in studying the becoming of activity, we acknowledge that a strategist's work is never 'done'; strategy is always an unfinished project under construction (Knights and Mueller, 2004).

Quick Reference Guide 1.2: Three paths in the becoming of activity

Activity is always under construction. While it is goal-directed, it never reaches a reified state:

- Activity may follow an inertial pattern by drawing upon the recursive templates of past activity, but this inertia is actively constructed as a state of becoming.

- Activity may follow a changing pattern as an ongoing process of becoming.

- Activity may follow a stabilizing pattern of becoming, constructing and reconstructing activity without sliding into inertia or occasioning change.

DISTRIBUTED AND COLLECTIVE STRATEGIC ACTIVITY

The recent surge of interest in practice theory has been attributed to an 'after modern' phase in the management sciences, which emphasizes the individual, fragmented, localized, pluralistic and contested, as opposed to standardized and collective nature of work (Lowendahl and Revang, 2004; Whittington, 2004).[2] This dispersed and fragmented nature of work highlights the problem of distributed activity.

The concept of 'distributed' arises from Hutchins' (1995) work on the role of distributed cognition in navigation. Complex social activities, such as navigation, require contributions from multiple actors, each of whom has only partial knowledge. Since no single actor can perform all the aspects of navigation, overlap of knowledge between actors is important, with each actor knowing enough about the adjacent activities to construct a responsive and useful contribution to the activity of navigating the ship. Contributions are the input of distributed individual actions into the flow of activity that comprises a social system. Weick and Roberts (1993) exemplify the relationship between distributed contributions and collective activity in their explanation of a flight deck as a complex social system involved in the activity of launching and recovering aircraft. No single actor is able to construct the activity in its entirety. Contributions to activity are distributed amongst a range of actors, very few of whom actually fly the aircraft. The launching and recovery of aircraft is thus an outcome of a stream of activity constructed by multiple, distributed actors, held together by their concept of a shared social system, the criticality of its goals, and their own reasons for contributing to the collective stream of activity.

These concepts have been adopted in organization theory, viewing organizations as distributed activity systems (Blackler et al., 2000; Jarzabkowski, 2003; Spender, 1995).[3] Firms are increasingly distributed. The multinational conglomerate is distributed across different time zones, geographic regions and national cultures, as well as being distributed across different products and markets represented in different divisions and business units. While this is an extreme example, most firms may be considered distributed. The problem for firms is that they are not like flight decks, with singular, critical, pre-established goals that can direct the contributions of a range of actors towards a collective activity. Rather, the distributed nature of the firm tends to create ambiguity of strategic purpose and activity, since different groups may have different interests and represent the appropriate goals and activities of the firm differently (Blackler et al., 2000). Distribution is thus a conundrum in terms of constructing collective activity from the multiple actors involved in any particular strategy. The organizations' challenge generally, and top management's challenge specifically, is to convince other actors to behave as if there is a shared social system into which they wish to contribute their own actions as part of a larger collective stream of activity.

The coordination of activity within organizations has long been a topic of organization theory (for example, Chandler, 1962; March and Simon, 1958;

Mintzberg, 1979). Hence there is a significant body of literature on the structural mechanisms of motivation and control, based on transactions that stimulate distributed actors to exchange contributions to the organization in return for perceived rewards (for example, Ferrary, 2002; Williamson, 1996). Other literature examines coordination from a social interdependence perspective, generating collective action through shared purpose, socialization and shared meanings (for example, Barnard, 1938; Daft and Weick, 1984; Ouchi, 1979). However, a practice lens, in keeping with the situated nature of activity, is less concerned with either the structural properties of control mechanisms or the interpretative properties of social interdependence than with their relational character, as they are realized in social practices of acting (Reckwitz, 2002). Fundamentally, practice is concerned with those structural and interpretative practices that render activity 'mutually intelligible' for distributed actors, producing a social structure that is sufficiently cohesive, stable and binding for collective activity to occur (Barnes, 2001; Suchman, 1987). The role of such practices in mediating mutually intelligible activity between actors is at the heart of practice theory (Garfinkel, 1967; Reckwitz, 2002). Strategy as practice, therefore, focuses upon situated activity as the common thread holding actors together, and seeks to understand the shared practices and interactions through which that activity is constructed (Spender, 1995). This is the basic 'premise' of the activity-based view (Johnson et al., 2003).

An issue that has, however, been largely ignored, even by the few practice studies that have begun to analyse the problem of distributed activity (for example, Blackler et al., 2000; Orlikowski, 2002), is its implications for top managers. While distributed means that strategy arises from the efforts of multiple actors, the fact that it is 'strategic' means that it is the responsibility of top managers. Hendry (2000) reminds us that, in our focus upon the micro issues of practice, we must not forget its 'strategyness'. Regardless of the provisional, emergent, divergent and grass-roots nature of distributed activity, top managers are charged with responsibility for 'the competitive appropriation of value by the organization or its stakeholders, in the form of revenue and profit' (Hendrey, 2000: 969). The managerial task is thus problematized by the notion of distribution. Top managers must be accountable to the board, the city, shareholders or, in the public sector, the state and the public, for the outcomes of their organization. And yet those outcomes arise from the activities of distributed actors within the firm, with their potentially divergent and competing interests.

A theory of strategy as practice must therefore deal with top managers as intentional actors who aim to pursue goal-directed activity. This does not assume that goals are always attained or imply a rational approach to strategy. Neither does it assume that strategy is top-down more than grassroots or middle-up-down. Rather, it acknowledges 'the centrality of management within the complexity of the processes that go to make up and influence organizations' (Johnson et al., 2003: 15). Top managers are placed at the centre of distributed activity, attempting to shape its collective performance, as in the earlier example of a senior university manager using committees, auditors and audit documents to shape divergent interests over commercial activity. The point is that top managers do have responsibility for the direction and outcomes of the organization, as indicated by their compensation relative to others in the organization. Indeed, the level of recompense for top managers is so high that it is currently subject to much public and shareholder scrutiny. Since the work of top managers is 'expensive work' (Whittington, 2003), we should better understand what they do to conduct that work. In particular, we should understand how they deal with the relationship between their responsibilities for collective activity and the fact of distributed interests and inputs to that activity.

Quick Reference Guide 1.3: The problem of distributed activity

- Activity is constructed by multiple, distributed actors who contribute individual actions into the wider flow of activity of their organization.

- Distributed actors have potentially divergent interests that make activity contested and prone to fragmentation. This generates problems for collective organizational activity.

- In order to generate collective activity, distributed actors must interact with each other using a variety of structural and interpretative practices. These practices are the focal point for understanding collective activity.

- Strategy as distributed activity is a challenge for top managers, who have responsibility for the collective output from the contributions of distributed actors.

STRATEGIZING: MANAGERIAL AGENCY AS PRACTICAL-EVALUATIVE WISDOM

In order to explore the challenges of constructing a collective strategic response in the context of situated, distributed and becoming activity, top managers are placed at the centre of this study. Top managers are not framed as all-powerful actors, fearless leaders or corporate heroes, but as skilled, knowledgeable and intentional agents (Giddens, 1984). Agency means to have choices and to be able to effect some action towards those choices, albeit that their outcome may have unintended consequences. Framing top managers as agents acknowledges the power relationships and resources through which they shape activity, whilst also acknowledging the reciprocity through which that activity shapes their ability to be agents. From a practice perspective this reciprocity is an active concept: 'Accounts of order and agreement that refer to practice presume not passive actors but active members, members who reconstitute the system of shared practices by drawing upon it as a set of resources in the course of living their lives' (Barnes, 2001: 17–18). In this section, managerial agency is explained as practical-evaluative agency. Exhibit 1.1 provides an example of practical-evaluative agency, as a strategy director reflects on the diversification process at RetailCo, a leading UK retailer. 'Strategizing' is then defined as practical-evaluative agency: the managerial agency involved in shaping and being shaped by situated and distributed activity in a process of becoming. Conceiving of strategizing as practical-evaluative agency provides a conceptual bridge between dichotomies such as strategic thinking and acting, and strategy formulation and implementation (Wilson and Jarzabkowski, 2004).

Exhibit 1.1: Diversification at RetailCo*

Practical-evaluative agency in a retail company

In this example, the Strategy Director explains the practical-evaluative agency involved in the diversification strategy formation at RetailCo, a leading UK retailer.

There are a few routine tasks, the most obvious of which is an annual planning process. And everything else is not routine and does require different types of analysis. Depending on what it is. Now there are some old favorites, but essentially you have got to sit down and think for each particular problem, 'What would be the most helpful way to tackle it?'

So we have said we want to be an international business. The thought process there in some ways is not very difficult. There is a limit to how much you can grow in the UK. If you want to be a growth business, where is it going to come from? Doesn't take a great deal of financial analysis to work that one out. But then in terms of 'OK, fantastic, international business', well that could be anywhere, couldn't it then? It wouldn't initially actually be financial criteria that would drive your first set of, sort of 'screens' for which countries do I go to. It's only as you get more and more specific about what you are looking at, does the financial analysis become relevant. And then you start to put numbers around them.

For most things we try to build a profit and loss (P&L). So whether that is understanding an acquisition target, or deciding to move into a new business area, we would essentially be trying to learn enough to say what are the different lines of its P&L. And then from there do a discounted cash flow (DCF) to value it.

If we are looking at entering a new product or services area, then we use reasonably typical market research. We then also look at what we already know analytically about this. On new geographic markets, you are still trying to understand how many people live in towns of over a hundred thousand and what's the demographic structure, and then how's the economy growing . . . I mean we don't sort of consciously sit there saying 'Right, why don't we look at this?' If that seems like an appropriate thing, then we might. But there's no standard 'Here's an idea, now let's subject it to the following process.'

And it's that way round because, um, if you try and get too detailed about the numbers when you don't really know very much about something, you might kill things too early, and you also, yeah, you kill things too early because you don't really realize that actually, if you stretched the margin by just another two percentage points, actually that can make all the difference.

*This is an extract from a series of interviews I conducted with strategy directors about their strategizing practices. It is anonymized for the purposes of confidentiality.

There are three dimensions of agency that inform a view of strategists as active participants in the creation of situated activity: iterative, projective and practical-evaluative dimensions (Emirbayer and Mische, 1998). These three dimensions help us to understand issues in shaping inertial, stabilizing and changing paths in the becoming of activity. The iterative dimension deals with actors' skilled reproduction of previous templates for acting without conscious thought; in effect the recursiveness noted above, which tends to emphasize the way that managerial agency is shaped by existing patterns of acting. This dimension of agency has been dealt with in practice theories such as structuration (Giddens, 1979, 1984) and habitus (Bourdieu, 1977, 1990) and privileges practical consciousness – displaying skilled agency through the doing of activity. It may not be thought of as agency, but more as actors mindlessly reconstructing the past, trapped by the routines of their context and the history of their own actions (Whittington, 1988). Iterative agency is thus associated with the value-laden connotations of inertia discussed above. Iteration is, however, far from mindless. It is an active form of social construction, involving intent, skill and knowledge in the selective recognition and implementation of ongoing activity. Strategists do indeed have known moves for product positioning, market entry, increasing capacity, divesting non-profitable businesses, or allocating resources. These moves are important heuristics that enable skilled strategists to do the work of strategy (Eisenhardt and Sull, 2001; Eisenhardt and Zbaracki, 1992). The selection and use of these routine moves may thus be seen as part of the process of stabilizing activity, as much as predisposing an inertial path.

The projective dimension is the one most commonly thought of as agency. This dimension involves the strategist as an agent imposing individual will on a projected future. The strategist as projective agent is a common concept in strategy: an actor with foresight who drives, drags or coaxes the company towards a better, brighter, leaner and more profitable future. For example, there is the cult of the charismatic leader, such as Jack Welch, who appears to have single-handedly masterminded success at GE. Entrepreneurial personalities, such as Richard Branson and Philip Green, continue to fascinate, with their strategies of bold moves, continuous growth and the seizing of opportunities (Mintzberg et al., 1998). The pervasiveness of projective agency as 'strategy' helps to sell management books that recount the tales of corporate heroes, leading their companies through transformation and turnaround. Neither should we be too dismissive of projective agency. As strategy is goal-oriented activity, projective agency is an important aspect of shaping those goals. Projected futures create momentum in current activity. Indeed, the ability to develop a future vision of the company is one important resource that top managers may use to build collective support for changing activity (Alvesson and Sveningsson, 2003). Nonetheless, it is only one form of agency and not necessarily the most 'strategic', since strategy involves getting things done as well as going places.

The final dimension of agency, and the one with which strategy as practice is most concerned, is the practical-evaluative dimension. Practical-evaluative agency is located within an Aristotelian perspective on practical wisdom. Practical wisdom involves localized exercise of judgment: the ability to 'get things done' within the particular contingencies and demands of the here and now (Emirbayer and Mische, 1998; Tsoukas and Cummings, 1997). This perspective on agency links both the iterative and projective forms, since the enacting of either type of agency involves the exercise of real-time judgments, taken 'in the face of considerable ambiguity, uncertainty, and conflict [where] means and ends sometimes contradict each other, and unintended consequences require changes in strategy and direction' (Emirbayer and Mische, 1998: 994).

When strategists project the future, they cannot know its outcome. Rather, to move towards those projections, it is necessary to draw on existing resources, which are likely to be those associated with iterative agency. For example, in Exhibit 1.1, the strategy director at RetailCo clarifies both the projective dimension 'We have said we want to be an international business' and also the iterative dimension, using typical strategy tools, such as P&L, DCF and market analysis, to analyse those projections. However, she emphasizes the oscillation between projected futures and iterative practices because of the uncertainty of the future and the recognition that these tools are only resources to be drawn upon in thinking and acting: 'If you try and get too detailed about the numbers when you don't really know very much about something, you might kill things too early' (see Exhibit 1.1). Practical evaluative agency is thus a way that managers bridge the gap between strategic thinking and acting and strategy formulation and implementation in practice. In both the introductory extract to this chapter and also Exhibit 1.1, we see that strategists actively bridge this gap between the doing of strategy and its future realization, formulating strategy as they implement, thinking as they act, and constructing and modifying strategy in the process. Practical-evaluative agency involves the skill and knowledge of the strategist in reconciling existing knowledge of the market and firm with its aspirations practically, through the performance of activity that involves multiple analyses, negotiations, truces, agreements, investments and commitments (Hendry, 2000). As Child (1997: 67) notes, strategic choice 'is mediated by a *consciously-sought adaptation to and manipulation* of existing internal structures and environmental conditions'. Such choice describes the essence of practical-evaluative agency, the ability of managers to consciously adapt, use and manipulate those resources that are to hand.

Of course, no discussion of agency is complete without a mention of power.

Agency is, after all, the exercise of power, in that 'to be an agent is to be able to deploy (chronically, in the flow of daily life) a range of causal powers, including that of influencing those deployed by others' (Giddens, 1984: 14). Power, as understood through a practice lens, is well encompassed by the notion of practical-evaluative agency. Typically, two interrelated types of power are posited: agent power and system power (Clegg, 1989). System power involves those structurally-based powers arising from existing social systems, such as routines, norms, roles and rules. Agents draw upon these existing structures to invest their actions with power. While all actors have access to the structurally-based powers of their system, asymmetries of information and access to resources give some actors greater ability to influence action in accordance with their own intentions. Actors, such as the top managers in the introductory extract, have power because of their hierarchical position, their access to the resources of power, such as committees and resource allocation mechanisms, and their ability to define for others what constitutes legitimate activity (Hardy, 1996; Whittington, 1992).

The point of legitimacy indicates that social systems also have power, developing continuity and influence that constrains or enables actors and favours the actions of some over others (Bourdieu, 1990). Therefore, power by an actor must 'be connected to issues of legitimacy, of the social organization of, and control over, resources' (Lave and Wenger, 1991: 37). Dominant actors derive power by drawing upon and reproducing the existing power resources in ways that consolidate the system and their power within it. In consolidating the system, they retain power over the prevalent meanings in a society (Lukes, 1974). Frameworks of meaning which favour a dominant social group are embedded within social systems to the extent that views that conflict with the routinized or habitually accepted power structures do not arise. Others act within these frameworks, even where the meanings constituted are not in their best interests, because they implicitly accept the social order of doing things. However, it is not appropriate to take an overly-deterministic view of either system power or to assume that power is primarily the property of one group of actors. Power is accessible by multiple actors (Pettigrew, 1973). Indeed, in the fragmented 'after modern' world which has fuelled the turn towards practice-based theorizing in strategy, the individuality of the actor is asserted, rather than compliance with a dominant framework of meanings (Lowendahl and Revang, 1998, 2004). For example, in the university context in this study, professional employees wield considerable power. Different actors' use of power may contest dominant frameworks of meaning, leading to change in the power structures as much as their reinforcement.

Power may thus be summarized in the following three points:

- Agency is connected to power. Power is the ability to draw upon the resources in the social system to lend meaning to action, which frequently reinforces that social system.
- While power is weighted towards dominant groups within a social system because of asymmetrical access to resources, it is not solely their province.

- Power is also accessible by other actors within a system. It is thus contested and open to change as well as reinforcement of the social system.

Power in practical-evaluative agency is the ability to draw upon existing resources of power, whilst also effecting change in power structures as part of the evolving and mutable nature of power constellations over time.

To conclude, practical-evaluative agency involves reflexive actors, able to understand their situated actions within the context of past actions and future aspirations and mediate between the two in ways that enable the stabilizing of existing practice as well as its becoming into future practice. To better understand practical-evaluative agency it is necessary to study both the iterative practices that strategists use to engage in activity as well as their intentions in using those practices to shape future activity. This does not mean that agency will result in the intended consequences. Rather, it is likely to generate the type of feedback that stimulates the exercise of further practical judgment. Any act of managerial agency is 'skilled improvised *in situ* coping' (Chia, 2004: 33): a performance at a point in time situated within a stream of such acts. Strategizing may therefore be defined as practical evaluative agency.

Quick Reference Guide 1.4: Strategizing and practical-evaluative agency

- Agency has three dimensions:

  - iterative, which involves selecting from existing templates for action;

  - projective, which involves imposing the strategist's will upon anticipated futures; and

  - practical-evaluative, which involves oscillation between the iterative and projective dimensions in order to 'get things done' within the uncertainties of any given situation.

- Strategizing is practical-evaluative agency: the skilled ability to use, adapt and manipulate those resources that are to hand to engage in shaping the activity of strategy over time.

AN ANALYTIC FRAMEWORK FOR STUDYING STRATEGIC ACTIVITY

In order to study strategy as situated activity, it is necessary to develop an analytic framework that can place top managers at the centre of the complex interactions involved in strategy as a situated, distributed and becoming activity. In this section, I propose an activity system framework as the basis for this analysis. This framework is informed by activity theory (Leontiev, 1978; Vygotsky, 1978), but it is not a faithful representation of activity theory in its entirety.[4] Rather, it draws upon activity theory principles of mediated interaction between actors and their social community in the production of shared activity. A brief introduction to the principles that underpin this framework is now provided.[5]

Shared activity is directed towards an outcome (Engeström et al., 2002). It is also distributed and collective, because different actors input their individual actions into the broader activity and outcomes of the activity system. Individual actors thus associate with a community in constructing outcome-oriented activity. Activity is a long-duration concept, a flow of activity over time. It is constructed by the interactions between actors and their community, and also contributes to those interactions. Activity is therefore posited as the essential level of analysis for studying the interactions between actors and their community. The activity level of analysis is helpful in developing an analytic framework because it separates the tightly interwoven interactions between actors and their community, directing attention to the activity that they produce as the level of analysis in which these interactions may be observed[6] (Blackler, 1993).

An activity system framework also proposes a unit of analysis – the practices of mediation involved in constructing activity. Mediation is a distinctive concept in activity theory that explains how individual actors, the community, and their shared endeavours are integrated in the pursuit of activity. Mediation occurs through structuring practices, such as role, division of labour, tools, and implicit and explicit rules that enable interaction between actors and their community (Engeström, 1993). Mediating practices are an important theme in the social theory of practice. As discussed above, practice theory aims to understand those structural and interpretative practices through which

Figure 1.1: An activity framework for studying strategy as practice

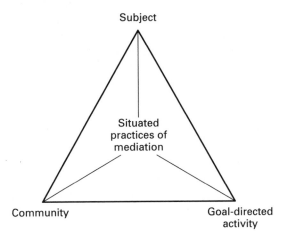

Subject

Situated
practices of
mediation

Community   Goal-directed
activity

distributed contributions are rendered mutually intelligible and collective. The activity system framework focuses upon these practices and their role in mediating the dynamics of interaction within the system.

Figure 1.1 illustrates the activity system framework to be used in this study. The organization is conceptualized as an activity system (Spender, 1995). It comprises three main elements of interaction: actors that are the subject of investigation, their community and the goal-directed activity in which they are engaged. Practices of mediation are situated in the context of the activity system and enable shifting dynamics of influence according to the issue at hand and the relative power of the different actors involved. Conceptualizing activity within an activity system enables us to generate an interdependent view, understanding how the actions in one part of the system affect actions in another part, with these interdependencies mediated by the practices. Each of these points in the framework is now briefly explained.

The subject is the individual or group of actors who form the focal point for the analysis. Any group of actors might be positioned as the subject, depending upon whether their contributions to activity are central to the research. Since strategy as practice highlights the practical-evaluative agency of top managers and their centrality in the complex and competing issues involved in constructing activity, top managers are the subject in this book. The actions of top managers are socially situated in relation to the community, comprising those distributed organizational actors with whom they interact in the pursuit of goal-directed activity. However, this community may have divergent goals and interests, emphasizing the distributed nature of activity and the complexity of the managerial task in shaping organizational activity towards common strategic goals. Goal-directed activity is organizational activity that is shaped through the interactions between actors and their community and directed at goals that are consequential for the organization as a whole.

Finally, the interactions between actors, their community and goal-directed activity are mediated by the practices available within the activity system. Such practices are situated, meaning that they reflect both the institutional properties of the wider society in which they are embedded and also the local interpretations of those practices as artefacts for action (Suchman, 1987; Whittington, 2002). Practices of mediation both lend meaning to and are imbued with meaning by the situation in which they are used. They enable interaction between the participants in the activity system and mediate shifting dynamics of influence in the construction of goal-directed activity.

This activity system framework furnishes the analytic requirements of an activity-based view of strategy as practice. It places top managers at the centre of the complex interactions involved in strategy as a situated, distributed and becoming activity. While this brief introduction may seem rudimentary, the framework will be further defined and located within the strategy literature in Chapter 2. It will then be empirically interpreted in Chapters 4 and 5, where it is used as an analytic tool to model the activity system dynamics involved in shaping strategy.

CONCLUSION: POINTS TO TAKE FORWARD

This chapter has developed the four core themes that, broadly, guide this activity-based view of strategy as practice. As these are broad themes of social practice, they are not analytic constructs. Rather, these four themes, which are summarized in their respective Quick Reference Guides, should be taken forward as sensitizing frameworks for thinking about the more empirically-grounded issues raised in the following chapters.

1 Strategy is situated activity. This means that it is embedded in context and socially constructed by actors in interaction with the situated features of that context.
2 The construction of situated activity is distributed amongst multiple actors with potentially divergent goals and interests. Distributed actions may be more or less aligned, depending upon the degree to which situated practices render them mutually intelligible and enable collective activity.
3 Such practices do not constitute a stable body of shared meanings, since activity is in a process of becoming, needing to be continuously constructed and reconstructed.
4 The situated, distributed and becoming nature of strategic activity is complex for top managers, who exercise practical-evaluative agency in both shaping and being shaped by that activity.

In practice, these four themes are complexly interwoven and difficult to disentangle analytically. An activity system framework has therefore been developed. This framework is conceptually underpinned by these four themes, but enables them to be operationalized empirically. The analytic uses of this framework will be further grounded in the strategy literature in Chapter 2 and empirically developed in Part II.

NOTES

1 For a more thorough discussion of social theories that underpin the practice turn, see Ortner (1984), Reckwitz (2002), and Schatzki et al. (2001), and for a discussion of their application to management theory, see Gherardi (2000), Jarzabkowski (2004a) and Whittington (2002).
2 For further discussion of the 'after modern' issues affecting the practice of strategy, see Cummings (2002), Ezzammel and Willmott (2004) and Lowendahl and Revang (1998).
3 For further discussion of organizations as distributed activity systems, see Blackler (1993, 1995), Orlikowski (2002), Spender (1996), Spender and Grinyer (1996) and Tsoukas (1996).
4 For the origins of activity theory, refer to its founder, Vygotsky (1978), and the development of the theory by his student (Leontiev, 1978). Additionally, Wertsch (1985) and Kozulin (1990) provide helpful interpretations of these works. For recent developments in activity theory, read Engeström (1987, 1993, et al., 1999) and Chaiklin et al. (1999). For application of activity theory in the management field, refer to Blackler (1993) and Blackler et al. (2000).

5 The activity system framework used in this book is a stripped down version of Engeström 's model. My framework is informed by activity theory and theories of situated action and distributed cognition (Nardi, 1996).

6 This focus is a distinctive point of activity theory, enabling analysis to go beyond the criticism leveled at many social theories of practice, that they conflate actor and society by associating them so closely that they are not analysable as separate entities (Blackler, 1993). For a more thorough discussion of the empirical problems of such conflation, see Archer (1995), Barley and Tolbert (1997), Barnes (2001) and Blackler et al. (2000).

2 LOCATING ACTIVITY IN THE STRATEGY LITERATURE

Key Points

- Level and unit of analysis
- Definitions of strategy and strategizing
- Grounding the activity system framework in the strategy literature
- Review of the strategy literature
- The three research questions

In this chapter the elements of the activity system framework proposed in the previous chapter are located within existing strategy theory. Each element is then defined in terms of its use in the empirical investigation in this book. In particular, three key terms are defined: strategy, procedural strategizing and interactive strategizing. These definitions are important for addressing the broad research agenda of the activity-based view, which was laid out in the introductory chapter: to explain how the strategizing practices of managers shape strategy as an organizational activity.

This chapter is in two main sections. The first section defines the key concepts in the activity system framework and explains how they are operationalized in this study. In this section the level of analysis, strategy, and the unit of analysis, strategizing, is defined. The second section takes the concepts and analytic constructs from the activity system framework and grounds them in a review of the strategy literature. From this review of the literature, three research questions are derived that will be addressed in the empirical study. First, the discussion of strategizing practices raises a question on the implications of procedural and interactive strategizing for shaping strategy. Second, analysis of five patterns of activity found in the strategy literature lead to the question: How are different activity system dynamics involved in shaping strategy as a pattern in a stream of goal-directed activity over time? Finally, the thought-provoking issue of multiple strategies is raised. While most strategy literature examines strategy as a singular construct, involving individual strategies, this study of universities involves multiple, potentially divergent strategies. Therefore, the third research question asks how patterns in multiple streams of goal-directed activity are shaped by association with each other.

ANALYTIC DEFINITIONS FOR AN ACTIVITY-BASED STUDY OF STRATEGY AS PRACTICE

In keeping with the activity-based view, strategy as goal-directed activity is the level of analysis for this study. It is, however, first necessary to define what is meant by the term strategy. This book builds upon and also goes deeper than Mintzberg's (1990) definition of strategy as 'a pattern in a stream of actions'. In his definition, actions are the outcomes of the organization over time. Specific strategic actions, such as entry into the television industry by the National Film Board of Canada (Mintzberg and McHugh, 1985), were the outcomes of activity – the realized strategy content. Such actions are therefore referred to as outcomes, in order to avoid confusion with the term 'action', which refers to instances of acting and is more clearly defined below. These outcomes arise from an organization's underlying stream of activity. Strategy is therefore defined as a pattern in a stream of goal-directed activity over time.

Goal-directedness acknowledges the future-oriented and consequential nature of strategy; it is purposive activity with goals that are consequential to the organization as a whole. However, this does not mean that activity will attain its goals. Rather, as different actors contribute to the stream of activity, new goals might arise to direct the activity. The level of analysis is thus a stream of goal-directed activity over time that is contributed to by actors at different levels of the organization, and which is consequential for the survival, reputation and profitability of the organization as a whole (see also Johnson et al., 2003; Spender, 1995).

This definition raises the question: What activity is strategic? Exhibit 2.1 provides a practical example of goal-directed activity. In this Exhibit, a top manager reflects on the iterative nature of activity construction that is neither strategic nor operational. It is a combination of the two, bringing strategic goals and operational actions into a stream of activity directed at developing some future set of conditions that are consequential for the organization. In putting strategy into practice, dichotomies of strategic and operational dissolve. Goal-directed activity is an organizational flow of both strategic and operational issues that 'get mixed and muddled up together'.

Exhibit 2.1: What activity is strategic?

Twiddling the modular programme

In this extract from an interview, a senior university manager explains changes being made in the teaching strategy to redeploy resources into other strategic activities. The specific change is to the modular teaching programme. This is a radical change that has been estab-lished strategically and its outcomes are consequential for the strategy of the organization as a whole. However, as an activity it iter-ates between the operational and the strategic level, in which strategic issues are operational and operational issues are strategic.

The modular programme is like trying to fly an aircraft; it will only fly if the computers are working. It is aerodynamically unsound unless you have constant adjustments going on. So there are a lot of good reasons for being cautious about the reform of this system. But if you want to produce part-time, proper part-time, because you want to open access . . . And you need to open access because you want to get people in from the region. And you want to do that because you want to build your regional strategy in a very short space of time. So actually twiddling this modular programme is absolutely essential for getting some of this stuff up here [at the strategic level] sorted out.

The worry is that we do some things down here [at the modular programme level] which actually have consequences up here [at the strategic level] that we didn't think about. It ought to be . . . in the old policy models that one learned about, you had the strategy and the policy and it filters down and levers clink and clunk and you do these bits at the bottom and there is the result. We all know that it is not actually like that, but nevertheless there is a residual worry that really maybe some of these things we are doing on our guts really, aren't necessarily congruent with the wider view. Except that I reassure myself with the thought that what we are trying to do on assessment, what we are trying to do on part-time, needs to be done anyway. It is in a sense creating the space which needs to be filled with the strat-egy. It is not in itself a set of strategies; it is the clink and clunk that you need to be attuned to. So people will talk about the strategy as being really twiddling the modular programme and tweaking this and that, or whatever. They won't necessarily be meaning in terms that you might understand by strategy at a much more macro directional level. They all get mixed and muddled up together.

Activity is too broad a level of analysis to adequately define the parameters of an empirical study. It is also necessary to identify a unit of analysis. An activity-based view places managers at the centre of the complex interactions that comprise activity (Johnson et al., 2003). Therefore, this study examines activity through the actions of top managers. Their terms of reference and the tools that they use to shape the stream of activity are central to this study. However, this does not imply a top-down perspective on strategy. Rather, in keeping with the practical-evaluative view of managerial agency developed in Chapter 1, this study analyses the interplay between top managers and those strategizing practices through which they endeavour to exercise agency over the shaping of strategy. Strategizing practices are discussed in greater detail later in this chapter. They refer to the institutionalized rules of strategy formation and their organizationally situated realization as administrative practices and social norms that mediate the shaping of strategy. This book examines how top managers use and modify such practices to shape activity and how their agency is in turn shaped by the practices available to them. Individual instances of interplay between top managers and these practices are defined as 'actions', while their ongoing interplay in the construction of strategy is 'strategizing' – a flow of practical-evaluative agency that shapes and is shaped by activity over time. Strategizing is thus the unit of analysis for this study.

These definitions and concepts will be applied in the empirical study using the activity system framework developed in the previous chapter. Figure 2.1 illustrates the activity framework as it applies to the analytic levels and constructs in this study, showing how they relate to each other. The activity system represented by this framework is the organization as a whole. Strategy is the stream of goal-directed activity arising from the activity system. Conceptualizing strategy within an activity system provides an interdependent view, understanding how the actions in one part of the system affect actions in another part, with these interdependencies mediated by the strategizing practices. This study aims to explain how the dynamics of the activity system shape strategy over time. These dynamics are broken down for analysis in the following way:

1 The subject of interest in this study is top managers.
2 Due to the distributed nature of activity, top managers need to interact with the organizational community, attempting to shape the way these 'others' contribute to the strategy of the organization.
3 Strategizing practices act as mediators that constrain and enable the interactions between top managers and their organizational community (arrow A in Figure 2.1). They also mediate the community's contribution and resistance to activity (arrow B), and provide vehicles for top managers to shape activity, even as they are shaped by it (arrow C).
4 The interplay between top managers and these practices is 'strategizing' – the unit of analysis for this study. The internal arrows indicate how different strategizing practices, taken together, mediate interaction between top managers, the community and goal-directed activity.
5 The dynamics of the activity system generates outcomes, namely the realized strategy content of the organization.

The value of this activity system framework is that it links the various components involved in shaping strategy over time. Using this framework, the dynamics of shaping strategy are modelled in the empirical chapters, showing how different strategizing practices confer influence to top managers, the community or the activity, under different circumstances. The framework thus draws together the analytic constructs used in this study, each of which is now located within the relevant literature.

Figure 2.1: An activity theory framework for strategy as practice

Subject:
Top managers

A: Practices constrain and enable interaction with the other about activity

C: Shape and are shaped by activity through practices

Strategizing
practices:
Institutionalized
rules and localized
practices

Outcomes:
Realized
strategy
content

Organizational   **B**: Contributes to and resists   Strategy:
community   activity through practices   Goal-directed
activity

Quick Reference Guide 2.1: Definitions of strategy and strategizing

- Strategy is a pattern in a stream of goal-directed activity over time.

- This activity generates outcomes that are the realized strategy content of an organization.

- Strategizing practices are the institutionalized rules of strategy formation and their locally situated realization as administrative practices and social norms.

- Incidents of interplay between top managers and these practices are 'actions'.

- 'Strategizing' is the ongoing interplay between top managers and the strategizing practices in shaping strategy over time.

LOCATING THE ACTIVITY FRAMEWORK IN THE STRATEGY LITERATURE

This section expands upon the relationships in Figure 2.1 by locating the dynamics of the activity system within the strategy literature and using this literature review to develop the three research questions. First, the relationship between top managers and their organizational community is examined.

Second, the institutionalized rules and localized practices that mediate this relationship and their association with activity are explained. Third, in order to explain how the dynamics of interaction shape activity, five patterns of activity found in the existing strategy literature are discussed:

- emergent activity;
- inertial activity;
- changing activity;
- realized activity; and
- unresolved activity.

This grounding within the strategy literature serves to define and interpret the activity framework and to derive the three key research questions that guide the empirical study in Part II.

SUBJECT: TOP MANAGERS

The actors at the centre of this study of strategy are top managers. They are referred to as an aggregate group, the top team, since this study does not look at the internal interactions between top managers but how they, as a group, interact with the organization and attempt to shape strategy (Denis et al., 2001; Pettigrew and Whipp, 1991). Of course, it would be possible to put, for example, a group of middle managers at the centre of a study, or a single individual, such as the CEO or the finance director, if we wished to understand how those practitioners interact with their community in the pursuit of strategic activity. However, this book specifically addresses the problem identified in Chapter 1, of practical-evaluative agency in the face of situated and distributed activity, by placing top managers at the centre of the complex interactions involved in the construction of strategy.

An activity-based view does not privilege the role of top managers. Undoubtedly, top managers are responsible for the outcomes of activity (Child, 1997; Pettigrew, 1992). However, due to the distributed nature of activity, top management must take into account the potentially disparate representations and divergent interests of other actors (Blackler et al., 2000; Floyd and Lane, 2000). Top managers' ability to interact with these others in the construction of collective activity is mediated by the situated practices of strategy-making. In this process, managerial agency both to influence others and also to shape activity is constrained and enabled by these practices. The ability to draw upon and modify these practices in the unfolding dynamics of activity construction is strategizing, the unit of analysis for this study. This literature review, therefore, does not deal with top managers per se, but examines the strategizing implications of their interactions within the activity system.

THE ORGANIZATIONAL COMMUNITY

Defining the community helps to situate an activity system in terms of the most relevant 'others' with whom top managers interact in their shaping of activity. The concept of community takes into account that all top manager contributions to activity are social, meaning that they are aware of others with whom they will need to interact in constructing activity (Wenger, 1998). For example, in the introductory extract from Chapter 1, top managers were acutely aware of the possible reactions of the community as they proposed changes to the research strategy. This community and its potential reactions thus provide important relational parameters for top managers' actions. The organizational community comprises heads of divisions or business units and lower level actors, such as middle and operating managers and other employees. It is not a uniform community but consists of distributed groups of actors who might have divergent interests about organizational goals and activity. The more distributed and potentially divergent the community, the greater the challenge for top managers to interact with them about any form of collective goal-directed activity.

Typical characteristics of particular communities may influence the nature of their relationship with top managers about activity. For example, in knowledge working organizations, such as accounting or law firms, or in the public sector, such as universities or hospitals, the community is comprised largely of professionals. Some specific features of professional work are therefore likely to be relevant, such as the autonomy and professional ties associated with work that is occupation rather than firm-specific (Denis et al., 1996; Hinings and Leblebici, 2003; Lowendahl, 1997). Autonomous knowledge workers are likely to have divergent interests and loyalties that are not necessarily directed towards a common strategic goal. This autonomy increases the distributed and potentially fragmented nature of activity. However, the preservation of autonomy is important because it is associated with the quality of work produced by professionals (Scott, 1965). This problem is compounded by the fact that the knowledge and capabilities of professional staff are not easily organized by formalization of structure (Podsakoff et al., 1986). Rather, they are mediated by mutual adjustments in and negotiations about the various practices available for managing within a given context. Top managers therefore have negotiated power and influence, attained by sensitivity to context (Denis et al., 1996, 2001; Strauss, 1978). By contrast, in a typical manufacturing firm, where features of work are low autonomy, task standardization and efficiency of production, top managers would be expected to have more routinized and directive formal procedures for interacting with their organizational community (Mintzberg, 1979). Top managers are thus likely to find that the problems of shaping distributed activity towards collective goals are exacerbated in professional organizations, such as the universities that form the empirical basis of this book.

The relationship between top managers and their community about strategy may be thought of in terms of shaping commitment and support for collective activity. It is necessary for top management to gain the support of the internal constituencies within their organization in order to shape collective activity (Denis et al., 2001). This is not a one-way process from top managers to the community. Rather, it involves commitment by organizational members to a stream of activity, and responsibility for its performance (Stone and Brush, 1996). To attain this commitment, the activity must be legitimate to the community; they must perceive it as important for the organization and for themselves. Additionally, the practices for shaping activity, such as resource allocation or control mechanisms, must be perceived as legitimate; they must perceive the practices as acceptable to their values. This is the most complete form of interaction between top managers and the community, in which there is agreement about the activity and also the way to perform it. More partial forms might involve the community legitimating a particular activity, but not the practices used to shape it. For example, professionals might resist formal control over activity (Alvesson and Sveningsson, 2003). Alternately, where top managers fail to accommodate the divergent interests of other actors, the legitimacy of the activity may be lessened, resulting in low organizational commitment. Top managers' skill in manipulating the dynamics of the activity system will therefore be important in generating commitment to strategy. Top managers must use the strategizing practices to influence how others perceive and contribute to strategy. These dynamics will be probed in greater detail in the five patterns of activity discussed below and will contribute to one of the research questions.

Quick Reference Guide 2.2: Interacting with the community

- The community comprises distributed actors from all levels of the organization.

- Top managers have to interact with these actors in shaping strategy.

- The community in professional organizations is typically more distributed and divergent in its interests than other contexts, posing particular problems for top managers in generating commitment to strategy.

- Commitment to strategy involves the community accepting both the legitimacy of the strategy – is it the right thing for the organization to do? – and also the practices for attaining the strategy – these practices are acceptable to 'my' professional values.

- Top managers' skills in strategizing are important in gaining this commitment.

STRATEGIZING PRACTICES

In order to analyse the dynamics of the activity system, it is necessary to understand those strategizing practices available to top managers to influence commitment to strategy. These practices are the institutionalized rules of strategy formation and their locally situated realization as the administrative practices and social norms involved in doing strategy within organizations. Their role in shaping activity is central, but can be overlooked because they are hidden in the everyday tasks that constitute a stream of activity. It is, however, these practices that provide the templates for acting, the resources for agency and the shared practices through which the dynamics of the activity system are played out. They are central to the mediation of activity, through both their innate properties and also the uses to which skilled actors put them. The relationship between these practices and top managers in shaping activity is 'strategizing' – the unit of analysis for this study. This section locates the institutionalized rules and localized practices for doing strategy in the existing strategy literature in order to flesh out their role in the dynamics of strategizing.

INSTITUTIONALIZED RULES: RATIONAL STRATEGY PROCESSES

Rules are the institutionalized norms, regulations and conventions that provide guidelines for managing strategy. In this book they are defined as those old staples, direction setting, resource allocation and monitoring and control, which are three strategy processes[1] that hierarchically coordinate the formulation and implementation of strategy. That is, a firm formulates a strategic direction and then implements it by allocating resources to the business units, and monitoring and controlling their performance to ensure consistency between formulation and implementation. In rational theories of strategic planning and design, these processes should be aligned for coherent strategic action (Ansoff, 1965, 1991). The managerial task is thus to oversee their alignment (Garvin, 1998).

The conventions of direction setting, resource allocation and monitoring and control reinforce perceptions about strategy making as a dichotomous process of strategy formulation and implementation. This linear and separate process has, however, been discredited from a number of angles over the past 25 years. For example:

- The action school has shown us that far from intentional setting of directions, strategies may emerge (Mintzberg and Waters, 1985) and actions may lead directions (Brunsson, 1982), while, from an interpretative perspective, direction setting actually involves retrospective sensemaking on prior actions (Weick, 1995).
- Resource allocation has been shown to lead the strategic decision process as much as to support pre-established directions (Bower, 1970; Burgelman, 1996).

- Monitoring and control remains problematic in strategic management. Multi-business firms struggle with the problem of financial or strategic controls, each of which creates different tensions between pursuing a corporate strategy or a business unit strategy (Campbell et al., 1995). Attempts to reinforce desired strategic behaviour at more micro levels are also problematic, tending to reward individualism rather than collective strategic activity despite complex strategic human resource systems and performance-related pay (Schuler and Jackson, 1987).

Given that direction setting, resource allocation and monitoring and control processes have been problematized by many authors, why do they persist as the rules that guide strategic activity? Well, for a start, despite derision and falsification of their practice, strategic management research has not given us any other rules to guide strategy. For example, we do not have rules for strategic emergence. Even Eisenhardt and Sull's (2001) 'simple rules' for conducting strategy in fast-moving environments are actually rules of monitoring and control and resource allocation to support organizational directions.[2] Second, strategy textbooks and case studies persist in reflecting these rational rules for strategy with their emphasis on strategic analysis, intentional choice and implementation (Hendry, 2000). Third, financial institutions and investors expect firms to be compliant with these rules (Whittington et al., 2003). In keeping with these expectations, institutionalized rules appeal to managers' needs for external legitimacy in making and articulating strategy. For example, most firms have a documented strategic direction, a resource allocation process and some systems for monitoring and control. The enactment of these rules provides evidence that the firm has legitimate strategy-making procedures, even if these are largely symbolic (DiMaggio and Powell, 1983). Therefore, while not providing a detailed blueprint, direction setting, resource allocation and monitoring and control are indeed the conventional processes, or 'rules' that guide strategy making. They reflect the institutionalized properties of rules, those norms or conventions that shape the broad parameters of practice. The variations that occur in applying these rules arise from the situated ways they are realized in the local practice of organizations.

Let us briefly examine that strategy literature on direction setting, resource allocation and monitoring and control which is pertinent to this book. Direction setting is perhaps the biggest conundrum in strategizing once we move beyond rational theories of strategy formulation. If directions are not established from the top of an organization through a rational planning procedure, what is top management's influence? Two main views apply:

- A strong body of empirical work dealing with this problem identifies top management's role in direction setting as an interpretative one: sensemaking about the environment and the organization, followed by a process of sensegiving to the organization (Gioia and Chittipedi, 1991). More recent studies in this vein suggest that the process of sensegiving is less top-down than reciprocal, with middle level managers purposively involved in interpreting strategic directions (Achtenhagen et al., 2003). In this vein, goal-directed activity is mediated through shared interpretative frameworks.

- There are studies suggesting that the top manager's role is more structural, using administrative practices to establish a structural context that determines existing strategy and exercises discretion over adopting strategies initiated at lower levels (Bower, 1970; Burgelman, 1996; Noda and Bower, 1996). The administrative practices, such as resource allocation, act as selection mechanisms for determining desirable strategies. From this perspective, goal-directed activity is mediated by organizationally-shared administrative practices.

The first of these perspectives conceptualizes direction setting as an interpretative process, while the second conceptualizes it as a structural process. As both of these views provide for mediated interaction between top managers and distributed actors, they are applicable from a practice perspective, which privileges neither interpretative nor structural mechanisms for constructing activity (Reckwitz, 2002). That is, in practice, goal-directed activity might arise from common interpretative frameworks or from shared administrative practices, or some combination of the two according to the specifics of the situation. For the purposes of this study, direction setting involves the shaping of goal-directed activity between top managers and distributed actors. Top managers have greater influence over shaping activity because asymmetries of power and information give them greater authority over resources for framing interpretations as well as access to instruments of structural control. However, top managers' influence is not hegemonic but fluid, because activity is shaped through distributed interactions. Direction setting is thus not a one-off, static occurrence, but is dynamic in nature, involving the shaping of goal-directed activity over time, during which different actors may have greater or lesser influence on the goals that orient the activity.

Resource allocation in this book refers to the allocation of physical, financial and human resources. Ideally, these resources are allocated according to areas of strategic priority, while resources are withheld in areas intended for strategic exit. However, as other studies have shown, resource allocation is composed of routinized and habitual practices, primarily formal but also social, which might dictate strategic priorities (Bower, 1970; Burgelman, 1983). For example, where resources are customarily allocated to an operating routine, such as the production of a line of products, the sunk costs of that activity continue to attract resources even when the organization attempts to move into other products (Miller and Friesen, 1984). Redeployment of resources to exit one activity and engage in another incurs both physical and behavioural costs that may be beyond the capacity of managers (Cyert and March, 1963). Thus operating routines may shape an organization's strategy via the resource allocation mechanisms. Resource allocation, therefore, does not reflect linear processes between strategic priorities and operational activity, because of the way it is realized in practice.

No consideration of resource allocation can be devoid of power relationships, since the allocation of resources is essentially the exercise of power

(Clegg, 1989; Giddens, 1984; Hardy, 1996). An examination of the practices for resource allocation in an organization highlight the power relationships between the top team, distributed actors and their influence over particular activities. For example, where there are multiple activities, some will attract greater resources than others, indicating either the power of the activity or the power of those who wish to influence the activity.

Monitoring and control is intended to monitor organizational performance towards pre-articulated goals and reinforce desired action through sanction and reward. Simons (1991) provides a four-level classificatory system of monitoring and control systems, belief systems, boundary systems, diagnostic systems and interactive systems. Belief systems have a normative role, communicating and defining those values and actions that are legitimate within the organization. Boundary systems are explicit codes of conduct and operating directives that clarify the parameters for strategic action. Diagnostic control systems are typically performance measurement systems that provide feedback on progress towards articulated goals. These belief, boundary and diagnostic control systems may become routinized and habitual, focusing organizational attention on the actions that they measure and legitimate rather than on the purposive pursuit of activity. However, formal control systems may also be made interactive through face-to-face interaction between the top team and other actors, so strengthening their dynamic association with activity (Simons, 1991, 1994). Control systems, like resource allocation mechanisms, are also involved, not only in implementing strategy, but also shaping its directions. Given the blurred distinctions between direction setting, resource allocation and monitoring and control in practice, we need to go beyond their theoretical distinctions and analyse the social dynamics by which they privilege the top team, other actors, or a particular activity in any given context.

LOCALIZED PRACTICES: PROCEDURAL AND INTERACTIVE STRATEGIZING

The above discussion of direction setting, resource allocation and monitoring and control illustrates that the conventions of strategy formulation and implementation breakdown in practice (Mintzberg, 1978). In order to understand the varied effects of such rules in practice, it is necessary to go inside them and analyse the firm-specific micro practices of which they are composed (Johnson et al., 2003). As illustrated in Figure 2.1, these practices play a key role in mediating the dynamics of the activity system. Drawing upon these practices, top managers interact with their community in an effort to shape strategy. However, as the diagram indicates, such practices are not neutral servants of the activity system or the user. Rather, they have localized, historically situated meanings and innate properties that may constrain or enable interaction, shape managerial agency and provide the community with vehicles to resist as much as contribute to activity. By studying the uses of those seemingly mundane practices that comprise much of the work of strategizing, such as budget allocations, committee meetings, trend analyses, forecasts, plans, performance measures and personal interactions, we begin to understand the localized dynamics of shaping strategy within an activity system. Their centrality thus cannot be ignored. However, they are not of interest in isolation. Rather, the dynamics of strategizing are captured by studying the relationship between these practices and those who use them to shape activity. This section locates the practices that mediate activity within the strategy literature and develops two key terms, 'procedural strategizing' and 'interactive strategizing', to explain two predominant ways that such practices might be used.

Specific practices are now discussed as procedural or interactive, which are two terms arising from the empirical study to explain those practices that top managers identified as important for interacting with others in shaping strategy.[3] Procedural strategizing deals with the use of formal administrative practices, such as plans, budgets and trend analyses and their associated committees and procedures, through which strategy is coordinated, documented and formally embedded within an organization. Interactive strategizing involves direct, purposive, face-to-face interactions between top managers and other actors. These interactions enable top managers to reinforce their own interpretations of activities as well as to negotiate these interpretations with others. These empirically grounded terms are now related to the strategy literature on administrative procedures and social interaction.

LOCATING AND DEFINING PROCEDURAL STRATEGIZING

Due to increasing awareness of the unplanned and emergent nature of strategy, there is a tendency to sideline formal practices as 'rational' and hence not reflective of practice (Hendry, 2000). Yet formal is important, since strategy is littered with formal practices, such as plans, budget cycles and committees, which serve as important and not necessarily rational tools for the conduct of strategic activity (Jarzabkowski, 2003; Whittington, 2003). Formal practices involve the various administrative practices and systems that are used to organize much of the work of strategy. For example, strategic plans and their associated budget cycles are annual procedures in most organizations. They involve other formal practices that bring together the necessary people to do the work of strategy, such as planning meetings and committees. At these meetings, yet more formal administrative practices are generated, such as quarterly reviews, trend analyses, forecasts and performance targets. These formal practices provide the externally legitimate, traceable realizations of the above institutionalized rules of strategy making. For example, generating documents that articulate strategic directions or generating forecasts and targets that measure and monitor internal performance. Use of these administrative practices to shape strategy is termed 'procedural strategizing'. An example of procedural strategizing at Intel is provided in Exhibit 2.2.

Exhibit 2.2: Procedural strategizing at Intel*

This example shows how administrative practices enable a strategy to persist, as well as how others can use these practices to resist and change a dominant strategy.

Throughout the 1970s, Intel's growth and profitability came from being one of the first companies to successfully manufacture and market Dynamic Random Access Memory (DRAMs). Strategic goals were therefore strongly focused upon Intel as a memory chip company. However, in the early 1980s Intel was losing market share in the DRAM business to fierce price-based competition from Japanese manufacturers. The truth was, Intel was no longer a leading memory chip company. However, DRAM remained the dominant strategy in the minds of top managers, particularly COO Andy Grove. As a result, DRAM continued to attract resources and investment, particularly in R&D, where DRAM commanded a third of the total R&D budget. Resource allocation practices thus propped up the declining activity until, in the years 1985–86, Intel had lost $255 million in the memory chip market and made the decision to exit the DRAM business.

When Intel exited from the memory chip market, top managers realized that despite the prevailing mythology that Intel was a memory chip company, middle managers had for some time been using the resource allocation practices to direct resources towards the more profitable microprocessor industry. Intel operated on a 'maximize margin-per-wafer' rule of allocating manufacturing capacity to products, meaning that more profitable products should be allocated greater manufacturing resources. While DRAM was able to bump more profitable products off the production line because of its status as the key strategy of the company, increasingly this meant sacrificing margin. As a result, during 1983–84 middle managers were able to use the practices for allocating manufacturing resources to divert capacity towards the more profitable microprocessor market. While the strategy of Intel remained the DRAM business, middle managers used the administrative practices increasingly to focus business unit activity on microprocessors. As Grove noted, top managers believed 'our strategic rhetoric, but those on the front lines could see that we had to retreat from memory chips.' Top managers maintained their commitment to the DRAM strategy through the resource allocation practices, while lower-level managers progressively used the resource allocation practices to divert activity away from this strategy.

*The Intel exhibit is developed from published research articles and case material authored by: Bartlett and Ghoshal, 1994; Burgelman, 1991, 1996; Cogan and Burgelman, 1990.

There are different perspectives on the purposes that procedural strategizing serves. The Bower-Burgelman vein of strategy process research has focused upon the interplay between top managers and the structural context (Bower, 1970; Burgelman, 1983, 1996; Noda and Bower, 1996). Structural context is defined as those administrative practices through which planning, resource allocation and monitoring and control occur, and which enable top managers to establish and maintain a link between corporate strategy and the actions of middle and operational level managers. Structural context enables top managers to determine the existing strategy and select from strategic initiatives arising from lower-level managers. It thus serves primarily as a selection and control mechanism for top managers to influence other actors' contributions to the strategy of the organization (Lovas and Ghoshal, 2000). However, strategy process research has surfaced an interesting paradox in the use of administrative practices. Top managers' influence over the way others contribute to activity lies in their control over the structural context but, paradoxically, once they embed activity in an administrative procedure, such as a resource allocation mechanism, they find it hard to alter or shape that activity. This is because administrative practices operate as selection and control mechanisms that, once established, require little active top management attention (Simons, 1991). Their role in shaping strategy is taken for granted in the structural context of the organization. As shown in Exhibit 2.2, administrative practices move from being a vehicle for influencing others' contributions to activity, to being the driver of that activity (Burgelman, 1991). The use of administrative practices is thus prone to inertia, simplifying into procedural routines that, as indicated in Figure 2.1, may shape the agency of top managers as much as enabling top managers to exercise agency.

These inertial and reciprocal shaping tendencies of formal administrative practices indicate that they are not the neutral 'servants' of top managers. Rather, they are historically situated in the organization. They become routinized, carrying strategic knowledge and patterns of acting across levels of the firm over time (Nelson and Winter, 1982). They thus convey a 'procedural memory' (Cohen and Bacdayan, 1994) of how to act, which top managers can draw upon as localized templates for shaping activity, indicating iterative forms of agency. This may not always be associated with the negative consequences of inertia found in the Bower-Burgelman studies. Indeed, in Noda and Bower's (1996) comparison of two telecommunications companies, formal administrative practices had an inertial effect in only one. Thus, as will be discussed in the empirical chapters, situation and use appear to be relevant indicators of when formal administrative practices are associated with iterative agency and negative consequences, such as inertia, and when these practices have more positive implications for shaping strategy.

Despite the somewhat deterministic views of routinized administrative practices implied in the above, organizational routines are socially enacted, mutable and subject to change (Feldman, 2000). An alternative view of such practices is thus as a means of enabling distributed actors to interact with each other sufficiently such that they can act collectively (Feldman and Rafaeli, 2002). Given the potentially conflicting interests of distributed actors, formal administrative practices and systems provide top managers with a vehicle for establishing a truce between the interests of different actors (Blackler, 1993; Jarzabkowski, 2003; Spender and Grinyer, 1996). Skilled strategists may use these practices to mediate activity, providing vehicles to coordinate the various fragmented perspectives of distributed actors.

This does not, however, imply that administrative practices are neutral, simply mediating interaction without effects of their own. They are not neutral on two grounds. First, as the Intel example shows, historical embedding of activity within formal administrative practices enables its persistence. Second, there is unequal access to formal practices. Top managers are more likely to attend the meetings, control the agendas and commission the figures with which formal practices deal. Ostensibly, therefore, they serve the purposes of top management. Frequently that is the case; formal administrative practices tend to accord more power over strategy to the top team than to other actors (Child, 1997; Hardy, 1996; Hickson et al., 1986). However, that power is far from blanket hegemony. Multiple actors have access to the formal administrative practices and can use them to influence activity, depending upon their particular claims upon or contributions to strategy (Pettigrew, 1973). For example, at Intel the eventual move out of memory chips arose from middle managers' use of the 'maximize margin-per-wafer' practice of resource allocation to shape activity towards the increasingly profitable microprocessor market (Exhibit 2.2). Administrative practices are thus vehicles for contested contributions that may change the course of activity as much as they are mechanisms of control or vehicles for truce.

KEY CHARACTERISTICS OF PROCEDURAL STRATEGIZING

In this study the use of formal administrative practices by top managers in order to shape strategy is termed 'procedural strategizing'. The above discussion has outlined three key characteristics of formal administrative practices in mediating activity:

- Administrative practices operate as selection and control mechanisms for shaping activity, with low managerial attention once they are established.
- They are historically situated templates that carry system knowledge about acting. They are thus important resources for iterative forms of agency, but may also be associated with negative consequences such as inertia.
- Top-down control and inertia are not inevitable effects of the mediating properties of administrative practices, as they may also be used by distributed actors to counteract control or to shape activity in their own interests.

Formal administrative practices may be seen as a subset of practices involved in strategizing. Specifically, they are involved in procedural strategizing, which under most circumstances can be carried out as an iterative process requiring little active attention from top managers (Cohen and Bacdayan, 1994; Simons, 1991).

LOCATING AND DEFINING INTERACTIVE STRATEGIZING

Social interactions take place around and even within the formal practices, such as planning meetings. These interactions incorporate social, political and behavioural dimensions of strategizing, such as the way people think, their forms of speech, their group interactions, and their use of the norms and symbols of the wider organizational culture to enact their own interests. While social and frequently tacit in use, such interactions have profound influences on strategy. For example, strategists' cognitive maps affect the strategic choices they make (Barr et al., 1992; Porac and Thomas, 1990). At the decision-making level, strategists' skilled use of language can influence which strategies are seen as legitimate and which are displaced (Samra-Fredericks, 2003). At the wider organizational level, linguistic, cultural and symbolic resources serve as important social media for constructing strategic change across different levels of the firm (Heracleous and Barrett, 2001; Johnson, 1987). Social interactions thus cover a diverse and interwoven range of behaviours. For example, a speech act is associated with a mental schema and, in use, may well draw upon cultural resources for interaction. The full range of such interactions is beyond the scope of this book. This book focuses upon a particular subset of social interactions that top managers in the empirical study identified as important for shaping activity: purposive face-to-face interactions between top managers and others actors about strategy. This phenomenon is termed 'interactive strategizing' (Achtenhagen et al., 2003). Interactive strategizing is now located within the strategy and organization literature and its various purposes are explained. An example of interactive strategizing at a Swedish bank, Östgöta Enskilda Bank (ÖEB), is provided in Exhibit 2.3.

Interaction as a form of mediation between distributed actors is theoretically informed by the notion of double interacts, those interacts and responses by which individuals contribute and react to collective activity (Weick, 1979; Weick and Roberts, 1993). Such interacts are situated, tending to follow locally established social norms. Social norms for face-to-face interaction, like other norms, are shared practices built upon mutual expectations between top managers and the community about the conduct of such interactions. As norms, they are relatively stable, providing patterns that guide the general character of interactions. However, norms are also actively constructed and reconstructed in every interaction (Bettenhausen and Murnighan, 1985). In particular, norms for face-to-face interaction need to be considered as double interacts, in which each interact is dynamic and may potentially be reconstructed according to the response received (Weick, 1979). Face-to-face interaction provides an opportunity for negotiation, communication and persuasion on both sides. It may mediate the influence of lower-level managers and their strategic agendas (Dutton et al., 2001) or those of top managers (Simons, 1991; 1994), depending upon their skill in face-to-face interaction. While norms of interaction exhibit stability in their conduct, the meanings they impart are not durable. Rather, they facilitate the interests of whichever party is more influential in negotiating or renegotiating meanings in any given interaction (Strauss, 1978). This active character of social norms of face-to-face interaction highlights their central role in mediating the ongoing shaping of activity between the top team and distributed actors.

Exhibit 2.3: Interactive strategizing at Östgöta Enskilda Bank*

This example shows the role of interactive strategizing in generating a collective strategy for a network of local banks.

Östgöta Enskilda Bank (ÖEB) was a medium-sized Swedish bank that, during the 1990s, developed a strategy of geographical expansion through a network of provincial local banks that would focus upon locally customized service. Each bank was to operate as a small, independent bank that offered personal service. Top management's challenge was to focus the local banks on the corporate strategy at the same time as enabling them to develop a local identity and approach: 'We want the customer to feel that all the decision power is in the local bank, even if the decision process on larger credits is standardized and centralized' (Local bank manager).

Top management put in place a centralized framework of standardized controls for issues such as risk-taking and credit decisions. While these provided procedural guidelines, the real key to the success of managing the strategy lay in top manager's use of interactive strategizing. Top managers engaged in formal and informal dialogues with local bank managers, including regular face-to-face meetings. These interactions gave top managers power to frame the strategic goals of the organization, for example by continuously emphasizing the ÖEB vision of a network of small banks operating locally. However, in the process of developing common goals, interactions comprised a two-way process. Top managers had a vision of the goals but needed to adapt these to the localized activity through which the goals could be realized. Strategic goals and appropriate local activity were progressively interpreted and reinterpreted through the dialogues with local bank managers: 'No manager from the centre came down to tell us how to do it. . . . They were very supportive and interested, but they let us do things based on our own thinking' (Local bank manager).

While top managers had greater power to frame the goals, lower-level managers had a strong input into the activity aimed at those goals, gradually developing a set of shared meanings about ÖEB as a network of largely independent local banks with common views on personalized customer service, profitability, risk-taking and credit decisions. Interactive strategizing gave top managers and their community the ability to shape activity in common directions: 'If we are successful in these regards, then we [at the centre] can allow almost any [degree of] local influence and freedom' (CEO).

*This example is developed from 'Leadership: the role of interactive strategizing' by Achtenhagen et al. (2003: 49–71).

On the one hand, face-to-face interaction is reciprocal and accords power to each party. However, as Exhibit 2.3 shows, this interaction features the power and information asymmetries that favour top managers' ability to frame goals and shape activity according to their own views (Achtenhagen et al., 2003; Ranson et al., 1980). This is because much top management communication within the organization is through administrative procedures that may be experienced by distributed actors in largely remote, formalized and controlling or coordinating ways. Face-to-face interaction is thus a particularly powerful social resource that top managers can use to focus organizational attention upon their own interpretations of strategy (Simons, 1991, 1994). Through face-to-face interaction top managers can directly communicate their own frameworks of meaning about activity in order to shape others' behaviour. Interactive strategizing is thus an example of deeply sedimented forms of power and control, in which a powerful group exercise their dominance by generating the frameworks of meaning in which others will act. That is, the dominant group interprets which activities are legitimate within a system, so that resistance by others does not occur because they have accepted the legitimacies and hence the norms of behaviour inherent in that system. It is a particularly powerful form of control because others control themselves in the interests of a system to which they have subscribed (Clegg, 1989; Lukes, 1974). This aspect of interactive strategizing may be conveyed in the quote from the CEO at ÖEB: 'If we are successful in these regards, then we [at the centre] can allow almost any [degree of] local influence and freedom.' As long as lower-level managers have accepted the meanings conveyed by the centre, they will conduct their localized activities in ways that are consistent with those meanings. Interactive strategizing may thus be a means of generating normative control over others through the development of a dominant set of meanings.

However, this aspect of interactive strategizing both assumes that meanings are durable and emphasizes the power of managers in framing those meanings. It tends to ignore the underlying principle of double interacts and the distributed, potentially divergent and becoming nature of activity. Interactive strategizing is premised on the distributed nature of activity and the need to align the divergent interests of the community around some common frameworks of meaning. From the perspective of double interacts, any interaction has the potential for renegotiation of meaning between parties (Strauss, 1978; Weick, 1979). Because activity is continuously being reconstructed over time by a number of distributed actors with potentially divergent interests, shared meanings are not durable but are, at best, a temporary state needing to be continuously reconstructed (Garfinkel, 1967; Neilsen and Rao, 1987; Suchman, 1987). Top managers must, therefore, work consistently at maintaining the agency afforded by interactive strategizing. For example, the process of developing the local bank strategy at ÖEB occurred through multiple interactions over time, with top managers having the greater power in framing the strategy, but lower-level managers also participating in shaping that strategy through the ongoing interactions (Achtenhagen et al., 2003). Interactive strategizing thus provides an enriched view of agency as one of interaction within a socially dynamic process of strategy construction and reconstruction (Emirbayer and Mische, 1998; Giddens, 1984).

KEY CHARACTERISTICS OF INTERACTIVE STRATEGIZING

Interactive strategizing is purposive face-to-face interaction between top managers and other members of the organizational community about strategy. Interactive strategizing has three interrelated characteristics that are relevant in mediating activity:

- Interactive strategizing has a normative character and thus may exhibit stability in patterns of interaction between top managers and their community. However, as social norms are not immutable, the meanings derived from such interaction may be renegotiated within the process of interacting.
- Interactive strategizing favours top managers' agency in shaping activity because it is an interpretative practice that tends to legitimate top manager's frameworks of meaning about activity.
- Dissemination of top managers' frameworks through interactive strategizing is neither durable nor inevitable. Top managers must work continuously at interactive strategizing in order to convey their own meanings and renegotiate those meanings in light of others' responses.

Face-to-face interaction may be seen as a subset of the strategizing practices available to top managers. By definition, interactive strategizing requires active top manager engagement in shaping strategy.

RESEARCH QUESTION: PROCEDURAL AND INTERACTIVE STRATEGIZING

Procedural and interactive strategizing are situated. They mediate interactions between actors within a given activity system. An important issue in the effectiveness of such practices for mediating collective activity is the way that they are used, recognized and understood by all participants. These practices are only relevant resources for shaping activity when other actors recognize their legitimacy, with legitimacy imparted by the cultural and historical aspects of the organizational context as well as the broader social institutions (Mantere, 2005; Whittington, 1989). The managerial challenge is to understand how to use and adapt these practices to shape collective activity from distributed actors, who may also use the practices to shape activity in their own interests. This discussion of procedural and interactive strategizing raises an important research question, which is addressed in the empirical study: What are the implications of procedural and interactive strategizing for shaping strategy?

Quick Reference Guide 2.3: Strategizing and the activity system framework

- Strategizing is the interplay between top managers and those practices that mediate interactions with the community about strategy. It takes two forms:

  - procedural strategizing, which is the use of formal administrative practices to shape strategy. It is a selection and control means of mediating strategy with low active managerial attention; and

  - interactive strategizing, which is the use of face-to-face interaction to shape strategy. It is an interpretative means of mediating strategy that involves active managerial engagement.

- Procedural and interactive strategizing do not confer top-down control over strategy to top managers. Rather, top managers may gain agency from procedural and interactive strategizing, but their agency is also influenced by those practices available. Additionally, other actors can use the administrative and interactive practices to shape activity according to their own interests.

- Strategizing confers different dynamics of influence around the activity system that shape patterns of activity in different ways.

STRATEGIZING, ACTIVITY SYSTEM DYNAMICS AND GOAL-DIRECTED ACTIVITY

In discussing the various components of the activity framework in Figure 2.1, such as top managers, the organizational community and the strategizing practices, it is important not to lose sight of the overall dynamics of the activity system. While the unit of analysis in this study is strategizing, such strategizing does not occur in isolation. Rather, strategizing is the way that top managers attempt to shape strategy within the existing power plays and influences over strategy within an activity system. There is thus a relationship between strategizing, activity system dynamics and patterns of goal-directed activity over time, which incorporates all elements of the framework. In this section, the dynamics involved in shaping goal-directed activity are examined in relation to the five patterns found in the strategy literature:

- emerging;
- inertial;
- changing;
- realized activity; and
- unresolved.

While these patterns do not display detailed or discrete relationships between elements of the activity system framework, they broadly illustrate the dynamics involved in shaping strategy and lead to a second research question.

EMERGING ACTIVITY SHAPES GOALS

First, a firm might engage in activity without an explicit goal; a common condition in action studies of strategy where the goal emerges from the activity. This occurs when an activity is essentially shaped from the bottom-up. For example, in Mintzberg and McHugh's (1985) study of strategy in an adhocracy, the National Film Board of Canada pursued strategies that it never articulated as goals. Nonetheless, strategies such as its four-year penetration of the television market were significant streams of activity, concentrating resources around a series of actions that developed enough coherence to become a stream of activity directed at entry into the television industry. This was a case of emergent activity within an adhocracy. An adhocracy is an extreme example of a distributed activity system, where managerial influence over a planned activity is minimal. The actions of the distributed community are thus a strong influence; emerging activity and goals from the bottom up. In such cases, initial interaction about activity is weak, with lower-level actors using existing practices to build momentum around the activity, perhaps unintentionally. However, as activity gains momentum it attracts resources, procedures and, eventually, top management attention. The activity becomes goal-directed, even if its goals have never been formally endorsed. Emerging activity is, therefore, an example of weak interaction between top managers and their community at the outset, which strengthens as the activity gains momentum and legitimacy. While it is apparent that the momentum of the activity and the increase in interaction must be associated with some changes in strategizing, the specific dynamics of strategizing that enable emergence are less explored. Nonetheless, evidence that goal-directed activity can emerge directs our attention towards the dynamics of the activity system and how strategizing is associated with that emergence over time.

INERTIAL ACTIVITIES: PERSISTENCE OF GOALS AND SUB-OPTIMAL PERFORMANCE

Inertial activities are embedded within existing historical, cultural and procedural relationships within the organization, sometimes referred to as the 'strategic context' (Burgelman, 1983) or 'strategy-in-use' (Gioia and Thomas, 1996). While these activities may start out with an explicit and valued goal, they have a tendency to inertia over time (Burgelman, 1991; Johnson, 1987). Inertia is associated with sub-optimal performance and decline, because the activity drifts from the original purposes of the goal, such as firm profitability, towards maintenance of the activity itself. The seditious nature of these activities is that, because they are embedded in the history, culture and procedures of the organization, they are persistent and difficult to change (Miller, 1993). The Intel example in Exhibit 2.2 shows how existing activity has a strong influence over administrative practices and goals, even where that activity is no longer valid to the growth or profitability of the firm. This pattern of activity is important for understanding the reciprocal nature of strategizing practices indicated in the activity system framework (Figure 2.1). Strategizing practices not only give top managers agency to shape activity, but also enable activity to shape the agency of top managers. In this particular example, procedural strategizing constrained managerial agency, as top managers persisted with the original goal-directed activity of dominating the memory chip market. This example shows how the dynamics of strategizing may become embedded in inertial patterns that mediate influence over top managers, as well as mediating their influence over activity.

CHANGING DIRECTIONS: PURPOSEFUL AND EMERGENT ACTIVITY

Change involves redirection of a stream of activity away from its initial goal towards a modified or somehow different goal. This change may be purposive and top-management led, as in Gioia and Chittipedi's (1991) study of strategic change in a university. In this example, the CEO and top managers established goals and then deliberately engaged in interactive strategizing throughout the organization – a process of sensegiving – in order to build momentum for change in the university. Interactive strategizing generated a coherent framework of meanings between top managers and the community, so enabling collective activity. In this example the process of changing directions was top-down, purposively designed by top managers and mediated through interpretative practices that generated commitment from the community and resulted in largely intended changes to activity. Strategizing practices mediated influence to top managers to shape change in activity.

Equally, however, changing directions might be associated with emerging, bottom-up activity that, while unintended, has positive outcomes. For example, Regnér (2003) illustrates how emergent activity can reconstruct top manager's intentionality and expand their definition of goal-directed activity. In a study of innovation in four Swedish firms, he found that lower-level managers in the peripheries of the firm were focused on exploratory activity with various products. This activity was neither espoused nor supported by top management and, hence, was not 'goal-directed activity' at its outset. While the activity of these peripheral workers was initially ignored or even suppressed, as it grew in revenue and importance top managers incorporated it into the goal-directed activity of the firm. They post-hoc rationalized this activity as intentional, ascribing goals and direction to activity that had initially emerged in a bottom-up way. Strategizing and changes in activity may thus occur through non-linear dynamic processes that indicate shifting influences over goal-directed activity.

UNRESOLVED STRATEGIZING: ALWAYS IN SEARCH OF GOAL-DIRECTED ACTIVITY

It is possible for an organization to engage in substantial strategizing in the search for a direction, without actually attaining sufficient goal-directedness to translate that activity into anything more concrete. For example, Maitlis and Lawrence (2003) studied an orchestra engaged in strategizing in order to develop an artistic strategy that would secure funding in an increasingly commercial environment. Their study spanned two and a half years, during which the top team and a variety of other stakeholders engaged in meetings, committees, plans, external and internal reports, and away days. Despite the considerable investment in strategizing aimed at developing goals that might orient further activity in the orchestra, neither directions nor activity eventuated; strategizing simply continued for the duration of the study and beyond. The authors term this failure because, at the end of their study, no outcome had been realized. However, this is not the same as inertia and failure in goal-directed activity, such as that described in Intel's memory chip strategy. Neither is it the same as an unintended goal emerging from activity. Rather, strategizing persisted in the search for unfound goal-directed activity. It is thus labelled 'unresolved activity' (Greenwood and Hinings, 1988).

This situation is likely to occur when the organization is so fragmented that all strategizing goes into continuous attempts to construct commonly understood meanings about activity, leaving little extra capacity to coordinate any goal-directed activity. Certainly the case described, a symphony orchestra, could be considered an extreme distributed form, similar to Mintzberg's (1979) adhocracy. It is distributed and fragmented to the extent that it is not possible for any actors to shape goal-directed activity. This pattern remains interesting because it shows the extreme implications of distributed activity, where there can be considerable investment in strategizing without gaining any influence over goal-directed activity.

REALIZING GOAL-DIRECTED ACTIVITY

While little dealt with in the literature, there is also the possibility of realizing goal-directed activity. That is, actively constructing and reconstructing activity in ways that prevent inertia and enable goals to be attained without actively occasioning change. Theoretical debates deride the over-simplistic connotations of achieving intended outcomes from activity (Mintzberg, 1990). However, for managers in practice, the pursuit and realization of existing goals are as much part of strategy as emergence, inertia and change (Hendry, 2000). Companies do, in fact, actively consolidate their existing strategy. We should therefore keep in mind that goal-directed activity may be realized through a series of outcomes based on the existing strategies. While these outcomes might not be precisely the realization of a planned strategy, nonetheless they arise from purposive accommodation and adjustment between top managers and the community about the goals and outcomes of activity, and hence need to be seen as intended or partially intended. In this situation, the dynamics of the activity system are likely to enable each party to have influence over activity and yet to be aware of and respond to subtle shifts by other players, in order that activity may be continuously realigned with existing goals. Strategizing in this situation is expected to mediate strong links within the activity system about strategy.

RESEARCH QUESTION: THE DYNAMICS OF STRATEGIZING SHAPE STRATEGY

In the above discussion, five patterns in the stream of goal-directed activity over time have been explained in terms of the dynamics of strategizing that shape strategy. Of course, the patterns outlined above are neither mutually exclusive nor discrete. Explanations of strategy over time may incorporate more than one of these patterns, because of the changing dynamics between strategizing and activity. The five patterns described clarify three aspects of these dynamics:

- any existing activity is embedded in existing patterns of strategizing that have powerfully constraining effects on the dynamics of the activity system;
- even embedded activity can change and, in the process, reconfigure the dynamics of the activity system; and
- influence over shaping activity is distributed rather than a property of top managers.

Changing influences over activity are associated with changes in the dynamics of strategizing. In order to understand patterns of strategy better, we need to understand the activity system dynamics of strategizing and their implications for shaping strategy over time. This leads to a second research question that is addressed in the empirical study: How are different activity system dynamics involved in shaping strategy as a pattern in a stream of goal-directed activity over time?

WHAT ABOUT MULTIPLE STRATEGIES?

In addressing this question, it is important to consider the issue of multiple strategies. So far, strategy has been explained as a pattern in a single stream of goal-directed activity. While this activity might emerge, decline or change, becoming in some way a new strategy, it is not complicated by the presence of multiple strategies. Indeed, the above discussion highlights the complexity of shaping a single stream of activity, given the dynamics of the activity system. However, in the empirical study for this book, complexity is compounded by the finding that universities pursue not one but four streams of goal-directed activity, research, teaching, commercial income and size and scope. The strategy literature tends to discuss strategy as a singular construct; that is, research examines a firm's strategy, the evolution of that strategy, or the substitution of that strategy by another strategy. Coexistence of strategies is not explored because, as a new strategy emerges and gains precedence, the existing strategy exits or subsides (for example, Burgelman, 1996; Lovas and Ghoshal, 2000). In this study, however, exit was not an option; the activities had to coexist. This finding may be attributable to the acknowledged divergent goals of professional contexts, such as universities and hospitals (Denis et al., 2001), although it appears that other diverse organizations, such as multinationals, must also face the problem of multiple activities which are not necessarily compatible and which may be in the interests of some actors more than others. The challenge for top managers is thus not only the shaping of single streams of activity, but also managing the relationship between streams of activity. This raises a final question, building on the first two: How are patterns in multiple streams of goal-directed activity shaped by association with each other?

Quick Reference Guide 2.4: Three research questions

- What are the implications of procedural and interactive strategizing for shaping strategy?

- How are different activity system dynamics involved in shaping strategy as a pattern in a stream of goal-directed activity over time?

- How are patterns in multiple streams of goal-directed activity shaped by association with each other?

CONCLUSION: POINTS TO TAKE FORWARD

This chapter has covered broad terrain in defining the key terms and concepts for this study, applying them to the activity system framework and grounding them in the strategy literature. There are four key points to take forward from this chapter.

1 In keeping with the activity-based view, the level of analysis is strategy as a pattern in a stream of goal-directed activity over time. The overarching aim of the empirical study is thus to explain how this pattern is shaped over time.

2 Strategizing is the unit of analysis for explaining how strategy is shaped over time. Two types of strategizing, procedural and interactive, were identified, based on the use of different strategic practices. Procedural strategizing involves the use of formal administrative procedures to shape strategy. Under most circumstances it can be carried out as an iterative process requiring little active attention from top managers. Interactive strategizing is purposive face-to-face interaction between top managers and other members of the organizational community about strategy. By definition, interactive strategizing requires active top management engagement in shaping strategy. As strategizing is the unit of analysis for this study, the role of procedural and interactive strategizing gave rise to the first research question: 'What are the implications of procedural and interactive strategizing for shaping strategy?' Chapter 4 in the next section will address this question through an empirical investigation of procedural and interactive strategizing.

3 Top managers' ability to shape strategy cannot occur in isolation. Due to the distributed nature of activity and the role of strategizing practices in mediating influence around the activity system, other actors also shape strategy. This is shown in the five examples of patterns in strategy:

- emerging;
- inertial;
- changing;
- realized activity; and
- unresolved.

The activity system dynamics of strategizing are fluid and can be associated with quite different patterns of goal-directed activity over time. This gave rise to a second question: 'How are different activity system dynamics involved in shaping strategy as a pattern in a stream of goal-directed activity over time?' Chapter 5 in the next section will analyse the different dynamics associated with procedural and interactive strategizing. It will also develop two further, empirically-informed categories of strategizing – preactive and integrative strategizing – to show the range of strategizing dynamics that shape patterns of strategy over time.

4 The final section of this chapter raised the thought-provoking issue of multiple strategies. While strategy research typically examines strategy as a singular construct – how a stream of activity emerges, develops, changes or fails – there is less research on how multiple streams of activity coexist and how they shape each other. However, in this study multiple streams of strategy were found. Therefore, a final question was raised: 'How are patterns in multiple streams of goal-directed activity shaped by association with each

other?' Chapter 6 in the next section addresses this question by analysing the association between core and non-core streams of activity.

This concludes Part I, which has provided a theoretical overview of strategy as practice, explained the activity-based view and located it within the strategy literature. The contributions of this section have been a theoretical underpinning to the activity-based view and the development of an activity framework for its study in Chapter 1. Chapter 2 has provided definitions of the key terms applicable to an activity-based view, such as strategy as a pattern in a stream of goal-directed activity, and identified the unit of analysis as strategizing. The dynamics of strategizing and its association with patterns of goal-directed activity have then been developed. Part II now enriches these terms, concepts and themes through an empirical study.

NOTES

1   The term 'process' used here is distinct from the strategy process school of research, which studies strategy as a sequence of events over time. References to strategy processes of direction setting, resource allocation, and monitoring and control are more narrowly defined and refer to internal coordination processes for managing the work of strategy (Garvin, 1998).
2   Four of Eisenhardt and Sull's (2001) 'simple rules' – how-to rules, boundary rules, timing rules and exit rules – are actually forms of monitoring and control pertaining to boundary systems, according to Simons' (1991, 1994) classification, whilst their priority rules pertain to resource allocation.
3   Practices are not, in and of themselves, a clearly defined analytic category. Which practices to study, therefore, represents a theoretically and/or empirically informed choice by the investigator. This study examines formal administrative practices and norms of face-to-face interaction, which are empirically derived and grounded in practice-based theorizing of these concepts as the interplay between structural and interpretative practices (Reckwitz, 2002). Other types of practices that mediate the construction of activity might also be legitimate choices for analysis, such as the study of discursive practices that informs a growing body of research (e.g. Academy of Management Review, 2004; Czarniawska, 1997; Hardy et al., 2000).

PART II: SHAPING STRATEGIC ACTIVITY IN PRACTICE

The aim of this section is to empirically interpret the concepts raised in Part I and contribute to an empirically-grounded development of the activity-based view of strategy as practice. Chapter 3 outlines the specific details of the research context, three UK universities. The three empirical chapters, 4 to 6, each address one of the three research questions developed in the previous chapter. Chapter 4 addresses the implications of procedural and interactive strategizing for shaping strategy. Chapter 5 takes this analysis further by investigating the different dynamics associated with procedural and interactive strategizing. It also develops two further, empirically-informed categories of strategizing, pre-active and integrative strategizing, to show the range of strategizing dynamics that shape patterns of strategy over time. Finally, Chapter 6 addresses the issue of multiple strategies, analysing the way that patterns in strategy are shaped by association with each other.

3 ESTABLISHING THE RESEARCH CONTEXT

Key points

- Doing strategy research in the university context

- Universities are not alone: contexts that share university characteristics

- Introduction to the empirical base: three UK universities

- Introduction to the four streams of activity: research, teaching, commercial income and size and scope

---

The empirical context for this research is the university sector. Specifically, three longitudinal cases studies of UK universities inform the discussion and the conceptual framework developed in this book. This chapter sets out the characteristics of the research context. The chapter is in three sections. The first section deals with doing strategy research in the university context; this section explains the critical characteristics of universities that add depth and complexity to the activity-based research agenda, making the case that more strategy research needs to be done in universities and similar critical contexts. The second section notes that universities are not unique; many public and professional service contexts share similar characteristics with the university context. Therefore, there is likely to be value in cross-fertilization, with research in one of these contexts being illuminating for the other contexts. Finally, the three cases that inform this study are introduced and described. Each case is pursuing four strategies, teaching, research, commercial income and size and scope, which adds an interesting dimension of complexity to researching strategy as goal-directed activity. These 12 strategic activities, four from each case, form the basis of the analysis in the following chapters.

DOING STRATEGY RESEARCH IN THE UNIVERSITY CONTEXT

In a theory-building study it is valuable to find extreme examples that will expose the phenomena under investigation (Pettigrew, 1990). The university sector exposes the core themes that underpin the activity-based research agenda for four reasons:

- the goal ambiguity and divergent professional interests that are typical of a university context highlight the complexity of distributed activity;
- over the past 25 years an increasingly competitive environment has placed greater responsibility upon top managers to ensure a collective strategic response from their university;
- despite their responsibilities top managers cannot act by management fiat but must take into account the divergent interests of an autonomous professional workforce, and
- universities pursue multiple strategies, which adds complexity in terms of the association between streams of activity.

These points are now explained.

First, universities are good examples of distributed activity because they typically have goal ambiguity associated with their constituents' divergent interests (Hardy et al., 1983; Cohen and March, 1974). University contexts pose problems for collective activity because of the different responsibilities and affiliations of their constituents. For example, while universities may have research excellence as an overarching strategy, the motivation for and content of research activity is the responsibility of different departments and, within those departments, different individuals whose affiliation is to their discipline more than to their institution. As such, top managers may have trouble generating any collective form of research strategy. Typically, because of the multiplicity of goals and interests, strategic decision making within universities has been viewed as a 'garbage can' involving random confluence between streams of choice, problems, solutions and actors (Cohen et al., 1972). Rather than being held together by shared activity, top management and other actors have a loose-coupled relationship, with different constituents pursuing pockets of activity in relative autonomy from each other (Cohen and March, 1974; Weick, 1976). As such, a traditional university context is an extreme form of a distributed activity system, in which actors are fragmented in their objectives with little attention to strategy as a collective organizational activity.

Second, these typical characteristics of universities are under pressure in OECD countries, where universities are increasingly exposed to a competitive environment due to declining state funding and increased market pressures (Clark, 1998; Slaughter and Leslie, 1999). Under these conditions, there is greater responsibility upon top managers to ensure that the university can make a collective strategic response to funding bodies and to the market (Birnbaum, 2000; Shattock, 2003): 'The university must speak with one voice and the central administration must be able to coordinate the university response' (Slaughter and Leslie, 1999: 230). This creates an uneasy alignment between the traditional distributed nature of the university and the need for top managers to coordinate strategies. For example, despite changing environmental conditions, professional actors persist in perceiving strategy from a personal or departmental, rather than university, perspective (Slaughter and Leslie, 1999; Welsh and Metcalf, 2003). While changing environmental conditions increase the centrality of the top management role, they do not lessen the problematic nature of shaping collective strategy within such contexts (Denis et al., 2001; Ferlie et al., 1996). Universities are thus ideal research contexts for placing top managers at the centre of 'the complexity of the processes that go to make up and influence organizations' (Johnson et al., 2003: 15).

Third, top managers cannot discharge their responsibilities for strategy through management fiat because universities are characterized by an autonomous professional workforce which is resistant to overt formal control (Cohen and March, 1974). As strategy cannot occur directly through top-down influence, strategizing practices that mediate managerial influence are important for shaping strategy. However, the strategizing practices available to top managers in these contexts typically have low sanctions for non-performance. Indeed, relevant sanction and reward in such contexts may be outside managerial control because the nature of professional work commands external, peer-based rewards and recognition. For example, high-quality research attracts rewards of prestigious publications and peer recognition. The bind for top managers is that this work is central to the strategy of the organization and yet the strategizing practices available to shape such work are weakly sanctioned and may be largely irrelevant to a professional workforce (Ferrary, 2002; Lowendahl, 1997). Professionals therefore have significant power in their interactions with top management (Denis et al., 1996). Top managers may achieve influence over others through their ability to construct an interpretation or ideology that others may understand and value (Gioia and Chittipedi, 1991; Mintzberg and McHugh, 1985). At the same time, however, external demands increase the need for 'rational' management techniques, such as formal planning and control mechanisms (Oakes et al., 1998). Top managers must thus balance competing demands for external legitimacy, through the use of formal administrative practices, whilst also meeting the need to gain value-based commitment from an autonomous professional workforce (Stone and Brush, 1996). The two types of strategizing defined in Chapter 2, procedural and interactive, are thus placed under stress, providing an ideal context in which to observe practical-evaluative agency.

Fourth, the multiple strategic directions that universities pursue compound the problem of collective activity. Historically universities have pursued research and teaching as two separate activities, which each give a distinct strategic character to the institution. For example, there are teaching-dominated institutions that also do some applied research and top-of-the-league institutions that focus primarily upon prestigious, 'pure' research (Slaughter and Leslie, 1999; Brewer et al., 2002). The compatibility of these two strategic activities is contentious (Marsh and Hattie, 2002), despite considerable rhetoric about their mutually reinforcing character (Neumann, 1992). A third strategic activity arising from competition for scarce public resources is commercial income (Clark, 1998; Shattock, 2003). These multiple strategies erode collective activity because they are inherently contradictory for many actors. For example, many academics perceive a fundamental dichotomy between commercial income and teaching, and between prestigious research and teaching (Slaughter and Leslie, 1999). Commercial activity in particular is typically perceived as a threat because it is associated with economic considerations, which are perceived as innately counter to professional values (Satow, 1975; Townley, 2002). Tensions between professional and managerial interests are reflected in the tensions between activities. These tensions further challenge the strategizing resources of top managers and their ability to shape strategy.

These four characteristics of the university sector expose important elements of an activity-based view, providing a valuable context for research into strategy as practice. Such research may also broaden our understanding of strategic management more generally. Unfortunately, universities, with some noteworthy exceptions (for example, Gioia and Chittipedi, 1991; Gioia et al., 1994; Hickson et al., 1986), have been neglected contexts for strategy research. Strategic management has been largely dominated by free market concepts of strategy and competition that predispose a focus upon private sector organizations. However, this overview of the issues involved in strategizing in the university sector indicates that considerations of strategy and competition are both relevant and complex to manage in these contexts. It is time that universities stopped being 'poor cousins' on the strategy research agenda. Broader insights about the complexities of strategy and strategizing may be derived from research into the university sector and from cross-fertilization between sectors. A key contribution of this book, therefore, is its potential to illuminate our understanding of strategy in an under-explored context, and to provide insights that may feed back into the wider strategic management discipline, particularly about the nature of competition in non-traditional contexts.

UNIVERSITIES ARE NOT ALONE: CONTEXTS WITH SIMILAR CHARACTERISTICS

The four points raised in the above section are not unique to the university sector. Many contexts share similar characteristics, principally those with professional workforces. Earlier studies focused on these organizations as professional bureaucracies, examining the structural characteristics of coordination and control when dealing with a professional workforce (Mintzberg, 1979; Scott, 1965). There is also a growing body of research examining the implications of strategic change in the hospital and health care sector (for example, Denis et al., 1996; 2001; Pettigrew et al., 1992). More recently there has been a surge of interest in leadership and management in professional

---

Quick Reference Guide 3.1: Universities as contexts for strategy research

- Universities are good examples of distributed activity systems because they typically have a fragmented professional workforce, pursuing divergent goals and interests with little concern for strategy as a collective organizational activity.

- Increasing competitive pressures and external demands have placed greater responsibility on top managers to coordinate a collective strategic response from the university.

- Top-down management is not an option in universities because of the autonomous professional workforce. Therefore, the strategizing resources through which top mangers have influence over strategy are placed under stress.

- Universities pursue multiple, contradictory activities that create tensions between professional and managerial interests. This increases the distributed nature of activity and further challenges the strategizing resources of top managers.

---

service firms, such as law, accounting, consulting and engineering firms (for example, Fenton and Pettigrew, 2005; Hinings and Leblebici, 2003; Lowendahl, 1997). Still other studies deal with the issues of managing change in a range of public and not-for-profit organizations, such as museums, orchestras and local government (for example, Greenwood and Hinings, 1993; Maitlis and Lawrence, 2003; Oakes et al., 1998). These organizations may be termed 'professional contexts'. They highlight a set of common characteristics that also apply within the university context:

- Multiple stakeholders with divergent interests and diffuse bases of power, which increases the distributed, fragmented nature of activity and generates problems for collective strategic action. For example, Denis et al. (2001) illustrate the problems of mobilizing strategic change within Canadian hospitals because of the need to align the divergent interests of multiple stakeholders at the strategic, organizational and operational level.
- Increasing external pressures upon top managers to coordinate a strategic response to the market. This is particularly prevalent in public sector contexts where the importation of private sector models has led to the rise of 'new public management' and an increasing emphasis on the managerial task (Ferlie et al., 1996; Oakes et al., 1998). It is, however, also an issue for professional service firms where market forces are more in evidence (Lowendahl 1997).
- Increasing tensions between external pressures for more formalized management and the internal problems of managing commitment from an autonomous professional workforce that has low tolerance for top-down

management and control. For example, Alvesson and Sveningsson (2003) examine the tensions between visionary leadership and bureaucratic controls in a life-sciences firm. Other studies show that normative controls are an increasingly important resource for top managers in shaping a cohesive corporate response (Robertson et al., 2003).

- Finally, these contexts are characterized by goal ambiguity, divergent interests and multiple identities. While little research has actually separated out the multiple goals and identities into separate streams of strategic activity and analysed the association between them empirically, there is considerable evidence that they constitute contradictory and competing rationalities that have consequences for managing these organizations (for example, Pratt and Foreman, 2000; Townley, 2002).

The contexts in which these characteristics apply range from universities and hospitals to law, accounting, consulting and knowledge-intensive software and biotech firms, among others. Each of these organizations has some specific features that are contextually unique. However, their common characteristics suggest that findings about strategizing in one of these contexts might have relevance to other contexts. Therefore, the findings from this book are expected to have wider application in a range of organizations that are based on a professional workforce.

OVERVIEW OF THE CASES AND THE RESEARCH METHOD

This section introduces the three cases on which this study is based. This book is based on a longitudinal study of three UK universities. While the data set is briefly outlined, issues of case selection, research method and analysis are incorporated in the Appendix. The main purpose of this section is to explain the separate activity streams that constitute the level of analysis for the following empirical chapters and give an overview of these activities in each of the cases.

The data presented are from a seven-year study incorporating six years of retrospective and one year of real-time data collection from 1992 to 1998 inclusive. Multiple sources of rich qualitative data were collected and these are documented in the Appendix. Each case involved essentially similar participants, listed in the Appendix. Participants have been given the following standardized titles and abbreviations: Vice-Chancellor (VC), Deputy Vice-Chancellor (DVC), Registrar, Deputy Registrar, Senior Academic and Governor.

The three cases are called Collegiate, Entrepreneurial and Modern to preserve their anonymity. Details of case selection and background are given in the Appendix. Each case was pursuing four streams of activity: research, teaching, commercial income and size and scope. Professional actors might have a variety of interests that they ascribe to these activities. However, top managers tend to view the activities strategically in terms of their consequences for the organization as a whole. Managerial views on the strategic nature of these activities were similar across all three cases. Strategic issues for these activities are:

- *Research:* Strategically, the goal of research activity is to achieve research excellence. External measures of research quality were particularly important during this study because of a four-yearly state Research Assessment Exercise (RAE), which ranked departments nationally and funded them accordingly. Research is also important for attracting an intangible resource: prestige (Gioia and Thomas, 1996). Prestige has indirect effects in terms of funding, attracting top students and retaining elite staff: 'Good universities have strong research profiles, for all the reasons I mentioned. It underpins teaching, it gives you a national and international reputation. It brings in resources' (Modern).
- *Teaching:* Teaching strategy is directed at quality and service provision in order to ensure high student recruitment. The emphasis on teaching quality increased during this study because of state Teaching Quality Assessments (TQA) and rankings. Top managers involve themselves at the strategic level of quality, service and teaching rankings, but this might also mean some involvement in operational issues of teaching (see, for example, Exhibit 2.1). However, their focus is oriented towards the strategic consequences of teaching practice: 'To improve the delivery of academic services: scholarships, the site and its facilities, student accommodation, staff-student ratios and student registration and orientation arrangements. All of these have a part in helping to ensure recruitment of the best students' (Collegiate).
- *Commercial income:* Commercial income is a relatively recent strategy for universities. It involves attraction of non-state resources. Income is generated through initiatives such as research grants and contracts, commercial services and facilities, commercialization of intellectual property, professional short courses and full-fee-paying student recruitment. This last point, full-fee-paying enrolment, particularly from overseas students, is one of the easiest ways for universities to generate further income using existing teaching activity, whereas the other forms of income generation involve a stronger commercial orientation (Shattock, 2003). However, all forms of commercial activity are increasingly important for supporting other university activities: 'The fact that the place looks good, the fact that the staff:student ratio is reasonable . . . a lot of that rests on additional income supplementing the government grant' (Entrepreneurial).
- *Size and scope:* Size and scope is a strategic issue dealing with size, growth and disciplinary balance, including investment in capital infrastructure to provide for size and scope goals. Market pressures have made it increasingly important for universities to think about the scope of disciplinary balance because less popular disciplines may not bring in enough revenue to be self-supporting. Strategically, this means universities must make a decision to either cross-subsidize these disciplines from more profitable disciplines or

to starve less popular disciplines of resources with a view to closure: 'It will be important to resolve the issues regarding under-recruiting subject areas . . . [and] consider the withdrawal of provision where, after due investment in marketing and reorientation [a discipline] is clearly no longer viable' (Modern).

Despite different cultural and historical orientations to the various activities, all three were pursuing research, teaching, commercial income and size and scope. There were, however, different specific issues for each activity in each case, which are now presented. Table 3.1 summarizes the main objectives and strategic issues that the activities presented in the cases, using data extracts to help contextualize these points.

Of the three cases, Collegiate was most typical of the traditional characteristics of a university. It has a strong ethos of professional autonomy and resistance to managerial control: 'We do not want too many efficiency experts telling us what to do.' This posed challenges for top managers in shaping strategy without overt control.

- *Research:* As a research elite institution, research prestige is Collegiate's main priority. While the performance of research was generally strong, the very top rankings in research were not being achieved by all departments. Thus, raising the quality of research performance in all departments was a key strategic issue for top managers, although managerial intervention was highly contentious for academic staff.
- *Teaching:* Because of its elite reputation, Collegiate attracted good students to academically well-regarded undergraduate and postgraduate programmes. In particular, high-fee-paying overseas students on one-year postgraduate programmes were an important source of revenue for the University. Hence, the key strategic issue in teaching was to improve quality and service delivery to match the cost of the courses.
- *Commercial income:* The year-on-year downturn in higher education funding over the previous 20 years was beginning to take serious effect on Collegiate during this study, increasing the importance of commercial activity. However, this was the most contentious issue for academic staff, who regarded commercial activity as fundamentally threatening to research.
- *Size and scope:* The key size and scope issue was to maintain the full range of academic disciplines by protecting less fashionable disciplines from the forces of the market. At the same time, zero growth was an imperative because of Collegiate's central city location. In order to balance the objectives of a full range of disciplines and zero-growth, it was important for Collegiate to maintain undergraduate and postgraduate ratios and ethnic balance in the student body. Maintaining these balances would prevent the reliance on overseas student fee income from dictating growth in fashionable disciplines and threatening survival in other disciplines. This proved to be a strategic problem as the University grew disproportionately each year.

At Entrepreneurial, top managers held the balance of power over shaping activity, but this influence was continuously negotiated between top management and the departments: 'There is this kind of dumbbell where you've got this strong department there, this strong centre here and there is a kind of a balance. A kind of almost shared purpose with, um, this sort of managerial centre balancing a quite, you know, quite autonomous department.'

- *Research:* Excellence in research was the core activity and, generally, strongly performed. However, some departments were not achieving the top rankings in research. Raising the performance of all staff to the same high level of research was the key issue in shaping the research strategy for top managers.
- *Teaching:* Teaching was also strategically important to top managers in terms of achieving high TQA rankings that would ensure strong student recruitment.
- *Commercial activity:* Entrepreneurial had a reputation for commercial activity, due to its ability to generate some 60 per cent of its income from non-state sources. This strong commercial performance arose from the initial response to downturns in state funding, where Entrepreneurial was one of the first universities to take external sources of income seriously as a strategic issue. Maintaining commercial performance was the key issue for top managers.
- *Size and scope:* Size and scope objectives were to achieve targeted growth in the Sciences, to grow other selected disciplines and to maintain small Arts and Social Science departments through cross-subsidy. Additionally, upgrading and growth of facilities and infrastructure to meet the future needs of the University were important strategic issues.

Modern was a former polytechnic that had a strong reputation for excellent and innovative teaching. Relationships between top managers and departments were generally pleasant and non-confrontational: 'Almost everybody you have any dealings with are pleasant, obliging, and if they can be, helpful.' However, top managers clearly held responsibility for shaping strategy: 'that's what senior management are charged with doing.' Tensions thus arose between the need to control strategy, whilst also maintaining good university relationships.

- *Research:* Formerly, research had not been a strategic objective, although some actors did pursue their own research. As part of its strategic agenda as a university, Modern was now endeavouring to develop and strengthen its research profile, which became a source of tension with some departments.
- *Teaching:* High-quality teaching remained the core activity throughout the study, although teaching activity needed to be modified in order to make more room for other strategic priorities.
- *Commercial activity:* Commercial activity was increasingly important because changes in the higher education funding model seriously affected Modern's state income. This became a key strategic issue for top managers. The emphasis on commercial activity also affected the size and scope goals.
- *Size and scope:* The main size and scope goal was financial viability in

Table 3.1: Characteristics of the cases and their strategies

Characteristics	Collegiate	Entrepreneurial	Modern
Market position	*Top bracket of research universities*	*Top bracket of research universities*	*Top bracket of teaching universities*
Identity	World class research: The 'vision is to be worldwide recognized, Collegiate on a world stage, top academics, influencing thought on a world stage.	Excellent research and commercially strong: 'It has a lot of distinction about it in terms of academic excellence. But, um, it also has something of a reputation as a go-getter.'	Excellent and innovative teaching: 'Modern's heartland is teaching and learning.'
Research strategy	*Objective:* 'We would like to, in very concrete terms, strategically we would like to go to number one in the RAE next time. That would be the overall objective.' *Issue:* 'It is not possible to know about departmental strategies of research and they what are doing.'	*Objective:* 'We mean business. We absolutely mean to invest on the research side of the University.' *Issue:* 'If you declare yourself to be a research-based university, and you mean it, then all your staff should go in to be assessed for their research work.'	*Objective:* 'Modern has got a good and developing reputation, but it's not going to maintain that unless it underpins it with research because good universities have strong research profiles.' *Issue:* 'On the research, we are going to have to provide much more central leadership and direction and push and be more directive.'
Teaching strategy	*Objective:* 'To improve the delivery of academic services.' *Issue:* 'Students are paying very high fees and they were entitled to a better deal. More attention had to be paid to them to make sure that they were getting value for the high fees that they were paying.'	*Objective:* 'We've got to make sure the teaching side is just as good as the research side.' *Issue:* 'Teaching is much higher up the agenda at the moment because of the state Teaching Quality Assessments and because of the external pressures.'	*Objective:* 'The University will action a number of reviews aimed at releasing staff [teaching] time for re-investment in the strategic priorities.' *Issue:* 'The last thing we want is for teaching to suffer, because we do very well on teaching, we pride ourselves on teaching.'

Table 3.1: *Cont.*

Characteristics	Collegiate	Entrepreneurial	Modern
Market position	*Top bracket of research universities*	*Top bracket of research universities*	*Top bracket of teaching universities*
Commercial strategy	*Objective:* 'The University can't afford its infrastructure. The excellence which we have is balanced precariously on too small a resource base and action MUST be taken on the resources in the near future.' *Issue:* 'There are people who strongly resent the idea that an academic institution should want or need to engage in [commercial] activities which they see as rather low status and dubious.'	*Objective:* 'Entrepreneurial has to make sure that the commercial activities maintain their momentum and deliver the financial returns, because those underpin everything we do.' *Issue:* 'The squeeze has been on so long that the business just has to be able to bulk up the better income streams and minimize or curtail less productive ones.'	*Objective:* 'The big challenge is to grow additional activities, additional income, that will generate surpluses that will allow us to improve our facilities, to provide support for new initiatives and so on.' *Issue:* 'Unless you can convince the departments that they need to make income, it's very difficult to get them to develop the courses.'
Size and scope strategy	*Objective:* 'Use of cross-subsidy to maintain our essential character is well-established, where core disciplines are threatened by transitory shifts of student fashion or external funding policy.' *Issue:* 'Incentives for growth have disturbed the balance between financial integrity and academic considerations, such as the composition and mix of the student body.'	*Objective:* 'Differential treatment is accorded to departments depending on their rating [in teaching and research]. Special allowance is made for small departments and there is a 10 per cent premium for bench sciences.' *Issue:* 'We have continued with the principle of maintaining the University's infrastructure... It has positioned us for the next thing. If you are always trying to catch up with your infrastructure... you change the structure of the university by just not doing things.'	*Objective:* 'We emphasize financial viability in a department.' *Issue:* 'Small departments are under pressure. Big departments are more powerful... generate more resources and are more central to the University.'

departments. However, this goal raised problems for top managers as the emphasis on financial viability began to threaten the existence of smaller departments.

This concludes the introduction to the data and the overview of the cases. These four activities in each case provided 12 streams of activity for analysis. This analysis examined the relationship between strategizing practices and patterns in the 12 streams of activity over time (see the Appendix). A representative sample of the empirical data on these activities is used to furnish practical examples and exhibits, which bring to life the key concepts in the following chapters.

CONCLUSION: POINTS TO TAKE FORWARD

This chapter has introduced universities as the research context. Universities are important contexts for doing strategy research because they expose the complexity of strategy as practice. Five key points have been developed to take forward:

1 Universities highlight the problems of distributed actors with divergent interests and goals, which, due to increasing environmental pressures, must be aligned in collective activity.
2 The pressure for collective activity illuminates the complexities of managerial agency. Strategizing resources are placed under stress because universities are professional contexts where top-down control over strategy cannot be assumed.
3 Universities pursue multiple strategies. In this study, four streams of strategy in each case were found: research, teaching, commercial income and size and scope. The presence of multiple strategies compounds the problems of distributed activity and further increases the complexity of the managerial task.
4 Universities are not unique. Many other professional contexts share the above characteristics of universities. Therefore, the results from this book are likely to be applicable to strategizing in other professional or non-traditional contexts, where broader definitions of competition are required.
5 Three empirical cases of UK universities, each pursuing all four streams of strategy, form the empirical basis of this book. The 12 activities generated from the three cases inform the discussion and conceptual frameworks developed in the following chapters.

The following chapters in this section will draw upon the data from these three universities to address the three research questions identified in Chapter 2.

4 IMPLICATIONS OF PROCEDURAL AND INTERACTIVE STRATEGIZING

Key points

- Practical examples of procedural strategizing
- Purpose and problems of procedural strategizing
- Procedural strategizing confers structural legitimacy on activity
- Practical examples of interactive strategizing
- Purpose and problems of interactive strategizing
- Interactive strategizing confers interpretative legitimacy on activity
- Activity system dynamics of procedural and interactive strategizing

This chapter looks at those practices that mediate the shaping of strategy. Specifically, it examines two types of practices that top managers articulated as important in shaping the flow of strategy, formal administrative procedures and face-to-face interaction. These practices were located in the strategy literature in Chapter 2. Their use by top managers to shape strategy was conceptualized as procedural strategizing, to account for the use of formal administrative practices, and interactive strategizing, to account for the use of face-to-face interaction practices. As strategizing is the unit of analysis for this study, this gave rise to the first research question: What are the implications of procedural and interactive strategizing for shaping strategy? This chapter addresses the question of procedural and interactive strategizing in four ways:

- it provides practical examples of the practices involved in procedural and interactive strategizing;
- these practical examples are used to explain the purposes of procedural and interactive strategizing in shaping strategy. They show how procedural strategizing structurally embeds and diagnostically controls strategy, while interactive strategizing generates shared frameworks of meaning and normative controls over strategy;

- the implications of procedural and interactive strategizing are more clearly illustrated by examining the problems they pose. Procedural strategizing is prone to the problem of goals–means displacement and strategic drift. Interactive strategizing faces the problem that frameworks of meaning are not durable and need to be continuously constructed; and
- the chapter addresses the central aim of this book by analysing the relationship between these two forms of strategizing and the way they shape strategy.

Procedural strategizing and interactive strategizing provide, respectively, structural legitimacy and interpretative legitimacy for activity. These strategizing types and their respective legitimacies involve different dynamics of influence over activity, which are modelled using the activity system framework. The chapter is in two sections. The first section examines procedural strategizing and the second section examines interactive strategizing.

THE PURPOSE AND PROBLEMS OF PROCEDURAL STRATEGIZING

Procedural strategizing is defined as the use of formal administrative practices[1] to shape the flow of strategy in an organization. In this section, the purpose and problems of procedural strategizing are explained. The purpose of procedural strategizing is to embed activity structurally and provide diagnostic controls. This is interpreted through a practice theory lens as conferring structural legitimacy upon activity, which is important for its persistence. However, two problems of procedural strategizing are also discussed. First, controls must be perceived as relevant within the local context, which in a professional context can be counter to their formal purpose, as exemplified in Exhibit 4.2. Second, embedding activity in formal administrative practices has a tendency to lead to goals–means displacement over time, in which focus is upon the practices rather than the activity at which they were directed. Finally, the activity system dynamics of using procedural strategizing to shape strategy are modelled, showing how it mediates influence towards the activity and the administrative practices.

PURPOSE: STRUCTURAL EMBEDDING AND DIAGNOSTIC CONTROL

The strategic planning cycle at Modern University, explained in Exhibit 4.1, incorporates a fairly typical range of formal administrative practices involved in procedural strategizing, such as the establishment of plans, budgets, performance indicators and operational reviews to shape strategy. This example illustrates two important purposes of procedural strategizing, structural embedding of activity and diagnostic control. Let us deal with each of these points in turn. First, structural embedding refers to the set of practices through which activity can be resourced, coordinated and become part of the formal activity of the organization. The value of procedural strategizing is that it embeds a stream of activity within a set of routine practices that formalize goals and indicate hierarchies, roles and responsibilities for conducting aspects of the activity directed at those goals. It becomes part of the formal structures of the organization. Once an activity is formally documented, has a resource stream attached to it, and allocated targets and responsibilities, it is difficult to deny its status as a strategy. Structural embedding moves the debate from *whether* an activity should be done to *how* it should be done. The activity is then able to persist in the taken-for-granted administrative practices of the organization.

Exhibit 4.1: Investing power in the plan

Procedural strategizing at Modern University

In 1995, Modern incorporated direction setting, resource allocation and monitoring and control into a tightly linked annual strategic planning cycle (SPC). There is managerial discretion in setting the initial parameters of this planning cycle, but low discretion for any actors once the plan is approved, as activities are perpetuated annually providing they meet performance targets. Throughout the period observed resources were decreased, while performance measures were refined annually, culminating in 13 statistical performance measures that 'emphasize those key indicators which top management currently consider the most important for benchmarking performance internally and externally' (SPC minutes, 1998/99). Despite its directive nature, the plan was rapidly embedded: '. . . the planning cycle has got embedded in the University culture . . . people have said, I want more direction, more central direction' (Deputy Registrar, Planning). This is evidenced in departmental planning agreements. For example, a departmental head 'sought University support in handling the problem of under-performing staff within the context of clear disciplinary procedures' (SPC minutes, 1996/97). The annual cycle is described below, with an example of how it embedded commercial activity over a four-year period.

- *October:* Strategic directions are considered by the top team, based on steers arising from discussions with the governors. Staff input is canvassed through a 62-point questionnaire.
- *November:* The questionnaire results form the basis for TMT (top management team) presentations at Staff Strategy Day on the directions for the year. Financial and student number parameters are then set, incorporating staff time savings and financial efficiency gains for the budget period. The TMT meets with heads whose budgets will be adversely affected by under-recruitment.
- *December:* The planning framework document is circulated to

heads. Each department is required to prepare a planning submission comprising: strategic planning statement; five-year budget plan; two-year operational plan; and draft planning agreement. The operational plan must also include a review of achievements over the previous year, supported by evidence, and an evaluation of the extent to which objectives have been met.

- *January/February:* The Finance Department works with heads of departments to develop and monitor budget proposals. Heads then submit six copies of the above documents to the TMT. A minimum of two TMT members and the Planning Registrar meet with each head to go through their plan in detail, ensuring it meets strategic directions. 'While there will be lots of discussion about strategic plans throughout the departments, there won't be influence on strategic direction from them. The plans will be expected to conform to the directions set by the University' (TMT meeting observation).

- *March/April:* All the bids and strategic issues arising from the above meetings, including any University-wide issues, are brought together in a single document for discussion by the TMT. The TMT meets four or five times in a short period to develop the financial, strategic and operating plans for the University, after which resource allocation and action plans are drafted.

- *May:* The budget, strategic and operating plans and planning agreements are considered by two academic committees and the Board of Governors. However, as the plan can only be altered through an addendum, the academic committees are really for dissemination rather than input. After this, final planning agreements are approved and circulated to all heads of departments.

Embedding commercial activity: Over a four-year period, the planning cycle was used to embed commercial activity. While initially 'entrepreneurial activity and income generation [were] not integrated into the ethos of Modern' (Coopers & Lybrand Report, 1988), in 1995/96 commercial activity was incorporated into the planning cycle. Departments were required to plan on achieving a 10 per cent increase in income by 1998/99. They responded with plans to increase full-fee-paying students and develop potential partnerships, consultancy and sale of intellectual property. In 1996/97 greater incentives for commercial activity were allocated in the planning cycle. At the same time, departmental operating plans began to show increased full-fee recruitment. The 1997/98 plan was much more commercially focused, with clear targets for recruitment, short courses and consultancy. At the same time sanctions were proposed, such as examining cost to income ratios and bringing more pressure on departments to increase their commercial appeal. In the 1998/99 planning round, the VC noted that 'We need to emphasize departments thinking of themselves as a business, developing income through various diverse activities and reinvesting that income.'

Departments were offered either a cutback in their overheads or a chance to make up income deficit through commercial activity. At the same time, key performance indicators were increasingly weighted towards commercial activity, with incentives being used to differentiate between high- and low-earning departments. Increasing diagnostic controls were intended to 'concentrate their minds. They'll have to pull their finger out or they'll end up with a loss-making course on their hands' (TMT meeting observation). Administrative practices could be used to differentiate commercial performance, 'pinpoint' non-performers and 'embed this in the University culture; that you will be held accountable for your performance' (TMT meeting observation).

The strategic planning cycle (SPC) at Modern is a particularly clear example of structural embedding. It is an annual routine that indicates strategic priorities, targets to be achieved, timeframes, and who is responsible for these achievements. For top managers, it is about 'accepting responsibility to manage the University' (Senior DVC), while for other actors it 'increases the links and views of what the strategic umbrella is' (Department Head). The power of procedural strategizing is evidenced in the way that these responsibilities, targets and the activities to which they pertain are rapidly taken for granted. For example, 'the planning cycle has got embedded in the University culture'. Once an activity is in the annual planning cycle, it will be perpetuated and, as the embedding of commercial activity shows, reinforced through adjusting targets and performance indicators. Strategy that is structurally embedded thus becomes part of the taken-for-granted administrative routines of an organization (Spender and Grinyer, 1996; Weber, 1978).

Procedural strategizing not only embeds activity, but also delegates much of the power for shaping it to the diagnostic controls inherent in administrative practices. Diagnostic controls provide feedback systems that monitor organizational outcomes and help to correct deviations from performance without active managerial attention (Simons, 1994). These controls shape strategy by shaping the actions of subordinates through performance indicators, rewards and sanctions (Marginson, 2002). As such, they require little direct engagement between top managers and other organizational members. For example, targets are established, imposed and monitored through the planning cycle, such as 'a saving of 10 to 20 per cent of formal teaching responsibilities and 10 to 20 per cent of assessment time' (SPC minutes, 1995/96). Control over the way others contribute to the strategy can be delegated to the administrative practices, using the budget model to 'penalize departments if they don't recruit to target' (DVC, Corporate). Other actors can also use the diagnostic controls to shape the actions of those around them, as exemplified by the department head who sought disciplinary procedures to control his staff. Similarly, rewards are available for those groups that meet or exceed targets. They are able to amass more resources. Diagnostic control thus further embeds activity by indicating what type of actions are desirable and attaching rewards and sanctions to those actions.

PROCEDURAL STRATEGIZING CONFERS STRUCTURAL LEGITIMACY

Procedural strategizing plays an important role in shaping strategy through structural embedding and diagnostic control. This form of shaping strategy may be understood in practice theory as conferring structural legitimacy. Structures are the collective systems within which people carry out their daily activities and practices. They are socially produced and reproduced by the routinization of daily practices within a social context (Giddens, 1984: 19). We may thus conceive of organizations as social structures, produced and held together by the routine practices that coordinate the daily activities of those within them (Ranson et al., 1980). While these practices are socially produced, they have greater duration than any individual and thus impart stability to organization, which is a key feature of the practice theory discussed in Chapter 1. Structural legitimacy refers to the social order displayed in stabilized structural practices, such as routines, hierarchies and roles.[2] Legitimacy is derived from taking part in and reinforcing that social order. A key feature of activities that have structural legitimacy is their persistence in practices and routines without continuous attention by individuals or groups of individuals (Clegg, 1989; Lawrence et al., 2002). Activity is institutionalized and taken for granted: 'the way we do things here'. If people wish to de-legitimize this activity, they will need to expend considerable effort to counteract the administrative practices that enable its persistence. Such efforts might, themselves, be perceived as illegitimate because they subvert the existing social order (Clegg, 1989; Giddens, 1984; Weber, 1978). Activities that have structural legitimacy have long duration because they are embedded in the persistent social order of the organization.

Procedural strategizing confers structural legitimacy because it embeds activity in routine administrative practices that convey formal responsibilities, rewards and sanctions for doing that activity. Structural legitimacy is an important concept in understanding how activity is shaped. It provides an activity with stability and persistence. Most importantly, it imparts legitimacy: the right of that activity to be part of the organizational profile and to be pursued. Exhibit 4.1 explains how commercial activity at Modern gained increasing structural legitimacy over each planning cycle. Indeed, by its fourth year in the planning cycle, top managers spoke of performance indicators and rewards as a way to 'concentrate their minds'. Administrative practices could be used to differentiate commercial performance, 'pinpoint' non-performers and 'embed this in the University culture'. Commercial activity thus gained structural legitimacy, becoming further embedded each year and strengthening its persistence through the administrative practices that it attracted. Of course, strategizing through formal administrative practices and controls alone cannot ensure others' cooperation in an activity. Nonetheless, structural legitimacy is a powerful means of generating commitment to activity (Clegg, 1989; Weber, 1978).

PROBLEMS: STRATEGIC DRIFT AND SITUATED RELEVANCE OF CONTROLS

The persistence occasioned by structural legitimacy, however, indicates the problems associated with procedural strategizing. There are two main problems with shaping strategy through procedural strategizing: strategic drift and the situated relevance of diagnostic controls. Strategic drift occurs when the formal administrative practices, rather than the activity at which they are directed, become the focus of attention. One of the strengths of embedding activity in administrative practices is that it becomes taken for granted. However, this has an inherent weakness because the debate moves away from goal-directed activity to the administrative practices themselves. For example, at Modern top managers noted that despite 'lots of discussion about strategic plans . . . there won't be influence on strategic direction from them' (Exhibit 4.1). The existence of plans contains the debate to the plans rather than the directions. Activity is thus shaped by the targets, metrics and measures devised rather than by its original goals. Unless these metrics are very accurate, carefully aligned to directions and regularly adjusted, activity is increasingly dictated by the practices in which it is embedded. This is termed goals–means displacement; the means for shaping activity displace the goals of that activity (Cyert and March, 1963). As it is questionable whether many activities can be so accurately measured and realigned, and as the practices themselves are taken for granted, the activity may drift significantly from its original goals. This problem is consequential; strategic drift is typically associated with poor firm performance (Johnson, 1987; Miller, 1991).

While the strategic drift effects of goals–means displacement had not set in with commercial activity at Modern, this activity was still being actively embedded. It was more evident with structurally embedded activities that had long historical duration in the case studies, which is consistent with the literature on inertia (for example, Burgelman, 1994; Miller and Friesen, 1984). Only Entrepreneurial avoided the drift associated with procedural embedding because administrative practices there had high managerial discretion built into their use. For example, on resource allocation 'Differential treatment is accorded to departments depending on their rating [in research and teaching]. Special allowance is made for small departments and there is a 10 per cent premium for bench sciences' (Resource Committee Minutes, 1995). Differential treatment and special allowance require managerial discretion, which involves ongoing managerial attention, taking procedural strategizing into a different dimension. This point will be picked up in Chapter 5, where different forms of strategizing will be proposed.

Exhibit 4.2: Legitimate controls counteract legitimate activity

Procedural strategizing and strategic drift at Collegiate University

Collegiate has a long-held size and scope goal of preserving a full range of academic disciplines, not allowing disciplinary balance to be dictated by 'transitory shifts of student fashion' (Planning documents, 1996). However, it is also constrained by space to a policy of zero-growth. In order for all disciplines to be maintained, it is vital that growth in one department does not squeeze out another. Size and scope goals thus acknowledge that student balance is also important. In particular, postgraduate to undergraduate ratios and ethnic balance need to be maintained, to prevent excessive growth in marketable postgraduate courses for high-fee-paying overseas students. Excess growth will threaten the cherished goal that 'the University wants to be represented across the whole range of academic disciplines' (Senior Academic 6). In order to shape size and scope activity, in 1992/93 the Resource Committee developed a diagnostic control: Minimum Quota Allocations (MQAs).

The MQA is a points-based staff resource allocation system for departments, based upon five yearly rolling reviews. Departments are given points for the number of students they have in addition to other measures. Within their allocation of points, departments may make staff appointments at their own discretion. The quotas are supposed to control size and scope by ensuring that less marketable departments can survive because they get enough points, while more marketable ones cannot grow excessively, ensuring the zero-growth and student balance goals. However, 'what tended to happen is that the allocation decisions about how much a department is going to get was sort of taken a bit in isolation so you weren't consciously trading off one against the other; 100 MQAs here meant less somewhere else' (Senior Academic 6). In order to manage the growing tensions between departmental resource needs, departments were allowed to gain additional MQA points, above those in their initial five-year allocation, by recruiting more full-fee-paying students. This system was unintentionally inflationary, with departments exploiting the MQAs to grow, increasing student numbers, distorting the student balance and threatening the range of disciplines.

Top managers pointed this out to the Resource Committee in 1995/96, showing them how the control system was inflationary, leading to a deficit, and distorting the scope of the institution in terms of UG:PG numbers, ethnic balance and market-led growth. As this totally counteracted the size and scope goals, which were collectively seen as important in order to avoid disciplinary scope being dictated by the fashions of the market, the Resource Committee adjusted the procedures so that departmental MQAs would be 'more rigorously linked to their performance in generating income, while taking account of other factors such as staff: student ratios' (RC Minutes,

1995/96). These tweaks to the procedures were not effective and excess student growth continued year-on-year, increasing distortion in size and scope goals: 'Each year we say we won't let the numbers change and we do' (RC meeting observation).

Despite attempts to control departmental growth through the MQA system, the Resource Committee was reluctant to develop more stringent diagnostic controls that would encourage more efficient use of resources and prevent departments from growing excessively. 'The Resource Committee is pretty spineless about resource allocation . . . it finds it pretty easy to dole out an expanding cake but much harder to change the angle subtended in the slice if it means one group getting less than it did before' (Senior Academic 5). While these diagnostic controls are ineffective, they have arisen because they are legitimate within the context of academic autonomy at Collegiate. They were devised on the basis of their legitimacy to other actors, albeit that this legitimacy is acknowledged as a bind. 'Ever since we started we tried desperately to find something to shut down. Some bit of macho management that could show we meant business and we never succeeded . . . in a sense because, being insiders, we knew what our limitations were' (Senior Academic 4). As a result, drift in size and scope activity persisted, recognizing too late how this was impacting upon the goals of that activity. 'There are an awful lot of strategic decisions which get taken simply by incremental drift, and we only realize in retrospect that they were strategic decisions' (DVC, External).

Exhibit 4.2 is an example of how procedural strategizing can be prone to goals–means displacement. It describes the diagnostic controls used to shape the size and scope strategy at Collegiate University. It is an extreme example, incorporating as it does the second problem of procedural strategizing, the need to use diagnostic controls that have situated relevance. As the example shows, the goals of size and scope activity were to maintain a multi-disciplinary institution with a balanced ethnic and postgraduate to undergraduate profile, all within the context of zero growth. This goal had structural legitimacy. It was documented in the annual strategic plans and interviewees subscribed to it as a goal. However, actions, year-on-year, were in contrast to the goal because of the weakly sanctioned diagnostic controls available to shape size and scope activity. At Collegiate, there is a culture of professional resistance to overt control. Diagnostic controls are thus weakly sanctioned and normative forms of control are more applicable. Diagnostic controls, such as the points-based Minimum Quota Allowance (MQA) system, have situated relevance because they do not incur penalties and are exercised in a negotiable way. These controls were, however, problematic in terms of goals–means displacement because they allowed departments to focus on the specific metrics of the quota allowances and use these to grow staff by growing students. Even when top managers realized that the controls were having unintended consequences, they found it hard to change them. This was not because departments were resistant to the size and scope goals, but because the controls were weakly sanctioned and therefore less able to align activity towards goals. However, they have situated relevance in the Collegiate context, whereas 'macho management' does not. The simple answer is to devise and impose a new set of controls that are more accurately aligned to activity. However, if the community does not accept these as relevant forms of control, their rewards and sanctions will not be effective (Ferrary, 2002). Eventually, Collegiate did develop a new set of controls, but this involved a move away from purely procedural forms of strategizing in order to fashion controls that were sensitive to the context.

Quick Reference Guide 4.1: Purposes and problems of procedural strategizing

- Procedural strategizing confers structural legitimacy on strategy through structural embedding and diagnostic controls.

- Structural legitimacy means that strategy is embedded within the routine practices that will enable its persistence without active managerial attention.

- Structural embedding has a tendency towards goals–means displacement, where action is directed at the practices, not the goals of the strategy. This is associated with strategic drift and poor performance.

- The longer that an activity has been structurally embedded, the greater likelihood that it will be prone to goals–means displacement and strategic drift.

- Diagnostic controls must have situated relevance, meaning that their rewards and sanctions must be perceived as relevant to the community. In professional contexts, situated relevance is associated with weakly sanctioned diagnostic controls that tend to shape strategy in unintended ways.

THE DYNAMICS OF SHAPING STRATEGY THROUGH PROCEDURAL STRATEGIZING

This section draws upon the above discussion to model the activity system dynamics of shaping strategy through procedural strategizing. These dynamics are modelled to capture and simplify the relationship between strategizing and patterns of activity. The activity system modelling in Figure 4.1 illustrates how procedural strategizing mediates influence over activity. There are three key points about procedural strategizing incorporated in the model:

Figure 4.1: Activity system dynamics of procedural strategizing

- Procedural strategizing confers structural legitimacy upon activity. Through structural legitimacy, the activity itself assumes primary influence in the dynamics of the activity system in terms of attracting targets, roles, responsibilities and other formal administrative practices that enable its persistence. Hence, activity is in bold type and dominates the two-way arrows of influence within the system.
- This structural embedding of activity tends towards goals–means displacement, according the formal administrative practices a secondary influence over the dynamics of the activity system, through their relationship with the activity. Practices are, therefore, also in bold type with a two-way link to activity.
- The strong relationship between administrative practices and activity shapes the way the community contributes to, or resists, activity and shapes the agency of top managers over activity, as captured by the two-way arrows to these parts of the system.

The overall dynamics captured by this modelling indicate the structural legitimacy of activity, which give it stability and persistence but also link it strongly to those administrative practices that shape its destiny. In this configuration of the activity system, the projective agency of top managers is marginalized and influence to shape strategy is iterative, relying upon existing patterns of activity and the formal administrative practices (Emirbayer and Mische, 1998). Figure 4.1 thus helps to capture the activity system dynamics of procedural strategizing that are involved in shaping strategy.

THE PURPOSE AND PROBLEMS OF INTERACTIVE STRATEGIZING

In this section, the purpose and problems of interactive strategizing are explained. Interactive strategizing is defined as purposive face-to-face interaction between top managers and other members of the organizational community in order to shape the flow of strategy.[3] It is a powerful strategizing resource because it involves direct communication and close attention by top managers (Simons, 1991, 1994). It is thus distinct from the largely self-perpetuating nature of procedural strategizing discussed above. Its main purposes are to generate frameworks of meaning and normative controls that confer interpretative legitimacy upon activity. Interactive strategizing is important for introducing new strategies, countering resistance by framing them as necessary and desirable. It is also important for reframing existing strategies and realigning them to their goals. The main problem with interactive strategizing is that the frameworks of meaning developed are not durable. They require ongoing interaction, during which the meanings themselves might be modified. This section concludes by modelling the activity system dynamics of using interactive strategizing to shape strategy, showing how it mediates influence towards top managers.

PURPOSE: FRAMING MEANING AND NORMATIVE CONTROL

The purposes of interactive strategizing are to build frameworks of meaning about strategy that might influence others' actions, making others 'self-conscious about their activity' (DVC, Entrepreneurial), 'bringing people around' (Planning Registrar, Modern) and 'getting others to think that they want what we want' (VC, Collegiate). Framing meaning about strategy constitutes a form of normative control, in which others fashion their own actions according to those meanings that are dominant within a community (Bartunek, 1984; Lukes, 1974; Ranson et al., 1980). Where there is a dominant framework of meanings, individuals will be self-controlling, subscribing to and aligning their behaviour with those meanings. Framing meaning is important in introducing new strategies into an organization, while framing meaning together with normative control are important for reinterpreting existing strategies and helping to align actions with strategic goals (Bartunek, 1984). These purposes of interactive strategizing are now explored empirically.

Exhibit 4.3: Making things happen through interaction

Interactive strategizing at Collegiate University

While Collegiate derives its identity and prestige from being a world-class research institution, research activity was showing some of the negative consequences and problems of structural embedding. Many departments were performing soundly, but not all were of the excellent standard required. Because of the Research Assessment Exercise (RAE), lower research performance has both prestige and also funding consequences. However, due to weakly sanctioned diagnostic controls, top managers had little overt control over lower performers. They set about a process of interactive strategizing to reframe and reinvigorate research activity. These face-to-face interactions were intended to 'get people to rally around the RAE' (VC in meeting observation) and to establish normative controls, 'Kind of saying to people, "Look, you've got to be more research active, otherwise you are effectively freeloading on everybody else"' (Senior Academic 1).

As part of this reframing, top managers wished to appoint a number of world-renowned research professors in targeted areas. 'The VC's aim is for all departments to get a 5 . . . Um, he's been trying to tackle this by bringing in world-class scholars in the weak areas' (Senior Academic 1). This action was contentious in two ways. First, the differential pay to attract such scholars does not accord with 'a community of equals' (Senior Academic 3). Second, this is not an area of top team discretion, being approved by the Appointments Committee. A series of face-to-face interactions were necessary to generate support for the action. The VC first talked with the chair of the Appointments Committee: 'He obviously turned to me and I made sure the Committee was well mobilized to deal with that' (Senior Academic 2). Negotiations with the key professors on the Appointments Committee emphasized the benefits to the elite reputation of the University, so framing alignment between the activity and the research goals. Interactions with key players triggered further interactions to generate support prior to the meeting: 'I did my best and persuaded colleagues' (Senior Academic 2). These interactions were effective in framing meanings with these key actors: 'We could have said no. Why did we say yes? We are very conscious of the RAE and the need to be 5-star. The VC made a very convincing case . . . And we thought this was a good thing' (Senior Academic 2).

The Appointments Committee was thus mobilized to appoint these world-class professors. However, it does not actually allocate resources. The VC also had to persuade the Resource Committee to approve the strategy and recommend the resources for approval to yet another committee, the Academic Board. A further series of face-to-face interactions were necessary with Resource Committee members to persuade them of the importance of the action. These interactions were again effective, with the action approved for resources at the meeting: 'He then had to go to the Resource Committee, but, because [Member] was on board, that wasn't too big a problem' (DVC, External). By this time, interactions had built sufficient momentum that it was also passed by the Academic Board. This ability to construct an action through skilled interactive strategizing gained the VC approval: 'Here's a VC who can actually make things happen' (Senior Academic 1).

An incident in reframing the research strategy at Collegiate University is described in Exhibit 4.3, which shows how interactive strategizing both frames meaning and constitutes normative controls. Research is the core strategic activity at Collegiate, which derives its identity and prestige from being a world-class research institution. As part of this, Collegiate aims to outperform competitors in the Research Assessment Exercise (RAE) and to be at the top of the league tables for research rankings.

However, as the Exhibit shows, the problems of structurally embedded historical activity were present in the way others contributed to research, so that some departments were not of the excellent standard required. Generally, top managers felt that research activity needed to be reinvigorated, so that performance in the RAE and bolstering the world class research reputation were brought to the forefront of people's minds and, therefore, actions. Interactive strategizing was a means of reframing the research strategy to other actors and guiding it away from potential strategic drift. They engaged in extensive interactive strategizing to interpret to others the importance of the RAE and make them self-conscious about their own performance. As part of this, the Exhibit recounts an incident of interactive strategizing to gain organizational consent to appoint world-class research professors. The incident shows the importance of interactive strategizing in making 'a very convincing case' and ensuring that others 'thought this was a good thing'. Both the surrounding frameworks of meaning, in terms of reasserting the importance of research activity within the wider organization, and the specific frameworks of meaning attributed to this single incident, enabled action to be taken. In the wider process, normative controls were constituted, encouraging others to assume self-control over their contributions to research activity 'otherwise you are effectively freeloading on everybody else'. Interactive strategizing was thus used in reframing and normatively controlling research activity, reasserting its importance in this particular incident.

Interactive strategizing can also be used to introduce a new strategy into an organization and give it credibility with the community. New strategies constitute change and, therefore, typically meet resistance (Denis et al., 2001). Interactive strategizing can counteract resistance by framing the activity as desirable or necessary. At Modern, which had been primarily a teaching-led institution, top managers undertook a major interactive strategizing exercise, Agenda for Modern, in 1994 in 'an effort to re-identify where Modern was going' (former DVC). This was initiated by top management but incorporated people from across the University, including senior managers, heads of departments, academics and administrators in a series of face-to-face interactions about changes to the strategic profile of the University. Subsequent consultative documents generated furthered interactions, engaging much of the University community in a phase of widespread interactive strategizing. The exercise served as a means of reframing teaching activity and introducing new activities, such as research and commercial activity that had not been historically accepted in the organization. For example, previously with research activity 'We took the view, strategically, that we couldn't be a research university' (former

VC). Interactive strategizing was a way of framing these activities as desirable and counteracting historical resistance to them. It gave both activities 'a kind of confirmation' (former VC). Research began to be seen as 'a vision thing, it's a "This University will, firstly, raise its reputation, profile through research"' (DVC, Finance). Commercial activity was framed as necessary: 'As the finances tighten, you have to steer the University in a particular direction, down the income generation route' (DVC, Corporate). While there was a continued emphasis on retaining teaching excellence, at the end of the year of interactive strategizing, commercial activity and research activity were incorporated into the strategic profile and strategic planning cycle of the University. Interactive strategizing may thus frame new activities as necessary or desirable, counteracting initial resistance to them.

The purpose of interactive strategizing is to frame meanings about strategy that provide normative control. It is a valuable aid in reframing existing strategies and in framing the desirability and necessity of new strategies. In the Collegiate example it was used to reinvigorate the research strategy and to try to counteract the negative consequences of structural embedding. In the Modern example, it was used to launch two new areas of activity that initially had low legitimacy with the organizational community, enabling them to become part of the administrative practices.

INTERACTIVE STRATEGIZING CONFERS INTERPRETATIVE LEGITIMACY

In practice theory, mutual intelligibility is at the heart of people's ability to act collectively (Garfinkel, 1967; Suchman, 1987). Interactive strategizing enables mutual intelligibility by framing common meanings and by establishing normative controls. This form of strategizing thus confers interpretative legitimacy upon activity. Interpretative legitimacy refers to those frameworks of meaning through which individuals understand what constitutes appropriate action in a community. Through interaction with each other, individuals construct those interpretative frameworks that confer meaning and legitimacy upon their actions (Brown and Duguid, 1991; Giddens, 1984; Lave and Wenger, 1991). This does not mean that each individual holds the same interpretations but that each individual understands what constitutes acceptable behaviour in this context and is thus able to act in ways that are intelligible to others (Neilsen and Rao, 1987; Weick and Roberts, 1993). Such meanings thus constitute a legitimating framework in which to act. Organization theory has shown how frameworks of meaning legitimate particular organizational configurations and structural arrangements (Bartunek, 1984; Greenwood and Hinings, 1993; Ranson et al., 1980). When an activity is interpretatively framed as legitimate to an organization, actions directed at it are legitimate, while non-action is not legitimate (Clegg, 1989; Hardy, 1996; Weber, 1978). For example, consider this extract about research performance at Entrepreneurial:

> I'll never forget the first RAE I saw, where a couple of departments performed poorly and worse than people expected . . . it was almost like vultures had descended upon them. There was no way the rest of the institution was going to put up with those departments letting the side down. (Governor, Chair)

In this extract, the framework of meaning is strong and widespread across the University. Excellence in research has interpretative legitimacy. Acting in ways that support that excellence is, therefore, legitimate, while not doing so is illegitimate, validating 'performers' in exercising normative control over 'non-performers'. The extract illustrates the strong relationships between interpretative legitimacy and normative control (Giddens, 1984). Interactive strategizing, with its emphasis on framing meaning and normative control, thus confers interpretative legitimacy on strategy.

Interpretative legitimacy is most commonly shaped by the dominant actors in an organization because of asymmetries of power and access to the resources through which meaning is framed (Lukes, 1974; Ranson et al., 1980). This is not, however, absolute, because of the diffuse sources from which power over meaning is derived (Whittington, 1992). For example, at Collegiate top managers acknowledge that their ability to frame meaning is an ongoing process of persuasion: 'If you are going to be in a position that we are, where we have very few real powers here . . . you have got to be able to carry people' (DVC, Academic Affairs). The ability to imbue activity with interpretative legitimacy is indeed weighted towards top managers, but only in so much as they are skilled at interacting with others to generate this legitimacy. Indeed, Suchman cautions against looking for structural invariants, normative rules of conduct or preconceived cognitive schema, emphasizing the emergent nature of action arising from the 'moment-by-moment interactions between actors' (1987: 179). Interpretative legitimacy is thus expected to be a source of ongoing construction, rather than a singular dominant framework of durable meanings (Weick, 1979).

PROBLEMS: FRAMEWORKS OF MEANING ARE NOT DURABLE

The ongoing construction of meaning is the main problem with interactive strategizing; frameworks of meaning are not durable. Interactive strategizing is underpinned by the theory of double interacts (Weick, 1979). The principle of a double interact is that an interaction generates a response, which then incurs another response. Each of these interacts is a moment of framing meaning, which is then framed and reframed through the series of interacts it triggers, each of which may shape or alter the initial meaning. Interactive strategizing is thus not a single incident of framing meaning but a series of incidents, each of which frames meaning about that incident. In these interacts, the dominant party will have greater influence in framing meaning. However, any interaction also has the capacity for renegotiating meaning, depending upon the responses it receives. In autonomous professional contexts, such as a university, divergent goals and interests mean that interpretative legitimacy cannot be taken for granted or assumed durable. Meanings require continuous renegotiation in order to impart any stability of shared purpose (Strauss, 1978). For example, in Exhibit 4.3, powerful academic staff 'could have said no' but did not because 'the VC made a very convincing case'. The ability to reframe strategy in any particular incident is dependent on the interactive strategizing associated with that incident. When a series of such incidents are taking place, meaning frameworks develop a degree of consistency that lends a feeling of stability to interpretative legitimacy. The strong framing of research excellence at Entrepreneurial, for example, may be partially attributed to the ongoing framing of meaning by top managers (see Exhibit 5.3). However, in each incident of interactive strategizing, frameworks of meaning are reconstructed, highlighting their impermanence and the need for chronic reconstruction (Neilsen and Rao, 1987; Suchman, 1987; Weick, 1979). Interpretative legitimacy is not, therefore, something that an activity attains and maintains. It must be reaffirmed on an ongoing basis, requiring top managers to engage in ongoing interactive strategizing.

THE DYNAMICS OF SHAPING STRATEGY THROUGH INTERACTIVE STRATEGIZING

This section draws upon the above discussion to model the activity system dynamics of shaping strategy through interactive strategizing. Figure 4.2 illustrates how interactive strategizing mediates influence over activity towards top managers. There are three key points about interactive strategizing incorporated in the model:

- In this study, interactive strategizing confers agency upon top managers to frame meanings about activity. Thus, top managers have the dominant influence over shaping activity, as indicated by the bold type.
- This agency is socially constructed through influencing the frameworks of meanings that others attribute to activity. Top managers are not all-powerful in this situation, as the nature of interaction also accords the community power to frame meanings. Thus the influence to shape activity, while privileging top managers, is not one-way but two-way, as the arrow indicates.
- These meanings constitute normative controls that link community actions to goal-directed activity. If the community accepts the interpretative legitimacy of an activity, this legitimacy constitutes normative controls that influence their contributions to the activity. However, meanings and, therefore, normative controls are not durable but must be continuously reconstructed through ongoing interactive strategizing. Hence the arrow to goal-directed activity is also two-way, to indicate the impermanence of interpretative legitimacy.

Figure 4.2: Activity system dynamics of interactive strategizing

Top managers

Face-to-face
interaction

Organizational
community

Strategy:
Goal-directed
activity

Quick Reference Guide 4.2: Purposes and problems of interactive strategizing

- Interactive strategizing is used to frame meanings that confer interpretative legitimacy on strategy.

- Interpretative legitimacy constitutes a form of normative control because it frames actions that contribute to legitimized activity as legitimate while those that detract from it are not.

- When introducing a new strategy into an organization, interactive strategizing is important for framing the new strategy as desirable or necessary in order to counteract the resistance to change that typically occurs.

- Interactive strategizing is useful in reinterpreting existing strategies, reasserting their importance within the organization and realigning actions with goals. This is particularly valuable with historically embedded activities that, without reinterpretation, tend towards goals–means displacement and strategic drift.

- Interpretative legitimacy is not durable. It must be continuously reconstructed through ongoing interactive strategizing.

The dynamics of this activity system model illustrate a distinctly different pattern to the dynamics of procedural strategizing shown in Figure 4.1. Interactive strategizing primarily mediates influence over activity towards top managers, affording them the projective agency discussed in Chapter 1, albeit that this agency is derived in consultation with their community.

CONCLUSION: POINTS TO TAKE FORWARD

This chapter has addressed the first research question on the implications of procedural and interactive strategizing for shaping strategy in four ways:

1 It has provided empirical examples of procedural and interactive strategizing in the exhibits and the text. Empirical examples are helpful in interpreting theoretical definitions and bringing them to life.
2 It has explained the purposes and problems of using these two types of strategizing to shape strategy:

- Procedural strategizing provides administrative practices that structurally embed strategy. It confers structural legitimacy on strategy, enabling its persistence through routinized administrative practices that require little managerial attention. However, the administrative practices used are prone to goals–means displacement. Hence, procedural strategizing tends towards strategic drift and poor performance over time.
- Interactive strategizing is used to frame meanings that confer interpretative legitimacy upon strategy. Interpretative legitimacy is associated with normative controls that encourage others to align their own actions to the strategy. Interactive strategizing is valuable for introducing new strategies into the organization and for reinterpreting existing strategies. However, the frameworks of meaning established are not durable and need to be continuously reconstructed through interactive strategizing. The impermanence of interpretative legitimacy thus requires ongoing commitment of managerial attention.

Taken together, procedural and interactive strategizing appear to counterbalance each other. Framing meaning counteracts goals–means displacement by reasserting the goals of an activity, while procedural strategizing provides the persistence that is lacking in frameworks of meaning.

3 These counterbalancing influences of the two types of strategizing are drawn together and captured by modelling their activity system dynamics. The activity system diagrams are useful for understanding how different types of strategizing mediate influence over strategy. They capture differences by illustrating how procedural strategizing confers influence on existing activity and administrative practices, while interactive strategizing confers influence over activity on top managers in association with their

community. Procedural and interactive strategizing thus seem to be polar types; the former imparting structural legitimacy, while the latter imparts interpretative legitimacy.

4 The key purposes and problems with using each type of strategizing have been pulled together into quick reference guides that explain procedural and interactive strategizing and their relationship with shaping strategy. These quick reference guides summarize the main contributions this chapter makes to an activity-based view of strategy as practice. The points, which are drawn from the empirical and theoretical discussion, highlight how different types of strategizing shape strategy in different ways. They thus provide important conceptual building blocks for explaining variation in shaping patterns of strategy, which will be developed in the next chapter.

Through these four points, this chapter has addressed the implications of procedural and interactive strategizing, explaining those phases of activity in which they will be most useful. In this analysis, the strengths of one type of strategizing appeared to counteract the weaknesses of the other. This became increasingly evident as the activity system dynamics of the two types were analysed, appearing as complementary polar types. Building upon this complementarity, the next chapter examines the linkages between structural and interpretative legitimacy afforded by different combinations of the two types of strategizing. From this investigation it will be possible to draw more robust links between types of strategizing and the way they shape strategy.

NOTES

1 Typical formal administrative practices associated with shaping strategic activity are strategic plans, budget plans, operating plans, management information systems, key performance indicators, trend analyses, quarterly returns, staff planning systems, asset utilization indicators and other such formal, frequently diagnostic mechanisms for documenting, coordinating, implementing and informing the strategy formation process. This book does not to go into detail on the merits of various formal administrative practices. However, Ansoff's (1965) text remains a good example of the types of formal practices available to support the strategy process. Helpful critiques of how these practices are put to use in organizations are Bower (1970), Burgelman (1983) and Simons (1991, 1994).

4 This form of legitimacy is also variously referred to as system integration (Lockwood, 1964) or systemic power (Clegg, 1989; Lawrence et al., 2002). Structural legitimacy has been used in this book, both to reflect the practice-based theory of structuration (Giddens, 1979, 1984) and to convey the sense of organizational structure that arises from strategizing through formal administrative practices.

3 While interactive strategizing might take other forms than face-to-face, in this study top managers identified face-to-face as important. The value of direct interaction through face-to-face has been noted in other studies, such as Orlikowski (2002), Sapsed and Salter (2004) and Simons (1991, 1994).

5 SHAPING STRATEGY AND THE STRATEGIZING MATRIX

Key points

- Strategizing involves different combinations of structural and interpretative legitimacy

- The strategizing matrix: pre-active, procedural, interactive and integrative strategizing

- The activity system dynamics of different types of strategizing

- Five patterns of strategy that are shaped by their movement through types in the strategizing matrix

- Practical examples of how strategizing types shape patterns of strategy

In Chapter 4 procedural and interactive strategizing were noted to be opposing but complementary types. These distinctions are based on the way that they confer structural legitimacy or interpretative legitimacy upon activity. Structural legitimacy enables an activity to persist through the administrative practices that it commands, but this is tempered by the problem of strategic drift from the goals of the activity. Interpretative legitimacy enables frameworks of meaning to be constructed between top managers and the community that affirm the relevance of goals, but these meanings lack durability. The two thus shape strategy in different and complementary ways, appearing as two sides of the same coin. This chapter examines the nature of these two types of legitimacy and how they combine to shape strategy. In doing so it builds upon the activity system modelling in the previous chapter to examine how different types of strategizing convey different influences over activity. It thus addresses the second research question: How are different activity system dynamics involved in shaping strategy as a pattern in a stream of goal-directed activity over time?

This chapter is in two sections. The first section addresses the first part of the research question by locating different activity system dynamics in different combinations of structural and interpretative legitimacy. These combinations are developed into a matrix of four types of strategizing:

- pre-active;
- procedural;
- interactive; and
- integrative.

These four types explain various phases of strategy development found in the empirical study. The activity system dynamics of each strategizing type are modelled within the strategizing matrix to facilitate comparison. The second section examines the second part of the research question by providing empirical examples of how different types of strategizing shape patterns of strategy over time. Five main patterns in shaping strategy are found in the empirical data:

- introducing localized activity;
- changing activity;
- stabilizing activity;
- unresolved activity; and
- inertial activity.

Empirical examples of each of these patterns are provided. The chapter concludes by drawing the two sections together and showing how strategizing types explain variation in strategy as a pattern in a stream of goal-directed activity over time.

THE STRATEGIZING MATRIX AND ACTIVITY SYSTEM DYNAMICS

This section develops a matrix of four strategizing types based on high and low combinations of structural and interpretative legitimacy. The four types are labelled pre-active, procedural, interactive and integrative strategizing.[1] Each type influences different phases of strategy development, involving different activity system dynamics. These dynamics are modelled within the matrix for easy comparison of different influences on the shaping of strategy. This section primarily establishes the conceptual framing of the strategizing matrix and activity system dynamics. Practical examples will be provided in the next section, where these concepts are used to show how different patterns of strategy are shaped over time.

The previous chapter drew out the structural legitimacy and interpretative legitimacy conferred, respectively, by procedural strategizing and interactive strategizing. Structural legitimacy refers to the social order displayed in stabilized structural practices, such as routines, hierarchies and roles. Legitimacy is derived from taking part in and reinforcing that social order. Structural legitimacy means that strategy is embedded within largely routine practices that will enable its persistence without active managerial attention. Interpretative legitimacy refers to those frameworks of meaning through which individuals understand what constitutes appropriate action in a community. Interpretative legitimacy constitutes a form of normative control over strategy because it frames those actions that contribute to the strategy as legitimate, while those that detract from it are not. While top managers have greater influence over interpretative legitimacy, it is constructed in interaction with their communities and so lacks durability, requiring ongoing managerial attention.

These two types of legitimacy are constructed differently and have different influences on strategy. They form the two axes of Figure 5.1, a matrix of different types of strategizing.[2] This matrix is based on whether strategizing types shape strategy through higher or lower combinations of structural and interpretative legitimacy. In placing these forms of legitimacy on separate axes, it is necessary to establish that they are discrete but complementary constructs. That is, can an activity have both forms of legitimacy, and can it also have one without the other? This chapter will show that structural and interpretative legitimacy are both separable and complementary, depending on the form of strategizing used.

PRE-ACTIVE STRATEGIZING

Pre-active strategizing involves activity that has low structural and interpretative legitimacy. This is typical of activities that are localized to pockets of the organization but have not yet attained status as mainstream strategies, which fall into two types:

- bottom-up strategies that are still emerging; and
- new strategies in a very early stage of development.

Bottom-up strategies in the emergent phase are typically pursued by localized groups, but not endorsed or legitimated as strategy in the wider firm (Johnson and Huff, 1998; Mintzberg and Waters, 1985; Regnér, 2003). However, as the second type indicates, strategies do not have to emerge bottom-up to be localized. Top managers also introduce new strategies into an organization. If these strategies are still in the very early phases of development, they may be localized to the top team, comprising pre-active strategizing because of the time and effort needed for an activity to attain interpretative or structural legitimacy. This is particularly likely if a new activity is contentious in the wider community. In this study, pre-active strategizing occurred in the early phases of new activities that were in some way contentious or counter to existing strategy, such as the research strategy at Modern University and the commercial activity strategy at Collegiate University. Pre-active strategizing is typical for activity that is localized, either because it is emergent or because it is a new strategy in the very early stages of its development. This strategizing is termed pre-active

Figure 5.1: The strategizing matrix and activity system dynamics

(Bold type and thicker lines denote higher influence over shaping strategy, while arrows denote flows of influence. Practices are central to indicate the way they mediate different activity system dynamics.)

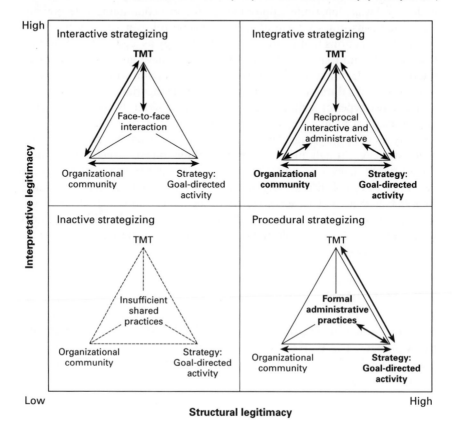

because it has not been activated either interpretatively or structurally in the wider activity system. Hence, as shown in Figure 5.1, the dynamics of influence over strategy are weak.

PROCEDURAL STRATEGIZING

Procedural strategizing involves activity that has high structural legitimacy but low interpretative legitimacy. It refers to strategies that are procedurally embedded, which accounts for the high structural legitimacy. However, the low interpretative legitimacy is typically associated with two ways of shaping strategy:

- activities with goals–means displacement; and
- activities that have 'hijacked' the administrative procedures.

First, activity may no longer have a relevant framework of legitimating meanings because of the goals–means displacement and strategic drift associated with procedural strategizing. In this situation, the interpretative legitimacy of the initial goals is no longer aligned to the procedural embedding of the activity. Rather, the structural legitimacy inherent in the administrative practices is dominant and there is a disconnection with interpretative legitimacy. This is typical with activities that have long historical duration in an organization and have thus drifted from their initial legitimating framework of meanings. The teaching strategy at Modern discussed in Exhibit 5.2, shown later in this chapter, is an example of a historically embedded activity that displayed high structural legitimacy but had lost interpretative alignment with the goals of teaching innovation. Such activities may begin with both interpretative and structural legitimacy, but because interpretative legitimacy is not durable they increasingly display both the strengths and weaknesses of structural legitimacy in terms of persistence as well as strategic drift.

The other possibility is an activity that has 'hijacked' the administrative practices, becoming procedurally embedded without ever generating interpretative legitimacy. This example is found in the unintended procedural embedding of the size and scope strategy at Modern, explained in the next section. A size and scope goal became embedded in the planning practices for ensuring financial viability in the teaching programme and commercial activity. It was unintended, but persisted because it had penetrated the administrative practices and gained structural legitimacy. A similar example is found in Exhibit 2.2 (Chapter 2), where middle managers at Intel used the practices for allocating manufacturing capacity to gain structural legitimacy for the microprocessor strategy before it had gained interpretative legitimacy with top managers or the wider organization.

In both of these situations, as illustrated in Figure 5.1, the activity system dynamics confer influence to shape strategy upon the activity itself and its embedded relationship with the administrative practices. Because interpretative legitimacy is low, the interaction between top managers and the community that establishes such legitimacy is also low. Where procedural strategizing is used to shape strategy, activity system dynamics are dominated by the relationship between existing activity and its administrative practices.

INTERACTIVE STRATEGIZING

Interactive strategizing involves activity that has high interpretative legitimacy but low structural legitimacy. This is typically associated with two ways of shaping strategy:

- new activities that are being introduced to the organization; or
- existing activities that are being reframed to shed the goals–means displacement of their former procedural embedding.

First, new activities encounter resistance because this is a typical organizational response to change, particularly where a new activity appears to threaten an existing activity. Such activities lack structural legitimacy because they have not yet been embedded within the organization. Interactive strategizing generates a framework of meanings that establish the desirability or necessity of the activity. The example below of introducing commercial activity into Collegiate explains how interactive strategizing is used to develop interpretative legitimacy for an activity prior to attempting to embed it structurally.

Second, interactive strategizing can reinvigorate frameworks of meaning in activities which have succumbed to goals–means displacement to the extent that their structural embedding is no longer relevant to their goals. Here interpretative legitimacy is being re-established in order to reframe the activity and realign it to its goals. As shown in Exhibit 5.1, interactive strategizing not only reasserts the interpretative legitimacy of an activity, it also exposes the inadequacy of the current structural embedding and establishes normative controls to counteract them.

Under interactive strategizing, the activity system dynamics will confer the majority of influence over strategy to top managers because of their power to frame meanings and build normative controls. However, as Figure 5.1 illustrates, interpretative legitimacy is neither durable nor one-way, involving reciprocal interaction between top managers and the community, in which the community have the ability to renegotiate meaning. Shaping strategy through interpretative legitimacy thus involves interaction between top managers and the community, weighted in top managers' favour. Because structural legitimacy is low, there is low use of administrative practices to embed the interpretations. Activity system dynamics thus lack durability, requiring ongoing managerial attention through interactive strategizing.

INTEGRATIVE STRATEGIZING

Integrative strategizing involves activity that is high in structural and interpretative legitimacy. Such activity has both the persistence of structural legitimacy and also the relevant meanings and normative controls of interpretative legitimacy. It is called integrative strategizing because it calls for high integration between interactive and procedural forms of strategizing. Face-to-face interaction is used to continuously frame and reframe the importance of goals, while administrative practices are modified on an ongoing basis to prevent goals–means displacement and ensure that diagnostic controls remain relevant to the strategy. Integrative strategizing typically shapes strategy in two ways:

• stabilizing activities, preventing them from sliding into strategic drift; and
• incremental change in activities.

The first of these was evident in the size and scope, commercial and early-phase research activities at Entrepreneurial, which were continuously stabilized and realized throughout the seven years of this study. Tight reciprocal links between interactive and procedural strategizing were important in stabilizing each of these activities. In particular, diagnostic controls, rather than imposing sanctions and rewards without managerial attention, frequently triggered interactive responses, which then triggered modifications to the diagnostics. The pattern of incremental change in activity occurs in much the same way, with progressive shifts in administrative practices and meanings aligning to shape change in activity. An example of this pattern is discussed in Exhibit 5.4, which looks at the research strategy at Entrepreneurial over a seven-year period. This Exhibit shows the reciprocal links between administrative practices and face-to-face interaction that are characteristic of integrative strategizing.

Quick Reference Guide 5.1: Understanding the strategizing matrix

Strategizing type	Activity system dynamics	Role in shaping phases of activity
Pre-active Low structural and interpretative legitimacy	Weak dynamics of influence	Activities that are localized because they are: • emerging bottom-up; or • in the early phases of development, particularly where they are potentially contentious
Procedural High structural and low interpretative legitimacy	Influence is conferred to existing activity and its administrative practices	• Historically embedded activities with goals–means displacement • Activities that have hijacked the administrative practices
Interactive Low structural and high interpretative legitimacy	Influence is conferred to top managers, in interaction with the community	• Introducing new activities in order to counteract resistance to change • Existing activities that are overly embedded, needing reframing and realigning with their goals
Integrative High structural and high interpretative legitimacy	Influence is primarily to top managers but tightly linked to interaction with the community, the activity and administrative and interactive practices	• Stabilizing activities to prevent slide into strategic drift • Incremental change in activities through ongoing reframing of meanings and modifying of administrative practices

As indicated in Figure 5.1, integrative strategizing is the most complete form of activity system dynamics, involving ongoing interaction between top managers, the community and the activity, mediated by a reciprocal relationship between face-to-face interaction and formal administrative practices. Top managers undoubtedly have the greater influence in these dynamics and thus in shaping activity. However, integrative strategizing involves strong interaction between all parts of the activity system in shaping activity.

IMPLICATIONS OF THE STRATEGIZING MATRIX

This section has answered the first part of the research question on how different activity system dynamics are involved in shaping strategy. It has done so by developing a matrix of four strategizing types based upon different combinations of structural and interpretative legitimacy. These four types – pre-active, procedural, interactive and integrative strategizing – involve different dynamics of influence that may be easily compared in Figure 5.1. Each explains a particular phase in the shaping of strategy, which is summarized in Quick Reference Guide 5.1.

Pre-active strategizing is difficult to trace, except retrospectively, because it involves localized activities that are not yet mainstream. Procedural and interactive strategizing are seen as polar types, with opposing activity system dynamics that procedurally perpetuate strategy through embedded structures or interactively alter it through human agency, primarily that of top managers. Strategy that is shaped by one or the other of these two types of strategizing will always be either lacking persistence or becoming overly embedded and inert. Integrative strategizing, on the other hand, brings the two together in a more tightly linked relationship between interpretative and structural legitimacy that can explain stabilizing activity and its incremental change over time. This strategizing matrix and its associated activity, system dynamics, thus contribute to an activity-based view of strategy as practice by explaining how strategizing shapes the phases of activity. The matrix also provides conceptual building blocks in understanding how strategy might be shaped as a pattern in a stream of goal-directed activity over time. The next section will use these building blocks to explore how activity is shaped by movement through the types in the strategizing matrix.

THE STRATEGIZING MATRIX AND SHAPING STRATEGY OVER TIME

In order to take the conclusions from the previous section further, it is necessary to trace how strategy is shaped over time by movement between the strategizing types. In this section five main patterns and some sub-patterns of shaping strategy, which were observed in the empirical data, will be explained with practical examples. The five patterns examine:

- introducing localized activity into mainstream strategy;
- changing existing activity;
- stabilizing activity;
- unresolved activity; and
- inertial activity.

The first four patterns are described using longitudinal empirical examples from the case studies. As the fifth pattern, inertial activity, was inferred in the empirical data but not observed longitudinally, it is described conceptually. All patterns are illustrated with activity system diagrams to illustrate how the dynamics of shaping strategy change with different strategizing types.

INTRODUCING LOCALIZED ACTIVITY INTO MAINSTREAM STRATEGY

Localized activities are particular to the interests of a group in an organization but are not mainstream strategy. These might be emergent activities or activities with top manager sponsorship that are at a very early stage of development. For such an activity to be introduced into the mainstream it must move from pre-active strategizing, where it has neither structural nor interpretative legitimacy, to one of the other types of strategizing. Two sub-patterns were found in the data, intended activity and unintended activity. These two are now described and explained, with activity system illustrations in Figure 5.2.

Intended pattern: pre-active => interactive strategizing

Intended introduction of localized activity involves a move from pre-active strategizing to interactive strategizing. This is typical of an activity that has top management sponsorship but has been localized during an early stage of development, perhaps because it is perceived as contentious in the organization. Commercial activity at Collegiate is an example of this pattern. Commercial activity was very important to top management: 'I worry continuously about our long-term survival. We have got to raise more free money' (Registrar). However, top managers were cautious about introducing commercial activity as a mainstream strategy, fearing widespread resistance to it as an illegitimate activity within a university context: 'There are people who strongly resent the idea that an academic institution should want or need to engage in [commercial] activities, which they see as rather low status and dubious' (Senior Academic 1). It thus remained a localized activity for some time, with only a few minor projects being taken up on a 'one-off' basis.

Increasingly, because of financial pressure, top managers needed to make commercial activity mainstream and legitimate with the community. They began a programme of interactive strategizing with people who could be 'champions for things' in order to generate interpretative legitimacy: 'This [commercial activity] can really work *but* only if it has strong support from the important constituents of the University' (Resource Committee observation). Interactive strategizing enabled the activity to be discussed at important meetings and to gain supportive comment from 'opinion leaders'. Commercial activity moved from pre-active strategizing as it gained tentative interpretative legitimacy: 'Income generation is on the rise as the academics begin to understand it' (Registrar). Interpretative legitimacy was strengthened as interactive strategizing introduced normative controls: 'It is not something you can go in like a bull in a china shop. What we are trying to do is to put the onus on departments to actually think of ways that they can generate more income' (Senior Academic 6). Commercial activity was thus shaped by moving from pre-active strategizing, where it was localized and had low structural and interpretative legitimacy, to interactive strategizing, where it began to gain interpretative legitimacy and vestigial normative controls, becoming part of mainstream strategy, albeit not persistent or durable at this stage. The pattern of introducing localized activity into the mainstream was intended and was initiated by top management.

Unintended pattern: pre-active => procedural strategizing

Unintended introduction of localized activity involves a move from pre-active strategizing to procedural strategizing. This is typical of activity that does not have top management sponsorship but can 'hijack' the existing administrative practices in order to infiltrate mainstream strategy. The size and scope strategy at Modern is an example of this unintended activity pattern. Initially, Modern had no articulated size and scope strategy. Decisions on issues of size and scope were made as they arose, 'very much on an opportunistic basis' (DVC, Corporate). However, as the University began to formalize other aspects of its activity more, such as controlling teaching resources and increasing commercial income through the strategic planning cycle, a goal for size and scope activity emerged as part of these administrative practices. In 1995/96 the financial planning minutes noted that 'It will be important to resolve the issues regarding under-recruiting subject areas . . . [and] consider the withdrawal of provision where . . . [a discipline] is no longer viable.' While it may be typical in a business context to exit from non-profitable areas, it is contrary to the principles of a university, where non-profitable departments may be important to the overall research or disciplinary profile of an institution (Slaughter and Leslie, 1999). Indeed, both other cases had an explicit size and scope goal to protect lower-earning departments from excessive exposure to market forces. However, at Modern the financial planning practices began to dictate a size and scope goal to the extent that in 1998 a department was closed because of under-recruitment. The activity had high structural legitimacy: 'The budget model penalizes them because if they don't recruit to target, then their budget is reduced which is why [Department X] ended up in this intolerable position, heading for a huge budget deficit' (DVC, Finance). However, it was unintended and lacked interpretative legitimacy with both the top managers, who wished 'to be able to tolerate some loss leaders' (TMT Meeting observation) and also the community, where 'small departments are under pressure' (DVC, Research). A size and scope goal of financial viability had emerged and unintentionally infiltrated the organization through the formal administrative practices. The activity went from pre-active to procedural strategizing by hijacking the administrative practices.

In Figure 5.2 the activity system dynamics of the intended and unintended patterns of introducing a localized activity into mainstream strategy are modelled. Unintended activities typically move from localized to mainstream strategy via procedural strategizing, gaining structural legitimacy despite lacking interpretative legitimacy. They are thus likely to lack top management support, emerging by way of the administrative practices either autonomously, as with the size and scope activity at Modern, or more deliberately by other actors using the administrative practices to their own ends (see Intel, Exhibit 2.2). By contrast, intended activities have top management support and thus move via interactive strategizing, establishing interpretative legitimacy as a means of introduction to the community. Once such activities have been introduced to mainstream strategy, their path through the organization will enter one of the other patterns discussed below.

CHANGING EXISTING ACTIVITY

Changing activity refers to modifying or reframing existing activity in some way, rather than exiting it in order to introduce a new activity. This is because strategic exit did not occur in this study. New activities that were introduced had to coexist with the existing strategies. Their introduction is discussed in the above pattern. This section, therefore, deals with activities that are already part of mainstream strategy but need some form of change. Three sub-patterns were found:

- re-framing activity;
- re-embedding activity; and
- chronically reconstructing activity.

Each of these sub-patterns is now explained and accompanied by a practical example. The activity system dynamics of the three patterns are then compared in Figure 5.3.

Reframing activity: procedural => interactive => integrative strategizing

In this sub-pattern, change involves reframing an existing activity. It typically occurs with structurally embedded activities that need reframing to counteract strategic drift. It thus occurs with activities that have high structural legitimacy but have 'come adrift' from their interpretative legitimacy. Change in the size and scope activity at Collegiate, recounted in Exhibit 5.1, is an example of this pattern. In the *first phase* size and scope displayed the negative symptoms of procedural strategizing, in terms of goals–means displacement lending structural legitimacy to actions that ran counter to the goals of the activity. In the *second phase*, interactive strategizing provided the means to reframe the activity.

Figure 5.2: Activity system dynamics of localized to mainstream strategy

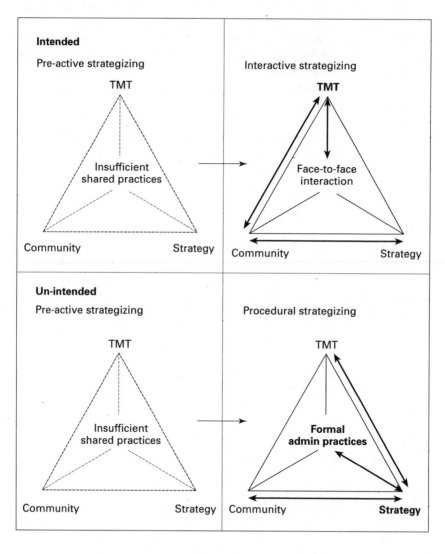

Through interactive strategizing the need for change gained interpretative legitimacy. Interpretative legitimacy for the change prepared the organization for a *third phase*, reframing and legitimating changes in the administrative practices in order to embed the changes. However, administrative changes could not simply be introduced and generate structural legitimacy for changes in activity. Rather, they had to be introduced with ongoing interactive strategizing to ensure the legitimacy of both the practices as well as the changes in size and scope activity. Thus, the third phase in reframing activity involved a shift from interactive to integrative strategizing, using a combination of administrative practices to embed changes in activity whilst supporting the change through ongoing construction of interpretative legitimacy and normative control. The reframing activity pattern shapes strategy through a swing from the strategic drift associated with persistent structural legitimacy to the interpretative legitimacy associated with managerial agency and change, followed by integrative strategizing to build coherence between reframed interpretative legitimacy and newly embedded structural legitimacy.

Exhibit 5.1: Changing for the greater good of the community

Reframing the size and scope strategy at Collegiate University

Phase 1: Procedural embedding
In Exhibit 4.2, the procedural embedding problems of size and scope activity at Collegiate were explained. It had succumbed to goals–means displacement. The community were focusing upon the Minimum Quota Allowance (MQA) method of allocating resources as a way of getting more departmental resources, rather than focusing on the goals of zero-growth, balanced postgraduate to undergraduate student numbers, balanced ethnic diversity and maintenance of the full range of academic disciplines. The MQA was a diagnostic control with situated relevance, being weakly sanctioned and appropriate to a culture of consensual rather than 'macho' management. As a result, activity ran counter to its goals, growing annually and distorting student ratios according to market forces, which also increased tensions about allocating resources between higher and lower earning disciplines. Size and scope activity thus displayed all the problems of procedural strategizing in terms of goals–means displacement, weakly sanctioned controls and strategic drift. It needed to be changed. Exhibit 5.1 picks up the story at this stage.

Phase 2: Procedural to interactive strategizing
Top managers realized that their size and scope strategy was being adversely shaped by the administrative practices: 'Incentives for growth have disturbed the balance between financial integrity and academic considerations, such as the composition and mix of the student body' (Resource Committee Meeting observation). They had 'to stop being rabbits in the headlights' (Governor) and reframe the size and scope activity. Reframing involved reasserting the goals of

student balance and zero-growth in order to maintain the full range of academic disciplines. However, this also needed to be reframed in terms of the cross-subsidization and financial viability issues associated with the goal. Mainly, reframing had to change the actions of the community in relation to the size and scope goals. Top managers used interactive strategizing, beginning by talking with members of the Resource Committee, showing them how the MQA practice was inflationary. Over a two-year period of interactive strategizing, members of Resource Committee became convinced that 'strategically the approach was slightly misguided . . . thinking that space was not a constraint when really it was' (Senior Academic 6). The need to change thus gained interpretative legitimacy, indicating the shift from procedural to interactive strategizing.

Phase 3: Interactive to integrative strategizing
Accepting the legitimacy of change, the Resource Committee began to work with the Finance Director to model resource allocation practices that might better shape the size and scope activity. Together they devised a new practice, Earned Points Score (EPS). EPS is 'meant to be a fairly flexible operation that deals with contraction and growth, that brings some kind of responsibility to departmental level' (Deputy Registrar). EPS represents the income earned by a department, net of various costs such as space and administrative charges, divided by the department's total MQA entitlement. EPS will provide the metrics to think 'here's a subject that we ought to keep in our portfolio, but can we afford to keep it at this size?' (Deputy Registrar, Planning). EPS for different departments will be disseminated to all departments to create greater transparency about performance. No formal sanctions will accrue to lower EPS departments and discretion in cross-subsidy will apply. However, transparency constitutes a form of 're-integrative shaming', so exercising normative control over the change. Interactive strategizing prepared the ground for changes in the activity as well as in the administrative practices that would be used to embed the change.

Interactive strategizing also had to be carried out with wider members of the community, both to convince them that their contributions to size and scope activity needed changing and also to accept the legitimacy of the new administrative practices. Widespread interactive strategizing by all members of the top team occurred in committees and with departmental heads and other staff, both showing people the consequences of distorted size and scope activity and introducing the new administrative practice, EPS, that would be used to embed change. For example, the Registrar pointed out to department heads that the old MQA systems were brought in to gradually get people ready for cuts that can now be phased in. The DVC for External Affairs emphasized that the new system would be easier to use. The VC explained that figures cannot be stable and consistent because of changes in the external environment. These interactions were effective in generating awareness: 'Judging by the number of phone calls I get, it's certainly concentrating minds' (Deputy Registrar, Planning). Top managers were both interpreting and legitimating the change in size and scope activity, and the practices associated with it. In doing so, they are developing both diagnostic and normative controls: 'The way EPS is constructed tries to encourage departments to act in particular ways' (Deputy Registrar, Planning). The top team realizes that, while they can change size and scope activity using EPS, they need to 'do it softly, not a hammer approach' (TMT Meeting observation). Thus, interactive strategizing shifted to integrative strategizing in the final phase. The new administrative practices embedded and controlled change in activity in tight links with interactions that ensured ongoing interpretative legitimacy for both the change in practices and in activity.

Re-embedding activity: procedural => interactive => procedural strategizing

This sub-pattern involves reframing and then structurally re-embedding change to an existing activity. As with the above pattern, it typically occurs with structurally embedded activities that need reframing to counteract strategic drift. The second phase, reframing the activity to gain interpretative legitimacy for change is also the same. However, in the third phase, the changed activity reverts to structural embedding in a new set of administrative practices, without ongoing attention to its interpretative legitimacy. Teaching activity at both Modern and Collegiate followed this path. Exhibit 5.2 recounts this pattern in teaching activity at Modern University. The first two stages are similar to the reframing pattern discussed above. An activity that has structural legitimacy has strayed from its initial interpretative legitimacy and needs reframing. The reframing incorporates radical changes but, having been the subject of widespread interactive strategizing, these changes have developed sufficient interpretative legitimacy within the University to move to another phase of change.

Exhibit 5.2: The more things change, the more they stay the same . . .

Re-embedding change in the teaching strategy at Modern University

Phase 1: Procedural embedding
Historically, Modern is known and has been widely acclaimed for its teaching innovation, having pioneered modular learning. However, increasingly teaching became procedurally embedded in the practices for administering the modular programme, which directed activity towards student-centredness and high pastoral care for students; 'Commitment to the students was tangible and well meant and a lot of people did more than they had to do to commit to that regularly' (Former DVC). While innovation initially legitimated teaching activity, through goals–means displacement, it drifted towards pastoral care:

'That is what it is about now. It is not about pushing back the frontiers of your subject, or new and creative ways of teaching about this that and the other; it is about loving their students and being loved' (DVC, Academic).

Phase 2: Procedural to interactive strategizing
Top managers felt that undergraduate teaching activity was now an overly dominant activity that was using all of staff time, leaving little spare human resource capacity for the other activities that the University had to pursue. During 1994, they engaged in a major inter-active strategizing exercise, Agenda for Modern, in order to reframe not only teaching but the whole strategy profile of the University, due to: 'A feeling that the university was too complacent, too elitist, perhaps unthinking in what it was doing, what it was delivering to students, whether it was giving value, whether it was really up to what the market was expecting of it at the time. So it was just a good look at what we were doing and where we were going to go' (DVC, Corporate).

Agenda for Modern was widespread, engaging departmental heads and lower level actors from across the University in a year of interactive strategizing during which teaching was reframed as over dominant on staff resources in its current form: 'We're trying to thin out teaching because we do over teach' (DVC, Research). At the same time, other activities such as research and commercial activity were introduced and framed as important to the strategic profile of the University. Teaching was thus framed as important in the context of also pursuing other activities, requiring change in existing ways of teaching in order to maintain quality but to lessen time. From top managers' perspective, this meant drawing on the initial roots of innovation in teaching and using it to develop more resource efficient and virtual means of teaching: 'We could be very good at becoming maybe the first of a certain sort of another breed again; we have also to have a strong virtual arm' (DVC, Academic). Reducing time devoted to teaching and reframing it to embrace new forms of teaching was seen as quite a radical change in strategy.

'In a university which prides itself on its modular scheme, it is noth-ing less than revolutionary! To muck about with it. And it is not just about conservatism, it is about the fact that it is so complex. . . . So there are a lot of good reasons about being cautious about the reform of this system. But if you want to produce part-time, proper part-time, because you want to open access . . . And you need to open access because you want to pull people in from the region. And you want to do that because you want to build your regional strategy' (DVC, Academic).

Phase 3: Interactive to procedural strategizing
Teaching was reframed within the context of reducing time given to the existing programme and increasing innovation in current forms of teaching. Staff time could then be redeployed into other strategic activities. Top managers set about embedding the change in the strategic planning cycle. In 1995/96 they proposed that departments plan 'upon achieving a 10 per cent reduction in cost' in preparation

for a 1996/97 'saving of 10 to 20 per cent of formal teaching responsibilities and 10 to 20 per cent of assessment time. These savings may then be used to redeploy resources into strategic priority areas.' The changed activity entered the annual diagnostic control practices, with departments required in their operating statements 'to confirm how they are implementing resource redeployment' of the 10 to 20 per cent reductions in staff time (1997/98 Planning Minutes). After three years of procedurally embedding the change to teaching activity within the planning cycle, top managers set about redeploying the saved resources by changing the teaching year from three terms to two semesters. 'My drive was to create some more space for academic staff. The undergraduate year was too dominant. There was clear agreement to that as a principle, but it had to be approved through the planning process' (VC). Drawing upon procedural strategizing, they embedded the next phase of the change in the planning cycle: 'the University will action a number of reviews aimed at releasing staff time for re-investment . . . specifically the University will review the length and shape of the academic year' (1997/98 Planning Cycle: 7).

However, at Academic Board, academic staff strongly resisted the change, eventually agreeing to scale down the teaching year, but only by moving from three 11-week to three 10-week terms. They saw this as the least disruptive option to their current way of teaching the modular programme: 'We didn't go for semesters in the end. Very strong feelings in the University about this' (DVC, Research). Top management was surprised about the strength of resistance: 'Why do they get so hot and bothered about these sorts of things? About whether we have semesters or terms or things like that?' (Senior DVC). This resistance indicated that the interpretative legitimacy of changing teaching activity had not been clearly established and, despite three years of procedurally embedded reductions in teaching time, there was no real change in the frameworks of meaning associated with teaching.

Resistance to change was clearly illustrated in a senior management meeting with department heads, where the focus of the agenda was upon optimizing the restructured academic year to free staff time for research and commercial activity. Departmental heads kept focusing upon the minutiae of the administrative practices for the changed year, directing attention to how they would have to alter their modules and assessment programmes to fit the shorter terms. They used the procedural embedding of the change to resist its broader goals: 'It is fine to talk about assessment, but you actually get people to try and think concretely about how we are going to reduce assessment load and there are a million reasons why it has to be exactly as it is at the moment' (DVC, Academic).

However, this case shows the problems of establishing interpretative legitimacy and its association with structural legitimacy. The framework of meanings established during the year of interactive strategizing did provide powerful momentum for change in the University. To this extent interpretative legitimacy was achieved. However, it was not durable and commitment to changed activity was weak. To be maintained, greater interactive strategizing was needed, continuously framing and reframing changes in teaching activity as both desirable and necessary. Instead, the change was implemented through procedural strategizing, progressively refining the administrative practices to shape a reduction in the teaching year. To some extent this worked, as reductions in teaching time occurred in accordance with the structural legitimacy imparted by formal directions and controls. However, as activity system dynamics indicate (see Figure 5.3), departmental heads used these practices to subvert the activity and resist the goals of the change, for example, focusing their energy on existing patterns of assessment rather than embracing innovative new teaching methods and redeploying saved time to other activities. In only three years, the activity drifted away from the interpretative legitimacy generated during the year of interactive strategizing. A radical change in teaching activity could not be sustained without ongoing construction of its interpretative legitimacy.

This does not mean that re-embedding is never an option. Teaching activity at Collegiate followed the same pattern, but was re-embedded more successfully because it was not a contentious issue for staff. Essentially, teaching was procedurally embedded in conservative delivery methods with low attention to student service: 'Teaching innovation is slow. Great emphasis given to the lecture and to formal examination' (Deputy Registrar, Academic). However, quality and service standards were inadequate to changes in state policy on teaching quality audits or to the University's financial dependence on high-fee-paying students. Interactive strategizing was successful in showing staff the problem: 'You do it by explaining the enormity of the thing and its significance' (Deputy Registrar, Academic). Change in teaching activity to encompass greater quality and service was framed as a necessity: 'The foreign students are paying very high fees and they were entitled to a better deal' (Senior Academic 1). The reframed teaching quality became embedded in administrative practices 'to improve the delivery of academic services' (Coordination Meeting Minutes) and in University promotion procedures, 'teaching is much more important' (Senior Academic 2), no longer requiring active top manager attention.

The difference in re-embedding these two activities lies in the scope of change (Wilson, 1992). At Modern, teaching was the core activity, with a strong professional identity for organizational members. Reframing it was not going to be simple because the changes were perceived as radical. On the other hand, teaching at Collegiate was procedurally embedded but not the core activity. The changes were less radical and less confronting to the professional identity of the community. Hence, interactive strategizing was able to reframe activity prior to procedurally re-embedding it. Re-embedding is thus an option for shaping changes in activity where the change is not perceived as radical. It is less successful for radical change to a historically embedded activity where establishing interpretative legitimacy may be a long-term process of framing meaning.

Chronically reconstructing: integrative => integrative => integrative strategizing

In this pattern, change involves reciprocity between reframing of existing activity and associated modification of administrative practices. It is about continuously constructing a connection between interpretative and structural legitimacy as an activity is shaped over time. It is therefore termed 'chronic', meaning that the pattern is recurrent (Weick, 1979). The research strategy at Entrepreneurial, described in Exhibit 5.3, is an example of this form of strategizing. In the earlier phases it encompasses the ongoing generation of research excellence, stabilizing research activity by ensuring that others' actions are continuously aligned to the research goals. However, in so doing, top managers also pick up a problem in research activity, the decline in research income, which is both a measure of research excellence and also of its commercial viability. They gradually shape the goals of research activity to encompass a greater dimension of commercial viability, eventually changing substantively to dual goals for research through ongoing integrative strategizing.

Exhibit 5.3: Leaving no stone unturned

Chronically reconstructing the research strategy at Entrepreneurial University

During the period of this investigation, UK university departments were assessed in a state Research Assessment Exercise (RAE) every four years for their research performance on a scale from 1 (poor) to 5* (highest international excellence). The metrics for ranking are complex, but include both the quantity and quality of publication output and, to a lesser extent, external research grants and contracts (RG&C) obtained. Departmental rankings impact upon university funding and reputation. State funding is awarded to a university in accordance with its research excellence in each subject area. Departmental research rankings contribute strongly to a university's overall reputation in league tables. Additionally, external RG&C are important to fund research, increase its financial viability and add to research prestige. Thus, excellent performance in the RAE was essential to Entrepreneurial's goal of being a leading research university. This did not have to include high income from external research grants, but it would certainly help, as well as bolstering the financial viability of research activity. The story is broken down into phases to show how integrative strategizing occurs as a recurrent pattern over time, which can gradually shape change in strategy.

Phase 1: After the 1992 RAE results were released, top managers reviewed substantial formal analyses of university performance, both internally and in comparison with sectoral standards. This procedural strategizing was aimed at determining what were the problem areas in research activity.

Phase 2: The diagnostics were used to inform interactive strategizing, conducting face-to-face reviews into eight lower-rated departments: 'it being the Committee's view that a rating of 3 was not an adequate research performance' (Strategy Committee Minutes, 1993). Reviews were conducted by top managers in conjunction with appropriate senior academics. Face-to-face interaction with department heads and lower-level staff was directed at focusing organizational attention on the research goals 'that has involved going into some discussions with individual members of staff about what their research plans are, individually' (Deputy Registrar, Finance). Quality research was framed as vital to the success of the University, emphasizing the importance of everybody participating in that success: 'Because we think we're a research university, everybody should be performing on the basis of the research model' (Registrar). Interactive strategizing thus reconstructed the importance of the research goals to the community, realigning others' contributions to existing goals.

Phase 3: Interactive strategizing was supported with adjustments in procedural strategizing. This involved putting together research plans with individual staff members, and lower-ranked departments also had annual research reviews established for all staff. Additionally, resources were allocated strategically for early retirements: 'that gave the University flexibility to bring in new people' (Senior DVC) and timescales were developed for a number of new appointments agreed between top managers and departments.

Around this same time, RG&C arose on the Strategy Committee's agenda as a strategic issue because diagnostic controls showed that rates of return were declining. Procedural strategizing was used to circulate information to departments on their performance in attracting research grants, highlighting the central research support available. During 1994/95, detailed analysis of the RG&C performance of individual departments was undertaken and linked to stronger diagnostic controls. This was supported with normative controls involving face-to-face interactions with departments about their performance. The primary strategizing mechanism was procedural, but supported by interactive strategizing to allocate resources in a discretionary way, based on face-to-face negotiations about performance.

Phase 4: In 1995/96 the Strategy Committee proposed the allocation of resources as research incentives to enhance departmental performance in the area of RG&C. The Research Committee was given the brief to interact with departments. After a number of face-to-face interactions, they developed a detailed implementation proposal. Thus, procedural and interactive strategizing went hand-in-hand in realigning research goals around greater RG&C productivity.

Phase 5: In the 1996 RAE, six of the eight departments that had been the focus of intensive integrative strategizing increased their rankings. Top managers believed that the improvement was due to their close attention to framing the importance of research in these departments and providing incentives and controls to support that framing. Thus the cycle of strategic actions was stimulated to begin again, particularly focusing upon those departments which did not perform as well as expected in 1996. These departments were subjected to quite strong normative controls arising from the interpretative legitimacy accorded to excellent research performance. For example, top managers felt validated in intervening directly in those departments: '. . . very centrally inspired by the VC and the Strategy Committee who said, yes, we want to get back up to grade 5. We're not content with grade 4 and we hate grade 3' (Deputy Registrar, Finance). These frameworks of meaning were also validated in the wider community: '. . . a couple of departments performed poorly and worse than people expected. And it was almost like vultures had descended upon them. I mean there was NO WAY the rest of the institution was going to put up with those departments letting the side down' (Governor).

Top managers first conducted extensive formal analysis of performance against the leading research universities across a range of indicators. Interactive strategizing then began again, with the objective of increasing the rating of all non 5* subjects by at least one grade for the next RAE. Analysis of performance and discussion with departmental heads led to the conclusion that appointing young staff may have inhibited the speed of improvement in some departments. According to priorities in the overall strategic profile of the institution, resources were allocated to appoint at higher levels. The process occurred as a series of interactive negotiations between top managers and departments: 'I have talked with the Chair of the department with a view to the way in which we arrange their package of resources. It is a central group striking an agreement with a department as to how things will operate' (DVC).

Phase 6: At the same time, the outcome of the interactive strategizing about RG&C led to modifications in the 1996/97 financial planning round, providing financial incentives to departments that increased RG&C income. To monitor the activity, return on investment in financial incentives for RG&C was modelled in the financial forecasts for the following years.

Phase 7: During the 1997/98 financial planning round, analysis showed that income from RG&C was up slightly in total but down £1 million in contribution, based upon the forecasted returns for 1999/2000. Further analysis showed that there had been a 3 per cent decline in contribution to central income from RG&C over the last three years. Comparison with competitor institutions illustrated that Entrepreneurial's performance in RG&C income was sliding down the scale.

Phase 8: Top managers realized that high RG&C performance needed to be framed as equally important to high research publication performance: 'It's not enough for research just to be good in itself. It has to have financial benefits as well' (Strategy Committee observation). They accepted that this was a significant change and that top managers needed to take responsibility for reframing research activity around the change: 'It's got to be authorized or recommended from the top.' They decided on a course of interactive and procedural strategizing to drive home the change to dual goals for research activity: research excellence alongside commercially viable research activity.

Phase 9: Procedural strategizing provided a basis of information for interaction with departments: 'the Research Office has broken down departments, individual by individual' (Senior DVC). Following this, top managers began talking directly with people in departments, encouraging 'people to do more bids' (senior DVC). However, this required significant reframing of research activity. Increased RG&C applications will increase the number of failures as well as successes in a culture that is success-oriented. 'Actually, this is working completely against what Entrepreneurial is like. You are going to have to write a lot of proposals in order to be successful but be unsuccessful in the process' (Senior DVC). Alongside the interactive strategizing to reframe the RG&C aspect of research activity, procedural modifications would ensure rewards to those who were able to bring in more external research funding. And so the reciprocal links between interactive and procedural strategizing continued . . .

The pattern of strategizing at Entrepreneurial is distinctive for the tight reciprocal links between structural legitimacy and interpretative legitimacy. This is brought about by a combination of interactive and procedural strategizing. This combination both reframes activity, reaffirming the legitimacy of research excellence and reinterpreting it to accommodate a commercial aspect, and also procedurally embeds the changes in continuously modified administrative practices. The combination is not a clear cause-and-effect chain of interactive and procedural strategizing, but a tightly linked reciprocity between the two that is termed 'integrative strategizing'. The administrative practices are typically used with managerial discretion, facilitating links to interaction. Thus, interpretative legitimacy for activity is continuously constructed and given structural legitimacy through administrative procedures that are continuously realigned to the interpretations. This pattern shows how integrative strategizing facilitates stabilizing of research activity, but also enables top managers to project change in the research goals and shape activity accordingly. The pattern requires continuous attention on the part of top managers, iterating between structural and interpretative forms of legitimacy to maintain their alignment as activity is incrementally shaped over time.

The activity system dynamics of these three patterns of changing activity – reframing, re-embedding and chronically reconstructing – are compared in Figure 5.3. The reframing and re-embedding patterns illustrate the shifting influences when an activity moves from procedural strategizing to interactive strategizing. The two are polarized, indicating that to shift from the structural legitimacy associated with procedural strategizing, it will be necessary to engage in intensive interactive strategizing. While interactive strategizing establishes new interpretative legitimacy, the strategizing type selected to follow interactive strategizing is critical in the way activity will be shaped over time. The re-embedding pattern highlights the low durability of interpretative legitimacy. Without continuous attention it erodes quickly. Even where new administrative practices are developed, without associated interpretative legitimacy the community can use structural embedding to resist the changes to activity. This re-embedding pattern indicates the problems of shaping change in strategy through either interactive or procedural strategizing because of disconnects between interpretative and structural legitimacy. Moving to integrative strategizing, as in the reframing pattern, enables change to be established by realigning its structural and interpretative legitimacy. The final pattern shows how tightly linked activity system dynamics with associated reciprocity between structural and interpretative legitimacy enable change to be shaped as part of the ongoing process of chronically reconstructing activity. In this pattern, change does not involve a radical shift in influence because top managers are continuously balancing the tension between the persistence of structural embedding and the impermanence of interpretative frameworks.

STABILIZING ACTIVITY

Stabilizing activity is one of the core practice themes identified in Chapter 1. While much strategy literature examines either the problem of strategic inertia or of strategic change, remarkably little research has been conducted into the stabilizing of strategy. There is a hidden assumption that stabilizing strategy will lead to inertia, while change is a necessary and somehow more strategic way of acting. However, practice theory explicitly addresses the problem of stabilizing activity, enabling its realization without inertial tendencies and without change (Chia, 2002; Wilson and Jarzabkowski, 2004). In this research, a stabilizing pattern was found.

Stabilizing activity: integrative => integrative => integrative strategizing

The pattern for stabilizing activity is the same as that for chronically reconstructing change in activity. This is because integrative strategizing is needed continuously to monitor activity and ensure that it is aligned to its goals, avoiding inertia even where active change in the goals is not desired. This pattern is described in Exhibit 5.3 with the earlier phases of shaping research activity at Entrepreneurial. The aim of integrative strategizing initially is to ensure that all actors contribute to research activity that aligns with the goals of research excellence, rather than to change the activity. This means continuously framing research excellence as an important goal to build others' commitment to it and establish normative controls, as well as aligning the administrative practices to that goal. This might require some actors within the organization to change their actions to align better with collective research activity, but it does not constitute change in the activity or goals themselves. It is thus about stabilizing research activity over time, which is, itself, effortful accomplishment to ensure that an ongoing activity retains interpretative and structural legitimacy (Giddens, 1984; Pentland and Rueter, 1994).

Figure 5.3: Activity system dynamics of changing activity

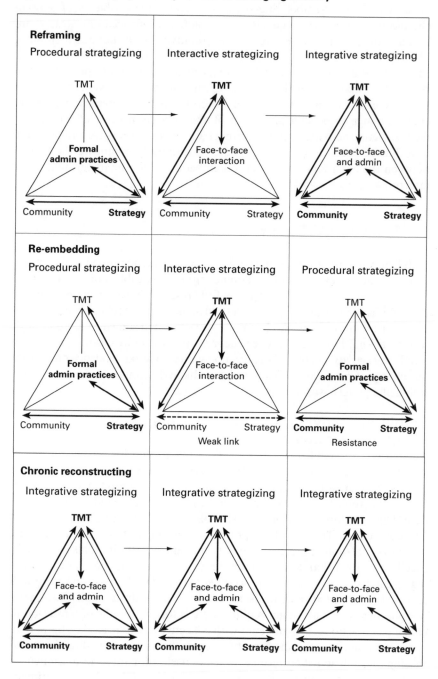

Other examples of stabilizing activity are not included here, for reasons of space. However, both commercial activity and size and scope activity at Entrepreneurial followed this same stabilizing pattern throughout the study. These activities did not require change but were continuously shaped through integrative strategizing to ensure that they could be realized. Thus the University realized its size and scope goals in outcomes over time, growing in the sciences, renewing capital infrastructure and cross-subsidizing and maintaining disciplinary balances. The activity directed at these goals needed continuous adjustment to the conditions of any given year but, overall, was about stabilizing a pattern of activity in order that it could be steadily directed at the size and scope goals. Similarly, commercial activity maintained its surplus year-on-year and its overheads to the University through goal-directed activity of new commercial initiatives and monitoring, growing, or scaling down existing initiatives. Similar to Exhibit 5.3, the distinctive feature in shaping both these activities was the intense managerial attention to both face-to-face interaction and modification of the administrative practices. Stabilizing activity requires continuous integrative strategizing to realign the interpretative and structural legitimacy of activity continuously in an ongoing pattern of goal-directed activity.

UNRESOLVED ACTIVITY

Another possible pattern is unresolved activity. The research activity at Collegiate indicated unresolved activity. Empirically, the pattern observed was one of attempting to change an embedded activity through interactive strategizing and being unable to do so with any persistence. Hence activity was unresolved. When this empirical evidence is taken in conjunction with the results from other strategy and organization theory research on unresolved activity (for example, Greenwood and Hinings, 1988; Maitlis and Lawrence, 2003), it is possible to conceptualize the broader pattern involved in unresolved activity. This pattern is now discussed.

Exhibit 5.4: If at first you don't succeed . . .

Unresolved research activity at Collegiate University

In this example top managers were trying to frame research as a more collectively managed activity, for which others should be accountable, rather than an individual activity. The problem is that research, while accepted as the core activity of the organization, is a very individual activity: 'Nobody monitors anybody else's research at Collegiate' (DVC, External). However, the increasing importance of the RAE and its implications for university funding have made this unsupportable for top managers: 'There is a hands-off feeling to research and yet senior people worry that actually this ties up quite a lot of our money in the future' (Senior Academic 4). While the goal is 'to go to number 1 in the RAE next time', there are few procedural means by which a more collective approach to research activity can be either encouraged or controlled. Research is currently procedurally embedded in committee structures that prevent overt control over research activity, based on a belief that 'a free, non-coercive atmosphere . . . is highly conducive to research' (DVC, External). Despite this 'non-coercive atmosphere', some departments and some individuals are not high performers in the RAE, affecting its collective outcome for the University.

Given the importance of external funding and the need to maintain the elite status, top managers feel that the University must develop a more coordinated and collective approach to research activity: 'The University needs to know about individual performers and what it can actually do with non-performers who aren't old enough for early retirement. We need a clear strategy of how to move people around in the actual RAE submission, mentor people on where they need to aim their publications, and have some punitive measures as well' (VC talking to departmental heads).

However, interpretative legitimacy for this change in activity and its associated administrative practices is difficult to attain. Indeed, the proposal of a mentoring scheme is met with suspicion as 'punitive and surveillance rather than mentoring and help' (DVC, External). The most that top managers are able to do is encourage normative control through interactive strategizing: 'Do it that way rather than threatening them in the sense that if you don't perform we'll squeeze you out in some way . . . a sort of moral persuasion' (Senior Academic 1). Interactive strategizing enables them to achieve some actions, such as the appointment of some world-class research professors, described in Exhibit 4.2 (Chapter 4), but top managers are not able to frame research as a collective activity that should be structurally embedded in diagnostic controls: 'It is not possible to know about departmental strategies of research and what they are doing' (VC in meeting observation). Interactive strategizing is ongoing, trying to generate momentum for collective research activity: 'What can we, the meeting, do to get people to rally around the RAE?' (VC in different meeting observation). However, no new administrative procedures are established and collectively managed research activity remains in a state of continuously trying to generate interpretative legitimacy.

Unresolved activity: interactive => interactive => interactive strategizing

In the unresolved pattern there is continuous effort to gain legitimacy for an activity without being able to embed that legitimacy structurally to enable its persistence. In Exhibit 5.4, which deals with top managers' attempts to change others' contributions to the research strategy at Collegiate, this pattern is explained. In this example, top managers are continuously striving to gain interpretative legitimacy for a more collectively managed approach to research activity. However, they are unable to establish any sufficiently collective framework of meanings that they can take the activity to another stage. Their efforts are focused on an ongoing process of interactive strategizing. The problem is that research is the core professional activity. Its protection is sacrosanct and any intervention encounters resistance from the community. In such situations, the problems of distributed activity discussed in Chapter 1 are exacerbated. The unresolved pattern thus appears to be associated with activities that are in some way contentious or a source of tension with the community. Interpretative legitimacy for such activities will be harder to establish.

The unresolved pattern highlights the impermanence of shaping activity primarily through interactive strategizing. As noted, one of the problems of interactive strategizing is that the interpretative legitimacy established is not durable. As Figure 5.4 shows, in the unresolved pattern strategizing is so focused on establishing sufficiently common meanings between top managers and the community that the link to activity cannot be maintained. Some actions might be achieved on a one-off basis, as with the world-class research professors at Collegiate, but these are dependent upon framing meaning in a single incident. Such incidents might be ongoing to try to attain some continuity of activity but, ultimately, an activity must also develop some structural embedding as a legitimate activity. An ongoing pattern of interactive strategizing, without moving to incorporate procedural strategizing as well, is indicative of unresolved activity.

INERTIAL ACTIVITY

A final pattern, inertial activity, was not observed over time in the empirical data. Nonetheless, it may be inferred from the difficulties with changing procedurally embedded activities in the cases, such as research at Collegiate and teaching at Modern. Taking these examples in conjunction with an understanding of how the strategizing types shape activity, it is possible to hypothesize the inertial pattern. Such theorizing is supported by the substantial body of strategy and organizational research into inertia (for example, Burgelman, 1994; Greenwood and Hinings, 1988; Miller, 1993). The inertial pattern is now explained and modelled in Figure 5.5.

Inertial activity: procedural => procedural => procedural strategizing

Inertial activity is typically associated with the problems of procedural strategizing. Activities that attain structural legitimacy tend to become overly embedded in the routinized administrative practices that enable their persistence and so are perpetuated without conscious effort. As noted, the problems with this are goals–means displacement and strategic drift. These symptoms of inertial activity were noted in the early-phase structural embed-

Figure 5.4: Activity system dynamics of unresolved activity

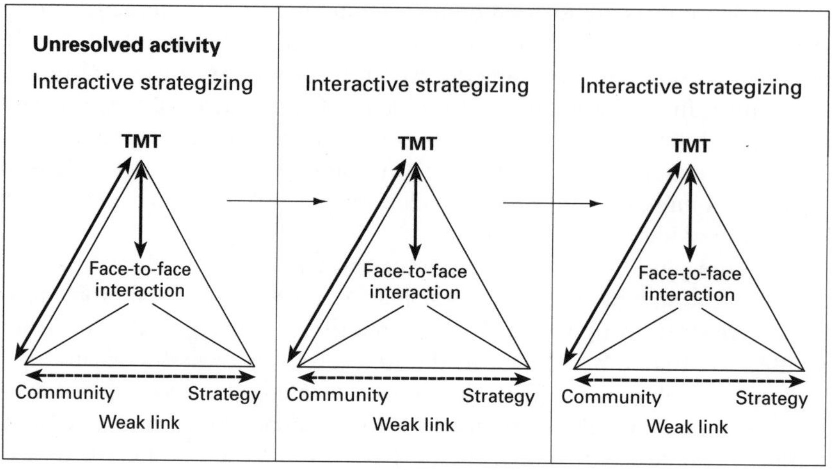

dedness of research, teaching and size and scope at Collegiate and teaching at Modern. Additionally, the Intel example recounted in Exhibit 2.2 (Chapter 2) shows the structural embedding of the memory chip strategy and its inertial path. Therefore, inertial activity is expected to follow the ongoing procedural strategizing pattern modelled in Figure 5.5. Shaping activity through continuous procedural strategizing exacerbates the negative consequences of structural embedding, and so is associated with inertia. Essentially, if structurally embedded activity is to avoid inertia, it needs at least periodic realignment with its interpretative base through interactive strategizing.

IMPLICATIONS OF STRATEGIZING TYPES AND PATTERNS OF ACTIVITY

This analysis of the five main patterns and their associated sub-patterns serves to answer the second research question on how different activity system dynamics are involved in shaping strategy as a pattern in a stream of goal-directed activity over time. The changing activity system dynamics involved in moving through different strategizing types have been modelled to show how different combinations of structural and interpretative legitimacy confer different types of influence over activity. This modelling and analysis highlights the main implications of the strategizing matrix for shaping patterns of activity. It shows how the interpretative and structural legitimacy that underpin this matrix are discrete but complementary concepts.

Figure 5.5: Activity system dynamics of inertial activity

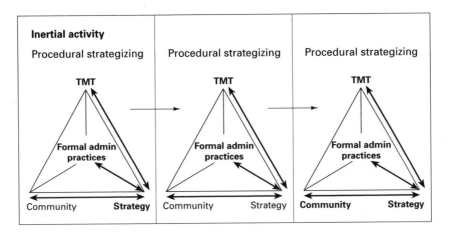

The different strategizing types shape activity by imparting higher or lower structural and interpretative legitimacy. Understanding how these forms of legitimacy shape activity provides a conceptual basis for explaining and describing patterns in activity:

- Pre-active strategizing involves an activity that has neither structural nor interpretative legitimacy and so cannot be considered mainstream strategy.
- Under procedural strategizing, an activity will gain structural legitimacy but, over time, will come adrift from the meaning through which it was initially legitimated. Prolonged procedural strategizing is thus associated with high structural and low interpretative legitimacy. Activity that is shaped through prolonged procedural strategizing will follow the inertial pattern and will need to be rebalanced by strong interpretative realignment.
- By contrast, an activity will gain interpretative legitimacy through interactive strategizing. However, interpretative legitimacy lacks durability, being constructed on each occasion of interaction. Activities shaped solely through interactive strategizing are dependent upon stringing together a chain of individually constructed incidents that will not necessarily show consistency because of the negotiated nature of each incident. Unless interpretative legitimacy reaches the stage where it also legitimizes the need to embed an activity structurally, it will lack persistence.
- As activities move from one or the other of these strategizing types, there is likely to be an intermediary phase, during which either existing structural embedding resists attempts at reinterpretation or newly framed meanings lend support to structural re-embedding. Eventually, however, the prolonged

use of one or the other types leads to a disconnection between the two forms of legitimacy.
- On the other hand, an activity may have both forms of legitimacy. Integrative strategizing is used to pay attention to both the continuous construction of frameworks of meaning and to the modification of administrative practices to assure ongoing alignment between structural and interpretative legitimacy.

These two forms of legitimacy are thus the key building blocks to the strategizing matrix and its associated activity system dynamics. They help to explain and describe strategy as a pattern in a stream of goal-directed activity.

CONCLUSION: POINTS TO TAKE FORWARD

This book aims to contribute to the conceptual development of an activity-based view by explaining how strategizing is involved in shaping strategy as an activity. This chapter has provided important empirical and conceptual building blocks in addressing this aim. These building blocks will be taken forward in developing a conceptual framework in Chapter 7. There are four main points to take forward from this chapter:

1 This chapter has developed a strategizing matrix of four types: pre-active, procedural, interactive and integrative strategizing. Each of these types involves different activity system dynamics that explain the different influences involved in shaping phases in strategy development.
2 This strategizing matrix is underpinned by two key concepts that comprise its two axes: structural legitimacy and interpretative legitimacy. Structural legitimacy refers to the social order displayed in stabilized structural practices, such as routines, hierarchies and roles. Structural legitimacy means that strategy is embedded within largely routine practices that will enable its persistence without active managerial attention. It is, however, prone to inertia. Interpretative legitimacy refers to those frameworks of meaning through which individuals understand what constitutes appropriate action in a community. While top managers have greater influence over interpretative legitimacy, it lacks durability, requiring ongoing managerial attention. These two forms of legitimacy have discrete but complementary influences on shaping activity.
3 Different combinations of structural and interpretative legitimacy, as imparted by the different types of strategizing, explain the patterns that strategy takes over time. Essentially, patterns in activity are shaped by the way that the tensions between these different forms of legitimacy are balanced. Integrative strategizing balances both forms of legitimacy in an ongoing reciprocal process. By contrast, procedural strategizing and interactive strategizing tend to shape activity as shifts between forms of legitimacy over time. Pre-active strategizing indicates activity that is not part

Quick Reference Guide 5.2: Shaping patterns of activity over time

Pattern	Shifts in strategizing	Issues in shaping activity
Introducing localized activity • intended • unintended	Pre-active to interactive	Has top management sponsorship. Interpretative legitimacy prior to establishing structural legitimacy
	Pre-active to procedural	Has hijacked administrative practices. Structural legitimacy prior to interpretative legitimacy
Changing activity • reframing • re-embedding • chronically reconstructing	Procedural to interactive to integrative	Interpretive legitimacy gained from interactive strategizing is established and aligned with structural legitimacy during integrative phase
	Procedural to interactive to procedural	Enables non-contentious change to be re-embedded, but not suitable for radical or contentious change where greater interpretative legitimacy is needed to gain commitment to change
	Ongoing integrative	Enables incremental change. Balances tension between persistence of structural legitimacy and impermanence of interpretative legitimacy
Stabilizing activity	Ongoing interactive	Continuously realigns structural and interpretative legitimacy in goal-directed activity, so avoiding inertia
Unresolved activity	Ongoing interactive	Activity is unable to maintain sufficient interpretative legitimacy to move to the persistence of structural legitimacy
Inertial activity	Ongoing procedural	Activity is overly embedded structurally, has lost alignment with its initial interpretative legitimacy and resists change

of mainstream strategy because it lacks either structural or interpretative legitimacy.

4 Using these strategizing types it is possible to explain variation in five patterns of shaping strategy over time, indicating that the concepts are conceptually robust. The five patterns explained are:

- introducing localized activity into mainstream strategy;
- changing existing activity;
- stabilizing activity;
- unresolved activity; and
- inertial activity.

These four points to take forward are empirically interpreted in the exhibits and examples given throughout this chapter. They are also summarized for easy access in the two Quick Reference Guides. The next chapter, 6, will draw upon these points to examine multiple, coexistent streams of activity and explain how these contextualize the different strategizing types used and the patterns that activity takes.

NOTES

1 Thanks to Ann Langley and Richard Whittington, who made these helpful suggestions about labelling the quadrants of the matrix.

2 This matrix is conceptually and empirically robust, having been derived from the data and located within the literature (see Appendix). The initial concepts in this matrix, the structural and interpretative legitimacy conferred, respectively, by procedural and interactive strategizing, are recounted in Chapter 4.

6 MULTIPLE STRATEGIES SHAPE EACH OTHER

> **Key points**
>
> - Universities have multiple strategic activities that must coexist
> - One activity is core because it is historically associated with the professional identity
> - The core activity is prone to the inertial pattern
> - Other activities need to establish a relationship with the core activity
> - Patterns of activity are shaped by their relationship with each other

'You might as well use your two main assets all year round, buildings and staff, to generate income when you're not teaching, which you're only doing for 30 weeks of the year' (Deputy Registrar, Commerce, Entrepreneurial).

In this quote, top managers perceive teaching and commercial income as two activities that can exist compatibly on the principle of maximizing the value of assets. From the perspective of a professional workforce, however, maximizing the value of assets in this way conflicts with research activity, which academics tend to engage in when they are not teaching. More fundamentally, maximizing commercial value may conflict with their beliefs about the academic profession and the purposes of the university. Different professional and managerial interests in shaping strategy are thus heightened in the context of multiple strategies.

At this stage, this book has looked at strategy as a single stream of goal-directed activity. However, universities have multiple strategies. Each case in this study was pursuing four strategies: research, teaching, size and scope and commercial activity. The strategy literature is reticent in examining the association between multiple strategies. Most strategy research examines the evolution of a single strategy, or alternately its substitution by another strategy. However, as Chapter 3 explained, universities and other professional contexts pursue multiple strategies that must coexist, since they cannot simply be substituted, one for the other; for example, ceasing to do teaching in order to focus on research.

Coexistence is not an easy situation to manage, as multiple strategies may not be equally compatible for all members of the community. For example, research into universities suggests that the compatibility of teaching and high-quality research is contentious. Similarly, many academics perceive a fundamental dichotomy between commercial income and teaching, and commercial income and research. The coexistence of multiple strategies thus adds to the complexity of shaping any individual strategy. This leads to the final research question: 'How are patterns in multiple streams of goal-directed activity shaped by association with each other?' This chapter addresses this question.

Three key points about the relationship between multiple strategies will be made:

- One strategy is the 'core' activity. This activity is core because of its historical embedding in the organization and its close association with the professional identity. Preservation of this activity will be important to the community.
- The core activity has high structural legitimacy and is, therefore, prone to the inertial pattern.
- There will be professional resistance to coexistence with any strategy that is perceived to threaten the core activity. Other strategies need to be established in relation to the core activity in order to enable their coexistence. Patterns of activity are thus shaped by their relationship with each other, and particularly with the core activity.

This chapter will deal with these three points in turn, showing their implications for the different strategizing types and patterns of activity found in the previous chapters. The analysis in this chapter thus serves to contextualize the theoretical points made in those chapters.

THE CORE ACTIVITY

In most organizations, there will be a core strategy; the strategy that in some way embodies what the organization is about, its identity (Albert and Whetten, 1985; Cummings, 2002). Often such an activity will have historical associations with the organization. For example, Intel's early success in the memory chip industry led to perceptions of itself as a memory chip company, and this remained the core strategy well beyond its commercial viability (see Exhibit 2.2, Chapter 2). The identity connotations of a core historical activity are thus powerfully persistent. Research shows that members associate strongly with their organization's identity and will respond to actions that threaten it (Gioia and Thomas, 1996). In this book, each case had a core activity that was associated with the professional identity. That is, the core activity was one that the professionals in the organization associated with strongly and regarded as properly a matter for professional, rather than managerial, concern (Alvesson, 2001; Fenton and Pettigrew, 2005; Hinings and Leblebici, 2003). The strategizing involved in shaping this activity was thus sensitive. This section first identifies those activities that were core to the professional identity in each case, and the issues this raised for top managers in shaping them. The strategizing implications of these issues are then drawn.

The core activity in each case was that activity most associated with the history and professional reputation of the university. Thus at Collegiate and Entrepreneurial it was research, and at Modern it was teaching. Chapters 4 and 5 have examined the patterns of each these activities over time. However, additional data are presented here to show the issues these activities raised because they were core activities. Four main issues associated with the tensions between professional and managerial interests are discussed and related to the strategizing types used to shape the core activity. These issues were more problematic at Collegiate and Modern, where the core activity displayed the problems of persistent structural legitimacy associated with procedural strategizing, even where top managers attempted to change them using other types of strategizing (see Exhibits 5.2 and 5.4). They were in evidence but less problematic at Entrepreneurial, where integrative strategizing was used.

SHAPING THE CORE ACTIVITY: ISSUES AND STRATEGIZING TYPES

As the activity associated with the history and professional identity of the organization, the core activity has a dominant claim over the contributions of the community. This means that they will undertake actions towards this activity which is, on the one hand, beneficial for collective activity. However, on the other hand, it can be used to resist changes in the way they contribute to the core activity as well as to resist contributing to other activities. This resistance is legitimated by the dominance of the core activity. Due to its historical durability in the organization, a core activity has high structural legitimacy. Therefore, focus upon the core activity and resistance to other activities are, themselves, legitimate actions because they preserve the core activity.

Teaching at Modern provides a good example of these three issues. Teaching is the core activity, being strongly associated with the success of the institution and its professional identity: 'Modern's heartland is teaching and learning' (DVC, Academic). Exhibit 5.2 explained the problems in trying to change contributions to teaching activity and to create more time for other activities. The community resisted the change. First, the core activity had the dominant claim on their time: 'We do teach a hell of a lot' (DVC, Research). This claim is legitimate because of the inherent structural legitimacy of the core activity: 'We should play to our comparative strengths, which is that we care for the students, not just in a pastoral sense, but also in teaching and learning' (Former DVC). Second, because teaching is a professional activity, professionals assume autonomy over their contributions to it, raising resistance to attempts to change the manner of those contributions. For example, 'It is fine to talk about assessment, but you actually get people to try to think concretely about how we are going to reduce assessment load, and there are a million reasons why it has to be exactly as it is at the moment' (DVC, Academic). Finally, the dominance of the core activity may be used to resist other activities, on the grounds that they might in some way damage the core activity: 'Research should not interfere with teaching quality. The last thing we want is for teaching to suffer' (DVC, Research).

Similar issues were noted at Collegiate, where the core activity was research. Exhibit 5.4 indicated the same type of problems in trying to change contributions to research activity. As the dominant activity, research commanded professional autonomy and resistance to control: 'Collegiate doesn't have a very directive process to research strategy. We haven't in the past and it would be very difficult to do it here anyway. I mean people in Collegiate wouldn't take very kindly to that. They didn't come to Collegiate to be treated like that' (Senior Academic 4). Because of the structural legitimacy of the core activity, resistance to other activities that might threaten it are also legitimate: 'diversion of effort' (Senior Academic 2) makes the University 'vulnerable to losing research excellence' (Senior Academic 1).

Shaping the core activity with procedural strategizing

In both these examples, as shown in the Exhibits from Chapter 5, the problems in changing contributions to the core activity lie in its structural legitimacy. As historical activities, they are largely shaped by procedural strategizing and, as Exhibits 5.2 and 5.4 show, where changes in these procedures are attempted through interactive strategizing, neither attempt is successful. The resistance that the community makes to these activities is also based in procedural strategizing. For example, at Modern staff used the problem of sunk costs to resist changing the teaching year, claiming the problem of 'transition costs in changing systems as well as the role of students and their rights, needs and potential to make a fuss' (Planning Committee observation). Similarly, the existing departmentally-based practices for managing research activity at Collegiate could be used to resist change: 'The DVC would be in a position to raise the research performance [of staff in a department] informally with the Head. The Head might say 'Well no, I don't think that at all' and that would be the end of it' (Senior Academic 2). In both these cases, the community could use the existing structural embedding to resist attempts to shape change in activity. The problem is that core activities have the history and structural legitimacy of persistent activities. They are thus prone to inertia. These inertial tendencies are increased by their strong association with the professional identity and professional resistance to intervention in such activities. Activities that are core to the professional identity face the paradox of being both highly legitimate to the community and, at the same time, being prone to strategic drift due to the goals–means displacement inherent in structural legitimacy.

This paradox is exacerbated because core activities tend not to break down totally due to the professional commitment to them. For example, at Modern staff continued to teach well, albeit that activity had drifted from the initial interpretative legitimacy of teaching innovation. Similarly, much research at

Collegiate continued to be of a high standard, albeit that there were few means of changing the contributions of those who were not performing well. This commitment, even where it is accompanied by managerial perceptions of drift and non-optimal performance, increases the sensitivity of attempting to change contributions to a core professional activity (Alvesson and Sveningsson, 2003; Lowendahl, 1997). There is an aura of 'If it ain't broke, don't fix it' with the core activity. For example, top managers at Modern acknowledged in changes to the academic year that 'there are a lot of good reasons about being cautious about the reform of this system' (DVC, Academic), while changes to research at Collegiate were tempered by considerations that 'I'm not sure that this is the best structure, but it is a structure which has made possible being high in the research ranking on a very narrow financial basis' (DVC, External). Top managers have concerns that changing the activity may damage its good qualities. Therefore, while top managers used interactive strategizing in an attempt to change both of these core activities, they found their own agency constrained by the legacy of procedural strategizing. Procedural strategizing enables the core activity to persist with low managerial attention, giving professionals autonomy over activity that is likely to be adequately, if potentially, sub-optimally performed. As illustrated in the activity system diagram (Figure 5.2), procedural strategizing thus provides a vehicle for the community to both contribute to and resist activity, as well as constraining and enabling the agency of top managers. Figures 5.2 and 5.4 illustrate that the shift to interactive strategizing may be insufficient to secure changes with a structurally embedded core activity.

Shaping the core activity with integrative strategizing

Entrepreneurial also had research as the core activity: 'We very clearly identify ourselves with other top research led universities' (Deputy Registrar, Finance). This activity had the same potential for dominance, resistance to change and resistance to other activities as displayed in the other cases. Top management is very aware of these issues. For example, they are sensitive to the potential for conflict and resistance when they intervene in departmental research activity: 'That leaves a constructive tension . . . and so I have to keep an eye on him [departmental head] while he keeps an eye on me and see how we go' (Former DVC). They illustrate this awareness in their relationships with the best research performers, acknowledging autonomy by 'inviting' them to put forward their own research strategies. Nonetheless, professional autonomy is not sacred: 'Professors still carry quite a lot of power and you don't interfere on their patch. On the other hand it's a kind of myth because the moment you need to interfere on the patch you do' (DVC, Quality). Professional commitment and autonomy are thus acknowledged, but the potential association with strategic drift and sub-optimal performance is not.

Balancing tension between professional interests and managerial interests in the core activity is maintained by integrative strategizing. As shown in Exhibit 5.3, the research strategy is a source of constant managerial attention through integrative strategizing. In this process, strong normative controls are continuously reconstructed to support diagnostic control over the core activity. The benefits of structural legitimacy are thus maintained and continuously realigned with interpretative legitimacy. Research is able to remain the dominant activity, but resistance to change and to other activities is countered by integrative strategizing. Indeed, as the next section will show, integrative strategizing moderates the dominance of research activity and its resistance to other activities by clarifying the interdependence of the multiple strategies.

This section has examined the issues and strategizing types involved in shaping the core activity in multiple activity contexts. As universities are professional organizations, the core activity is historically embedded in the reputation and professional identity of the organization. This raises four important issues about the tensions between professional and managerial interests in shaping the core activity:

- Activities associated with the professional identity have high autonomy in their performance.
- Even where they are performed sub-optimally, core professional activities tend not to break down because of professional commitment.
- The core activity dominates the contributions of the community.
- The community is resistant to change in the core activity and resistant to other activities that might divert their attention.

Quick Reference Guide 6.1: Characteristics of the core activity

- The core activity is historically associated with the reputation and professional identity of the organization.

- The core activity commands professional autonomy and surfaces tensions between professional and managerial interests.

- The core activity dominates the contributions of the community. They resist change to the core activity and resist activities that threaten the dominance of the core activity.

- The core activity is typically associated with procedural strategizing due to its historical duration, its inherent legitimacy as an activity, and the autonomy that such activities attract.

- Community commitment to the core activity is typically high, so that the activity is unlikely to break down even if its actual performance is sub-optimal. Interventions into the core activity must be exercised with caution, for fear of damaging the professional qualities associated with the activity.

- Procedural strategizing and caution over intervening in the core activity lead to inertial patterns of activity and increase resistance to change.

The problems associated with these issues are exacerbated because of the structural legitimacy of the core activity and the tendency to use procedural strategizing to shape it. Such strategizing has strengths in enabling the activity to persist with low managerial attention, so facilitating professional autonomy. However, it also has the weaknesses of procedural strategizing in terms of enabling the community to resist change in the core activity and shaping the agency of top managers over the activity. In this latter, sunk costs and goals–means displacement lead to inertia in the core activity. This inertia is likely to favour professional interests over managerial interests in the core activity. By contrast, at Entrepreneurial the core activity was shaped by integrative strategizing and avoided the problems found in the other cases. As the activity system diagrams in Chapter 5 indicate, integrative strategizing balances professional and managerial interests in the core activity, tending more towards managerial interests.

COEXISTENCE: ESTABLISHING A RELATIONSHIP WITH THE CORE ACTIVITY

This section examines how strategizing types are associated with coexistence between multiple strategies. While professionals may be primarily interested in the core activity, for managers all four activities – teaching, research, commercial and size and scope activity – are important, therefore they cannot allow the core activity to dominate but must shape coexistence between activities. Coexistence is based upon whether an individual strategy is perceived as a threat to or a support for the core activity. Top managers thus attempt to counter perceptions of threat and establish supportive relationships between the core and non-core activities. This section will first discuss the types of tensions that arise between activities, and then show the implications of procedural, interactive and integrative strategizing for their coexistence. While pre-active strategizing is also a possibility because top managers may be hesitant to mobilize a counter activity, this section deals with the active forms of strategizing.

TENSIONS WITH THE CORE ACTIVITY

Commercial activity is typically perceived as a threat in professional contexts because it has an economic rather than a value-based rationality (Denis et al., 2001; Satow, 1975; Townley, 2002). Commercial activity is associated with economic considerations, which are perceived as innately counter to professional values. This threat was apparent in all three cases. For example, at Collegiate the community were 'not given to commercially induced whims or undermining of academic standards' (Senior Academic 5). Indeed, there was concern that 'if [commercial activity] fed through into their mindsets, they would lose their research rating' (DVC, External). At Modern, commercial activity was initially perceived as an inappropriate activity for a university: 'Entrepreneurial activity and income generation are not integrated into the ethos of the University' (Coopers & Lybrand Report, 1988). Even at Entrepreneurial, which 'has something of a reputation as a go-getter, entrepreneurial' (Former Deputy Registrar), some doubt had initially been expressed over commercial activity: 'Commercial activity is bound to be a bit close to practice, otherwise people wouldn't pay for it, so it gives you a different kind of academic, which at one time used to sit unhappily' (Former DVC 2). Nonetheless, all three institutions, particularly Entrepreneurial, managed to establish commercial activity as a mainstream strategy that could coexist with the core activity.

Teaching and research typically have a less contentious relationship with each other than with commercial activity. However, this does not mean they are compatible for the academic community. For example, at Collegiate, even after reframing the importance of service and quality in teaching activity, it was clearly inferior although not a threat to the core activity, research: 'Teaching is much more important but . . . the main criterion is still the quality of one's research' (Senior Academic 2). At Modern there was increasing tension over research, which was perceived as a threat to the core teaching activity: 'If you invest resources and time [into research], you detract from the amount you're putting into the learning and teaching' (DVC, Corporate).

Only Entrepreneurial managed to generate a complementary relationship between teaching and the core activity, research: 'We're trying to support this idea of an excellent university and it's research led, but also does well by the students and produces good students who go on to get good jobs. And that just permeates everything that you do' (Deputy Registrar, Quality).

Size and scope is not an activity that directly counteracts or threatens the core activity. However, as the label implies, it shapes the size, student balance, and disciplinary scope of the university. Therefore, the way that it is conducted can have serious and possibly unintended implications for shaping other activities. For example, at Modern, the financial imperative in size and scope activity began to threaten departmental viability, indirectly threatening other activities by placing small departments under threat, regardless of their importance to the disciplinary balance of the University. Similarly, at Collegiate lack of control over the size and scope activity began to affect research appointments and teaching requirements in different departments.

> Department X would like to make a good appointment to boost their research rating . . . Department Y have got students coming out of their ears and no-one to teach them. So there is always tensions emerging . . . What tended to happen is that allocation decisions about how much a department is going to get was sort of taken a bit in isolation, so you weren't consciously trading off one against the other (Senior Academic 6).

Again, Entrepreneurial was able to manage these tensions and create alignment between size and scope activity and the goals for teaching, research and commercial activity. For example, while the [Modern Language] department 'got

5 in the RAE', it is small and 'could be wiped out tomorrow without it really impacting financially, in any way' (DVC, Quality). However, top managers use integrative strategizing to accommodate relationships between commercial activity, research, and the size and scope goal of cross-subsidy: 'The Arts get more than their fair share. But they have to because of the funding, the opportunities to make sure they work. And they have performed extremely well [in research]' (Former DVC 1).

As these examples show, coexistence is fraught with tension due to the divergent goals and interests associated with multiple strategies, particularly in their relationship with the core activity. Table 6.1 summarizes the complementary or threatening relationship between the core and non-core activities in each of the cases, and the principle type of strategizing involved in establishing that relationship. The strategizing type used has implications for the relationship with the core activity. These main implications of procedural, interactive and integrative strategizing are now discussed.

Table 6.1: Strategizing types and relationships to core activity

Institution/ Core activity	Relationship with core activity	Principle strategizing type in relationship
Collegiate/ Research	• Teaching: complementary but inferior • Commercial: initially threatening then gaining tentative complementarity • Size and scope: initially unintended threat then gaining tentative complementarity	• Interactive (frame complement) to procedural (embed complement) • Interactive (frame complement) to integrative (reconstruct complement) • Procedural (unintended threat) to interactive (frame complement) to integrative (reconstruct complement)
Modern/ Teaching	• Research: increasing threat • Commercial: initial threat then complementary • Size and scope: unintended threat	• Interactive (frame complement) to procedural (fail to embed) • Interactive (frame complement) to procedural (embed complement) • Pre-active to procedural (unintended embedding)
Entrepreneurial/ Research	• Teaching: Initially complementary but inferior, then equal status due to TQA • Commercial: initial threat then complementary • Size and scope: complementary	• Procedural (embed complement) to integrative (reconstruct complement) • Integrative (frame and reconstruct complement) • Integrative (reconstruct complement)

PROCEDURAL STRATEGIZING AND RELATIONSHIPS WITH THE CORE ACTIVITY

Procedural strategizing can establish either a complementary or a threatening relationship with the core activity, depending on whether the activity being structurally embedded is essentially non-threatening or lends itself to clear administrative practices and diagnostic controls (Chapter 4). It was effective in embedding the complementarity between teaching and research at Collegiate and between commercial activity and teaching at Modern. In both these cases, the relationship of the non-core activity to the core activity could be embedded through administrative practices and controls that clarified the relationship to the core activity. For example, improving teaching quality and service at Collegiate was complementary: 'to project its image as an elite institution offering high-quality and high-relevance research-led teaching' (Academic Board observation). Teaching quality and service needs to be at a 'standard comparable with other elite universities' (VC in meeting observation). It is not threatening to research activity and can be embedded in administrative practices to improve student services and teaching quality audits. Thus, after initial reframing it is possible to construct a complementary relationship with the core activity through procedural strategizing.

Commercial activity at Modern lent itself particularly well to procedural alignment with the core teaching activity. Many sources of commercial activity are teaching related, such as full-fee-paying students, short courses, and international, regional and commercially tailored teaching partnerships: 'We're currently talking to all the departments about their strategic plan and what they envisage in terms of international recruitment. I mean, we say to them, we want to double numbers' (DVC, Finance). These sources of commercial activity are relatively easy to embed in administrative practices such as budget allocations, targets, quotas and performance indicators, as noted in Exhibit 4.1. It is also possible to allocate relevant incentives for commercial activity, such as greater resources. Hence, many departments could meet commercial activity requirements through expanding their teaching activity. Indeed, the University met its overall targets for expanding teaching-related commercial activity in half the projected time period for the 1997 to 1999 planning rounds. Procedural strategizing helped to create strong structural alignment between teaching and commercial activity, making commercial activity nearly as dominant as teaching.

Procedural strategizing is less valuable at establishing relationships with the core activity, where the activity in question is both a threat and is not easily aligned through diagnostic control. For example, research activity at Modern was also embedded through procedural strategizing: 'We're keeping a very close check on what they are doing in terms of publication, what they're doing in terms of income, what they're doing in terms of PhD students because those are the things that count in the RAE. We're monitoring this very closely' (DVC, Research). On the one hand, it is possible to set targets for research output. However, output indicators could not easily ensure research input by the community. Furthermore, these outputs could not be easily aligned to teaching activity and were a threat to its dominance as the core activity: 'The main concern that staff have about doing more research is not having enough time to do it. We're trying to thin out teaching because we do over teach' (DVC, Research). However, the community did not want to thin out teaching. They began to use the administrative practices to resist research, particularly where they could show strong alignment between teaching and commercial activity. For example 'Why are we doing research? If it is money, then [a department] already does make good money, and if it is to enhance teaching, then their commercial profile is enhancing their teaching' (Department Head in meeting observation). In contrast to commercial activity, procedural strategizing was not able to embed the interpretative legitimacy of an activity such as research and, particularly, could not establish measures and metrics that would align it to the core teaching activity. In such situations, increasing administrative practices and diagnostic controls are likely to increase the community's perceptions of threat to the core activity (Alvesson and Sveningsson, 2003). Procedural strategizing thus embedded a deeper division between teaching and research.

Procedural strategizing has four implications for establishing relationships with the core activity:

- It is useful where activities are non-threatening and can be relatively easily embedded in administrative practices and controls.
- It is particularly useful for activities that attract clear measures and rewards that align well with the core activity, such as the association between teaching and commercial activity at Modern.
- It is less useful for establishing associations with activities that are perceived as threatening.
- It is less useful for activities that do not lend themselves to relevant targets and measures that align well with the controls for the core activity.

INTERACTIVE STRATEGIZING AND RELATIONSHIPS WITH THE CORE ACTIVITY

Interactive strategizing was not the sole means of constructing a relationship with the core activity in any of the cases. Nonetheless it was an important intermediary step, particularly in introducing new activities that were potentially threatening to the core activity. This is particularly well exemplified in introducing commercial activity at Collegiate, where interactive strategizing was used to frame the necessity of commercial activity (see Chapter 5, p. 109). Commercial activity was framed as non-threatening to research activity: 'You have to make sure they see how it is not at variance with the core business [research] and also how it can benefit them' (Registrar). Such interactive strategizing is not trivial. For many academics commercial activity constitutes a serious threat, as the following extract from a meeting observation shows:

> A leading academic queries: 'Is this going to be a situation where academics are bludgeoned into teaching these [commercial] courses to the detriment of research and promotion opportunities?' The VC responds that no bludgeoning will occur but that they must be allowed to explore all the options, as 'This is part of the changing framework of higher education.' Another academic says: 'As long as we stick to highly academic courses we'll do well in the market. We have good strengths. Let us build upon those and not chase our tails on something not central to our ethos and tradition of excellence.'

Interactive strategizing is vital to establish interpretative associations with the core activity, particularly where an activity is seen as a direct threat. More than simply denying the threat, the new activity will gain interpretative legitimacy by demonstrating that it can support rather than detract from the core activity. In order to demonstrate this, it is important to move to some procedural mechanisms that can begin to embed the desirable associations between the activities. Interactive strategizing alone is not adequate. At Collegiate, top managers progressed to integrative strategizing, developing rudimentary incentive systems to deploy resources from commercial activity into research support: 'This is then linked to the incentive, research time' (Resource Committee observation). At the same time they framed the supportive links between the two: 'There is more of a will towards income generation now . . . they are beginning to see some benefits in resource gain' (Registrar). Integrative strategizing not only enabled administrative practices, such as incentives, to establish links to the core activity, but also retained the high levels of managerial attention necessary to ensure the complementarity retained interpretative legitimacy.

Interactive strategizing thus has three implications in establishing relationships with the core activity.

- it is useful in framing potentially threatening non-core activities by minimizing perceptions of threat to the core activity;
- it is useful in framing an activity as supportive for the core activity, which will give that activity increased interpretative legitimacy; and
- support for the core activity needs to be substantiated, indicating that, once sufficient interpretative legitimacy is established, a move to another strategizing type will enable structural links between activities.

INTEGRATIVE STRATEGIZING AND RELATIONSHIPS WITH THE CORE ACTIVITY

Integrative strategizing was used to shape all the activities at Entrepreneurial. Integrative strategizing was valuable for managing tensions by establishing interpretative and structural links between the core activity and other activities. In doing so, it minimized the dominance of the core activity and gave other activities a complementary status as vital to the overall quality and reputation of the University. In particular, commercial activity, which is typically a key source of professional divergence over goals, was shown to support the other activities.

> People seem much less worried about it [commercial activity] now . . . that's happened because there has been an increasing recognition that those activities are part of the resource base of the University. I think there are still academics around who are not exactly sympathetic to those activities, but they can see the financial benefits. I think a small Arts department; if there weren't these activities you might find your department had been closed down. So I think it's as simple as that really (Former DVC 2).

Rather than being a threat, commercial activity supports research, teaching and size and scope activity. This support is structurally embedded. For example, in the resource allocation mechanisms 'special allowance is made for small departments' (Resource Committee Minutes, 1995). At the same time, profit-sharing mechanisms with departments, including a 'super surplus' retained by high-income generating departments, reinforce the structural legitimacy of commercial activity and increase departmental buy-in: 'Commercial activities give you autonomy, flexibility and a stronger link. You're more of a stakeholder' (DVC, Quality). There is high managerial discretion in the allocation of resources, ensuring that they are clearly linked in the community's mind to benefits in other activities, such as research, but also expecting a return from the community for the investment:

> We're backing our 5* departments. We're planning a £5 million building for one of them, which means that in return they have got to agree to pursue strategies in regard to both students and research that will benefit the University financially as well as academically. (VC in Strategy Meeting observation)

The interactions involved in discretionary allocation of resources helps create interpretative links between activities. For example, the department receiving the £5 million building was the target of a series of face-to-face interactions with top managers. These were intended to ensure that the department would not only do its high-quality research, but also develop new commercial activities in return for the investment made. While there was initial resistance, 'It's very difficult to persuade our colleagues in that department that they should do anything different' (Strategy Meeting observation), through persistent interactions the department eventually made 'a psychological breakthrough' (Commercial Meeting observation). They accepted the importance of making a contribution to commercial activity and proposed a number of specific commercial initiatives they could undertake.

This integrative pattern occurs with teaching and size and scope activities and their relationship to the core activity of research as well. For example, 'the proudest thing I think the University has achieved in the last 5 years is its national rankings for teaching. Now that's a heck of an achievement in parallel to its rankings for research. But the point is that in both areas we're in the top bracket' (VC). In this way, research remains the core activity, but other activities are seen as complementary to its performance. The interpretative legitimacy of these other activities is thus strong; the perception is that, without them, research would also suffer: 'In this place, the self-evident fact is that the academic strength of the University is growing as a direct result of its financial success' (Governor). Integrative strategizing is seen to balance the interests of different actors about the different activities, generating a collective purpose within which the four activities are aligned: 'A kind of almost shared purpose with, um, this sort of managerial centre balancing a quite, you know, quite autonomous department' (Deputy Registrar, Academic).

Integrative strategizing thus has three implications for establishing a relationship with the core activity:

- it enables non-core activities to be framed as complementary to the core activity and to develop demonstrable structural links to support this interpretative complementarity;
- it lessens the dominance of the core activity and its inherent resistance to other activities; and
- it lessens the tensions between top managers and the community about the different professional and managerial interests inherent in multiple activities.

IMPLICATIONS OF STRATEGIZING TYPES AND MULTIPLE STRATEGIES

In addressing the association between patterns in multiple streams of goal-directed activity, this chapter has delved into some of the aspects of strategizing in a university context raised in Chapter 3. The issues involved in shaping associations between the core and non-core activities highlight the complexity of strategizing in the context of situated and distributed activity. The core activity is a situated concept, embedded in professional norms and realized in specific professional contexts, such as the university sector and, within that, different universities. It is important in understanding the relationships between activities because it provides evidence of the divergence between managerial and professional interests. These divergent interests affect not only the core activity, but also the viability of other activities. If these oppose the core activity, they reinforce divergence between managerial and professional interests. The other activities analysed here tended to reflect a mix of such interests. For example, teaching and research are typically professional interests, although this is dependent on the historical situation, as the example at Modern illustrates. Nonetheless, there is clearly a managerial agenda in the strategic performance of these activities, such as attaining the overarching excellence that attracts external resources. Other activities, such as commercial activity and size and scope, are overarching strategies that reflect managerial interests, although their performance affects all members of the organization. The complexities of distributed activity are thus well reflected in the context of these four activities. They bring together a range of potentially divergent professional and managerial interests, albeit that no activity is exclusively professional or managerial. Multiple strategies highlight the tensions between top managers and distributed actors in shaping some collective strategic purpose for any single activity and illustrate how the pattern of one activity can affect the pattern of another.

Different types of strategizing serve different purposes in coping with the tensions within and between activities. Procedural strategizing is important for embedding relationships within administrative practices that give structural legitimacy to the associations between activities. Interactive strategizing is vital in framing the benefits of association between activities and persuading others that these benefits are in their own as well as others' interests. The two are related. Without structural links, activities remain tenuously connected by frameworks of meaning that construct interpretative links between activities. As the distributed community have divergent interests, the strong perceptions of conflict between activities will challenge these interpretative links. They are contested, not stable. Where a distributed community perceives structural benefits in the links between activities, they may be prepared to subjugate their divergent interests to the common benefits they can attain.

Integrative strategizing combines the effects of these two strategizing types in establishing both structural and interpretative links. As the example at Entrepreneurial indicates, integrative strategizing can establish 'a kind of almost shared purpose' that reflects predominantly managerial interests in shaping activity towards organizational goals, but takes account of community interests and co-opts their contribution to those activities and goals. This minimizes the tensions between activities that arise from the divergent interests that different activities represent. Through integrative strategizing, structural associations reinforce interpretative links and help to counteract the contested frameworks of meaning that are inherent in multiple strategies. Such contests will, however, remain. Multiple activities do not align easily because they do represent different interests. Hence, structural and interpretative legitimacy for each activity and for its association with the other activities will need to be continuously reconstructed.

CONCLUSION: POINTS TO TAKE FORWARD

This chapter has helped to contextualize the concepts developed in the previous chapters. It shows how the contingencies associated with multiple activities impact upon the application of the different strategizing types. The analysis in this chapter thus increases the robustness of the conceptual building blocks being developed in this book. Specifically, this chapter has raised four implications about multiple activities that impact upon the types of strategizing that are likely to be used:

1   The core activity is that activity most associated with the history and professional reputation of the organization. Because of its historical duration, its inherent legitimacy as an activity, and the autonomy that such activities attract, the core activity is typically a source of procedural strategizing.

2   Due to the reliance on procedural strategizing, the core activity has inertial tendencies. These inertial tendencies are strongly resistant to change in the core activity. Therefore, interactive strategizing, particularly of a short duration, is unlikely to be sufficient to reframe the core activity and counteract inertia. Integrative strategizing is thus indicated to shape changes in the core activity, combining longer-term reframing of the activity with ongoing modification of its structural embedding.

3   Non-core activities are likely to be perceived as threatening to the core activity, particularly if they are based on an economic rationale that competes with the value rationale of the core activity. It will be difficult to associate threatening activities with the core activity using procedural strategizing. Intensive interactive strategizing is important for generating interpretative associations that frame such activities as supportive and non-threatening to the core activity.

4   Multiple strategies increase the contested and distributed nature of an activity system because different activities represent divergent goals and interests. For example, in the professional contexts in this book, this divergence was based on tensions between professional and managerial interests. Frameworks of meaning are therefore contested and lack durability. Interactive strategizing alone is insufficient to counteract the ongoing challenges to the interpretative legitimacy of different activities and the association between them. Structural substance to this legitimacy, in the form of common benefits, must be built in through procedural strategizing. Given that both structural and interpretative legitimacy are required, and that the two need ongoing alignment, integrative strategizing is indicated for managing associations between activities.

These four points about shaping the association between multiple strategies help to contextualize the application of the four strategizing types proposed in Chapter 5. They also show how patterns of activity are shaped by the contextual contingencies of whether an activity is the core activity or is perceived as threatening to the core activity. Such detail furnishes a more situated understanding of how different types of strategizing apply to the shaping of activity.

This Chapter completes the empirical section of this book. Part III, comprising Chapters 7 and 8, will draw together the points raised within the book and move the strategy as practice agenda forward by theorizing the activity-based view.

Quick Reference Guide 6.2: Strategizing types and the coexistence of activities

- Multiple activities reflect different managerial and professional interests. Their alignment is thus an ongoing source of tension.

- Procedural strategizing links activities that do not threaten the core activity and may be easily aligned with it through the metrics and measures of administrative practices and diagnostic controls. The links give structural substance to the common benefits to be attained from multiple activities, but cannot frame complementary meanings, particularly with activities that are perceived as threatening.

- Interactive strategizing is essential to construct interpretative links between activities that are potentially threatening to the core activity. Interactive strategizing can frame the common benefits to be attained by pursuing multiple activities, but cannot structurally embed them.

- Integrative strategizing builds interpretative links between activities and structurally embeds them, constructing a concept of 'common purpose' within which potentially divergent activities can be aligned.

- Multiple activities will always be prone to contested interpretations and actions because they represent divergent interests. Hence, structural and interpretative realignment will need to be continuously reconstructed.

PART III: THEORIZING AN ACTIVITY-BASED VIEW OF STRATEGY AS PRACTICE

This section draws together the themes from Part I, which located an activity-based view in both practice theory and the strategy literature, and the empirical interpretation and development of those themes presented in Part II. The aim of this section is to contribute to the theoretical development of an activity-based view. Chapter 7 is concerned with assembling the conceptual building blocks for a strategizing framework. It deals primarily with the unit of analysis, strategizing, and how it shapes the level of analysis, strategy as a pattern in a stream of goal-directed activity. Explaining this relationship has been the main aim of this book. Chapter 8 looks more specifically at the dynamics of the activity system framework developed in Chapter 1 and expanded upon in Chapters 2, 4 and 5. Chapter 8 will return to the practice theory underpinning an activity-based view to explain the value and limitations of this analytic framework. It concludes the book by emphasizing the major contributions of an activity-based view of strategy as practice.

7 DEVELOPING A STRATEGIZING FRAMEWORK

Key points

- Building the strategizing framework:
  - structural and interpretative legitimacy are complementary concepts
  - these concepts underpin a matrix of four strategizing types that shape phases of activity
  - the strategizing matrix explains variance in a typology of activity patterns
- Multiple activities have implications for the strategizing framework

This book began by articulating a recently developed activity-based view of strategy as practice. The activity-based view conceptualizes strategy as activity and exhorts us to conduct empirical research that can explain how that activity is shaped in practice. In this book the activity-based research agenda has been addressed by developing a set of empirically and theoretically grounded concepts that describe and explain how strategy is shaped over time. These concepts have explanatory power that can contribute to the theoretical development of an activity-based view.

The aim of this chapter is to build these concepts into a strategizing framework. It will do so by looking at the three questions derived in Chapter 2, which were the subject of the three empirical chapters, 4 to 6. The frameworks and findings from each of these chapters are addressed and distilled to the three main concepts that inform the strategizing framework. First, structural and interpretative legitimacy are established as complementary concepts. Second, the strategizing matrix is conceptually refined to the four strategizing types – pre-active, procedural, interactive and integrative strategizing – and the various combinations of structural and interpretative legitimacy that they confer upon activity. Third, moves between these strategizing types are developed into an activity typology that explains variance in five different patterns of strategy

> ## Quick Reference Guide 7.1: Overview of definitions and conceptual building blocks
>
> • Strategy is a pattern in a stream of goal-directed activity over time (Chapter 2).
>
> • Strategizing is the interplay between top managers and those situated practices that mediate the shaping of strategy over time (Chapter 2).
>
> • Procedural strategizing is the use of situated formal administrative practices to shape strategy. It confers structural legitimacy on activity, but is prone to inertia (Chapter 4).
>
> • Interactive strategizing is the use of face-to-face interaction to shape strategy. It confers interpretative legitimacy on activity, but this interpretative legitimacy is not durable (Chapter 4).
>
> • There are four types of strategizing, pre-active, procedural, interactive and integrative strategizing, which differ according to the way that they confer structural and interpretative legitimacy on activity (Chapter 5).
>
> • Movement between strategizing types explains five patterns in shaping strategy over time: introducing localized activity, inertial activity, changing activity, stabilizing activity, and unresolved activity (Chapter 5).
>
> • In the context of multiple strategies, different strategizing types and activity patterns apply according to whether an activity is the core activity or whether it threatens the core activity (Chapter 6).

as a stream of goal-directed activity over time. Finally, these strategizing types and activity patterns are contextualized by their relationship with other streams of activity. The chapter concludes by proposing that the strategizing framework developed throughout this book and elaborated in this chapter contributes towards the theoretical development of the activity-based view.

PROCEDURAL AND INTERACTIVE STRATEGIZING AND FORMS OF LEGITIMACY

Chapter 4 addressed the first research question: What are the implications of procedural and interactive strategizing for shaping strategy? Procedural strategizing is defined as the use of formal administrative practices to shape strategy. Under most circumstances, procedural strategizing can be carried out with little active attention from top managers. Interactive strategizing is defined as purposive face-to-face interaction between top managers and other members of the organizational community about strategy. By definition, interactive strategizing requires active engagement from top managers. Respectively, procedural and interactive strategizing confer structural and interpretative legitimacy on activity. These two forms of legitimacy are core components of the conceptual development in this book. They have different purposes and problems in shaping activity, which were empirically described in Chapter 4, and which are now summarized in terms of their core concepts.

PROCEDURAL STRATEGIZING AND STRUCTURAL LEGITIMACY

The main purpose of procedural strategizing is to confer structural legitimacy upon activity. Structural legitimacy refers to the social order displayed in structural practices, such as routines, hierarchies and roles, which legitimizes activity and enables it to be carried out in ways that reinforce the existing social order (Clegg, 1989; Giddens, 1984; Weber, 1978). Because structural legitimacy is typically a recursive, self-reinforcing process, it has long duration. A key feature of this legitimacy is that it persists within the structures, without continuous attention from individuals (Lawrence et al., 2002; Lockwood, 1964). Therefore, activities that have structural legitimacy become embedded in the organization and persist over time with low managerial attention. Procedural strategizing confers structural legitimacy upon an activity through structural embedding in two ways.

First, procedural strategizing involves the use of formal administrative practices to structurally embed activity. The strategic planning cycle at Modern University (Exhibit 4.1) was a particularly strong example of embedding activity through procedural strategizing. On an annual basis, the planning cycle indicated the targets to be achieved and the timeframes and responsibilities for these targets. The exhibit explained structural embedding of the commercial strategy over four years of the planning cycle. While commercial activity initially had low legitimacy in the organization, as it became embedded in these practices, the debate moved from whether there should be commercial activity to what the targets and timeframes for that activity should be. Administrative practices confer this structural legitimacy because, once an activity is formally documented and has a resource stream attached to it, it is difficult to deny its legitimate status within the organization. The activity becomes part of the taken for granted routines of the organization. If actors wish to de-legitimize it, they will need to expend considerable effort to counteract the structural embedding that enables its persistence (Weber, 1978). The value of procedural strategizing is that it embeds a stream of activity within a set of routine practices that formalize goals.

Second, procedural strategizing provides diagnostic control over activity. The administrative practices that embed activity also control it. In the planning example at Modern, there are feedback loops that monitor activity and provide rewards and sanctions according to the ability to achieve targets. These controls occur through the planning practices, without direct managerial intervention (Simons, 1991, 1994). For example, the resource allocation model 'makes harsh decisions' based on the financial viability of a department (see, for example, Modern, Exhibit 4.1). Top managers do not need to 'decide' or intervene to penalize a department. They can allow the control mechanisms to do it. The persistence of activity without the attention of individuals is an indicator of structural legitimacy (Lawrence et al., 2002). Procedural strategizing thus contributes to structural legitimacy by embedding activity in diagnostic controls that enable its persistence without active managerial attention. Of course, strategizing through formal administrative procedures alone cannot ensure cooperation in an activity. Nonetheless, because it imparts structural legitimacy, procedural strategizing is a powerful tool for generating commitment to activity (Clegg, 1989; Weber, 1978).

However, the structural legitimacy attained through procedural strategizing is also associated with a key problem in shaping activity, namely strategic drift. Strategic drift highlights the taken for granted nature of embedded activity. Once an activity is embedded in administrative practices, the debate moves away from the goals of the activity to the practices for achieving the activity. As these practices are modified, activity is increasingly shaped by the targets, metrics and measures devised, rather than by its original goals. As the example of size and scope strategy at Collegiate University showed, academics focused on the staffing quota mechanisms. They used and modified these quotas in ways that distorted the size and scope goals, growing excessively in some areas and threatening the balance of the institution (see Exhibit 4.2). Thus procedural strategizing has a negative consequence of goals–means displacement and strategic drift in an activity. The longer an activity has been structurally embedded, the more likely it is to display these negative consequences.

Finally, there is a contingency in using procedural strategizing to establish structural legitimacy for an activity. Simply embedding an activity in administrative practices will not be sufficient to ensure its structural legitimacy because these practices may not be relevant to the community. This was evident in the size and scope strategy at Collegiate (Exhibit 4.2). In order for controls to shape behaviour, they must have situated relevance, meaning that they must be relevant forms of control to the community in which they are used. If the community does not see the sanctions and rewards inherent in a set of diagnostic controls as relevant, they will not comply with them (Ferrary, 2002). At Collegiate, this gave rise to weakly sanctioned controls that embedded the size and scope activity on a path of strategic drift. The problem of situated relevance may be particularly applicable to professional contexts, where diagnostic controls are perceived as less relevant by the community. The situated relevance of controls is thus a contingency that impacts upon procedural strategizing and its capacity to accord structural legitimacy to an activity.

INTERACTIVE STRATEGIZING AND INTERPRETATIVE LEGITIMACY

The main purpose of interactive strategizing is to confer interpretative legitimacy on activity. Interpretative legitimacy is powerful for shaping activity in two interrelated ways: common frameworks of meaning and normative controls. Individuals understand how to act by participating in and constructing those frameworks of meaning that confer legitimacy upon action. Through such frameworks, individuals' actions are mutually intelligible to each other, enabling them to act collectively (Garfinkel, 1967; Suchman, 1987; Weick and Roberts, 1993). In framing some activity as legitimate, frameworks of meaning also establish what activity is not legitimate. They thus constitute a form of normative control, in which individuals adopt self-control in the interests of the wider community (Giddens, 1984; Lukes, 1974). The research strategy at Entrepreneurial University provided an example of how interpretative legitimacy constitutes a normative control that both enables collective activity and sanctions behaviour that does not contribute to that activity. In the Research Assessment Exercise (RAE) rankings, departments that performed 'worse than expected' had 'let the side down'. Other actors were thus validated in descending on them 'like vultures'. Interpretative legitimacy is a powerful way of shaping activity. It is not, however, durable. Frameworks of meaning are constructed through the interactions between individuals. While these interactions favour the meanings of the dominant group, this is not absolute because of the diffuse sources of power from which meanings are derived (Neilsen and Rao, 1987; Pettigrew, 1973; Whittington, 1992). Frameworks of meaning need to be continuously reconstructed through interaction: 'Mutual intelligibility is achieved on each occasion of interaction with reference to situation particulars rather than being discharged once and for all by a stable body of shared meanings' (Suchman, 1987: 50–51). Interpretative legitimacy thus shapes activity through common frameworks of meaning and normative control, but this shaping is not durable, requiring ongoing attention by individuals.

As interactive strategizing involves face-to-face interaction between top managers and their subordinates, it is a particularly powerful communicative resource for constructing interpretative legitimacy about activity. It was valuable in shaping activity in two main ways: introducing new strategies and reframing existing strategies. With new strategies, the aim of interactive strategizing is to establish a framework of meanings that are sufficiently convincing that they enable collective activity. For example, in introducing the commercial and research strategies at Modern, top managers undertook a year of intensive interactive strategizing throughout the University to give the new strategies 'a kind of confirmation', framing the desirability, 'a vision thing' as well as the necessity of these strategies: 'you have to steer the University'. Such interactive strategizing legitimates activity and helps collective activity by 'bringing people around' (see, for example, Chapter 4, p. 94). Interactive strategizing is also valuable in reconstructing existing activity. Existing activity frequently exhibits the negative consequences of procedural strategizing, in terms of goals–means displacement and strategic drift. As shown with the research strategy at Collegiate (Exhibit 4.3), top managers can use interactive strategizing purposively to raise consciousness of an embedded activity and ensure that its associated practices are continuously realigned to the goals of research excellence. In this example, interactive strategizing was used to make others 'very conscious of the RAE', and encourage collective activity by getting 'people to rally around the RAE'. It also stimulated normative control by indicating to lower performers that they 'are effectively freeloading on everybody else'. Interactive strategizing is thus a valuable resource for shaping the interpretative legitimacy of a strategy. It establishes frameworks of meaning that legitimate and provide normative control over activity.

However, interactive strategizing also illustrates the problems with constructing interpretative legitimacy. The concept of interpretative legitimacy assumes a common framework of meanings. This does not imply durability of meaning, which is not consistent with practice-based theory (Reckwitz, 2002; Suchman, 1987). Rather, interpretative legitimacy needs to be continuously reconstructed. As Exhibit 4.3 on reframing the research strategy at Collegiate showed, frameworks of meaning were constructed around the action of appointing world-class research professors because top managers made 'a convincing case' and others were persuaded that the action was 'a good thing'. Throughout such interactions, these actors were aware that they 'could have said no'. Indeed, Exhibit 5.4 showed the ongoing attempts to reframe the research strategy at Collegiate through interactive strategizing. While top managers successfully framed meaning around the action on research professors, they had by no means reframed the entire research strategy. Each specific incident of interactive strategizing must, therefore, establish sufficiently shared meanings for that action to occur (Weick, 1979). Interactive strategizing enables top managers to impart interpretative legitimacy to activity, but this legitimacy is neither stable nor hegemonic in terms of the overall stream of activity. Indeed, the very need to use interactive strategizing is indicative of the fragile nature of top manager influence and their need to reconstruct their agency continuously through interaction with others. Interpretative legitimacy is thus not durable, requiring ongoing managerial attention in order to shape activity.

Finally, the impermanence of interpretative legitimacy indicates a contingency in using interactive strategizing to shape strategy. Interpretative legitimacy has to be continuously renegotiated because of divergent interests over activity between top managers and their community. The greater the potential divergence within the community, the more that frameworks of meaning will be open to different interpretations. The more that frameworks are open to different interpretations, the lower their durability. The lower the durability of meanings, the more that interactive strategizing must continuously re-establish a common framework of meanings. Universities, in keeping with other professional organizations, are contexts in which professional interests are likely to diverge from managerial interests over activity (Alvesson and Sveningsson, 2003). These contexts thus indicate a situated contingency that impacts upon the uses of interactive strategizing. In professional contexts, where high divergence of activity is expected, increased interactive strategizing will be required to construct interpretative legitimacy, and this is likely to be less durable.

The main points arising from Chapter 4 that inform an activity-based theory of strategy as practice are the purposes of procedural and interactive strategizing in shaping goal-directed activity. Procedural strategizing confers structural legitimacy on an activity, asserting its right to exist and to command a set of mediating practices that enable its persistence. Interactive strategizing confers interpretative legitimacy on an activity, enabling collective activity through common frameworks of meaning and normative controls. The two forms of legitimacy, structural and interpretative, may be seen as polar types, conferring legitimacy in ways that serve almost opposing purposes and so counteract the weaknesses in each other. For example, structural legitimacy gives an activity high persistence with low managerial attention, but is prone to strategic drift from its goals. By contrast, interpretative legitimacy ensures that goals are framed as desirable and relevant but, has low durability and requires high managerial attention. The two are thus discrete but complementary concepts, which are important building blocks to take forward in explaining the way that activity is shaped. Table 7.1 draws together these characteristics of structural and interpretative legitimacy as the basis for the strategizing framework developed in this chapter.

The above discussion also highlights the situational contingencies that affect the application of these two forms of legitimacy. Specifically, structural legitimacy is affected by the situated relevance of the practices in which activity is embedded. Practices that have situated relevance may not adequately reflect the

Table 7.1: Characteristics of structural and interpretative legitimacy

Characteristics	Structural legitimacy	Interpretative legitimacy
Strategizing type	• Procedural strategizing	• Interactive strategizing
Source of legitimacy	• Structural embedding in routine practices that reinforce roles, hierarchies and responsibilities	• Frameworks of meaning and normative control
Role in shaping activity and strategic drift)	• Activity has high persistence (structural embedding) • Goals lose relevance (goals–means displacement	• Activity has low persistence (meanings are not durable) • Goals have high relevance (framed as desirable and necessary)
Managerial attention	• Low managerial attention	• High managerial attention
Contingencies of use	• Controls must have situated relevance to embed activity • In professional contexts, weakly sanctioned controls have situated relevance but can embed activity on unintended paths	• Divergence of interests challenges the durability of meanings • In professional contexts, high divergence requires higher interaction to continuously construct common meanings

goal-directed nature of activity and so, over time, subvert its course. This is exacerbated in professional contexts where controls are typically weakly sanctioned in order to be relevant to the autonomous nature of professional work. As noted in Chapter 2, more hierarchical or formally structured contexts, such as traditional manufacturing organizations, may have different associations with forms of structural legitimacy that are beyond the scope of this book. In interactive strategizing, the more potentially divergent the community, the more that ongoing interactive strategizing is needed continuously to reconstruct a common framework of meanings. Again, this is exacerbated in professional contexts, which typically have divergent interests that require higher levels of interactive strategizing to confer interpretative legitimacy upon activity. Therefore, in developing a strategizing framework it is important to take into account those situated contingencies that impact upon the construction of interpretative and structural legitimacy. These contingencies are incorporated in Table 7.1 and are returned to in the discussion of multiple streams of activity below.

TYPES OF STRATEGIZING AND PATTERNS OF ACTIVITY

Chapter 5 addressed the dynamics involved in different types of strategizing and their mediating role in shaping strategy. The chapter built upon the complementary relationship between structural and interpretative legitimacy conferred by procedural and interactive strategizing. Four types of strategizing were developed, according to how each type combined structural and interpretative legitimacy. These essential points about strategizing arising from Chapter 5 are distilled into a strategizing matrix, Figure 7.1, using structural and interpretative legitimacy as the two axes. This matrix illustrates the four types of strategizing established: pre-active, procedural, interactive and integrative. These strategizing types are now explained in terms of the different phases of strategy that they shape. They are then further applied to explain variation in patterns of strategy over time, deriving a typology of five patterns.

Pre-active strategizing deals with activity that has neither interpretative nor structural legitimacy. These are localized activities that may be relevant to particular groups within the organization. However, they have not established either a set of formal practices that enable their persistence, or a set of relatively common meanings that enable them to enter mainstream strategy. Pre-active strategizing is typical of emerging, bottom-up activities that are being pursued at the peripheries but have not been endorsed as strategy at the organizational level (Johnson and Huff, 1998; Mintzberg and Waters, 1985; Regnér, 2003). It may also be associated with top-manager endorsed strategies that are in a very early stage of development but have not been promoted in the wider organization. This was found with new strategies that were likely to be contentious and a source of organizational resistance. For example, the commercial strategy at both Collegiate and Modern was initially localized to the top team and a few interested parties. Because commercial activity was perceived as counter to the professional identity

Figure 7.1: The strategizing matrix

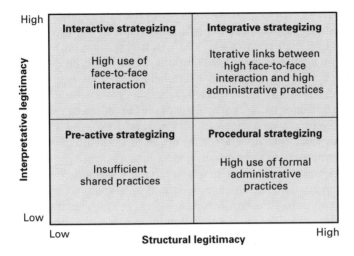

of these organizations, top managers exercised caution in the early stages, not introducing the strategy into the mainstream. Activity that is a source of pre-active strategizing must move into one of the other strategizing types in order to generate enough legitimacy to become a strategy in its own right.

Procedural strategizing involves establishing high structural legitimacy for activity by embedding it within the formal administrative practices of the organization. It is typical with activities that have a long organizational history, such as research at Collegiate and teaching at Modern, where the legitimacy of the activity is taken for granted. These examples show how an activity can have high structural legitimacy but can also drift and lose interpretative legitimacy. For example, at Modern teaching activity drifted from its initial legitimacy as 'pioneering' and 'innovative' on which the University had established its reputation, becoming embedded in the administrative procedures of the modular programme (see Exhibit 5.2). Procedural strategizing is thus likely to be associated with inertial patterns that subvert the goal-directedness of activity. However, without procedural strategizing, the activity will not attain the structural legitimacy necessary to persist. It is therefore important in the establishment and embedding of new activities, granting them a structural foothold in the organization. As all activities require some structural legitimacy to persist, procedural strategizing is necessary but tends towards negative consequences of strategic drift over time, needing to be reframed at least periodically (Barley and Tolbert, 1997).

Interactive strategizing involves establishing high interpretative legitimacy for an activity through face-to-face interaction between top managers and others in their community. It is important in introducing new strategies that need to counteract typical resistances to change and generate sufficient interpretative legitimacy to become mainstream strategy. It is, therefore, most likely to be the type of strategizing used to move activities from the pre-active strategizing quadrant, as shown with commercial activity at Collegiate (Chapter 5, p. 109). It is also valuable for changing an existing strategy that has become overly embedded and needs to be reframed and realigned with goals, as shown with the research activity at Collegiate (Exhibits 4.3 and 5.4). In this situation, interactive strategizing might involve reframing the meanings surrounding an existing activity to legitimize a change in the activity (Bartunek, 1984). However, as the examples from Collegiate illustrate, interpretative legitimacy is not durable, needing to be continuously reconstructed, particularly where the community is distributed and holds divergent interests. Interactive strategizing alone is not sufficient to establish and perpetuate activity. Rather, the degree to which interpretative legitimacy has been attained is, to some extent, evidenced in its capacity to furnish a framework of meanings that enable an activity to move to another strategizing type, where it can attain the persistence associated with structural legitimacy.

Integrative strategizing involves establishing both high interpretative and high structural legitimacy for an activity. Integrative strategizing can continuously construct interpretative legitimacy through ongoing interaction, structurally embedding these interpretations as well as counteracting the tendency to inertia involved in structural legitimacy. In this process there are iterative links between face-to-face interaction and formal administrative practices; reconstructing frameworks of meaning to ensure they continuously re-establish relatively common understandings of goal-directed activity and modifying formal practices on an ongoing basis to better reflect those goals. Integrative strategizing typically involves either ongoing realization of existing activity, preventing drift through continuous renewal, or ongoing incremental change in activity through continuous modification. Both of these uses of integrative strategizing were evident in the research strategy at Entrepreneurial, continuously renewing the research strategy to ensure its realization, while increasingly developing a commercial aspect to that strategy (Exhibit 5.3). Integrative strategizing is a very dynamic state of interplay between structural and interpretative legitimacy.

The strategizing matrix developed in this study illustrates four different configurations of structural and interpretative legitimacy, which have different applications in shaping phases of activity. These four types of strategizing, and the phases of activity to which they apply, are summarized in Table 7.2.

A TYPOLOGY OF ACTIVITY PATTERNS

These four strategizing types are critical to theorizing the relationship between strategizing and strategy as a pattern in a stream of goal-directed activity. By tracing the movement between these types of strategizing longitudinally, it was possible to show their influence on patterns of activity in the empirical data. Drawing upon evidence from the empirical data, a typology of five patterns and some sub-pattern variations in shaping strategy are now proposed and located within their relevant literatures. These five patterns, which are illustrated in Figure 7.2, are:

Table 7.2: The strategizing matrix and its application to phases of activity

Strategizing type	Legitimacy	Application to phases of activity
Pre-active	Low structural and interpretative	Localized activity, either: • bottom-up, emerging strategies; or • intended activity in a very early phase of development
Procedural	High structural, low interpretative	• Activities with a long organizational history • Necessary for embedding new activity • Prone to inertia over time
Interactive	High interpretative, low structural	• New activities that are becoming mainstream • Reframing existing activity that has succumbed to drift • Not durable
Integrative	High structural and interpretative	• Ongoing renewal and realization of existing activity • Incremental change in activity

- introducing localized activity;
- inertial activity;
- shaping change in activity;
- stabilizing activity; and
- unresolved activity.

Pattern A: introducing a localized activity

As this pattern is concerned with introducing a localized activity, it only involves moving from pre-active strategizing. The focus is on the pattern by which a new activity that is localized to only some actors and has neither structural nor interpretative legitimacy is introduced into mainstream strategy. Once an activity moves into another type of strategizing it is no longer localized. How it progresses in the organization after this depends upon which of the other patterns, explained below, it moves into. Two sub-patterns are possible in moving from pre-active strategizing, intended and unintended. First, the intended pattern involves moving from pre-active strategizing to interactive strategizing. This is most likely to occur where the activity is intended and has the sponsorship of top management. Top management uses interactive strategizing to create a favourable framework of meanings about the activity in order to 'launch' it in the wider community and counter possible resistance (Gioia and Chittipedi, 1991). This pattern was exemplified in initiating the commercial and research strategies at Modern and the commercial strategy at Collegiate (Chapter 5, p. 109). An intended pattern of introducing a localized activity is likely to have been either initiated by top management or to have their sponsorship.

Figure 7.2: An activity typology: patterns in shaping activity over time

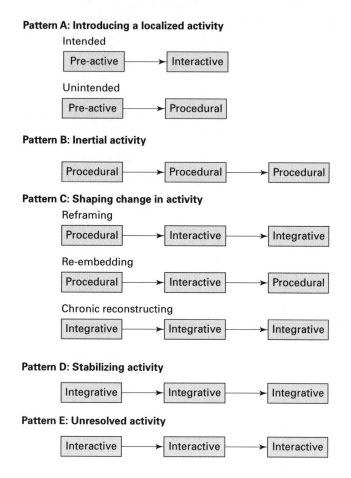

The second, unintended pattern involves a move from pre-active strategizing to procedural strategizing. This is most likely to occur when the activity 'hijacks' existing administrative practices to establish itself in the organization. It is therefore unlikely to have the sponsorship of top management, who would have recourse to establishing the interpretative legitimacy of an activity prior to developing its structural legitimacy. The activity might, therefore, emerge as an unintended consequence of the administrative practices (Lowe and Jones, 2004). An example of this is the size and scope strategy at Modern, which was unintentionally embedded in the resource allocation practices for administering teaching and commercial activity (Chapter 5, p. 110). Alternately, lower-level managers might deliberately use the formal administrative practices to insinuate an activity into the organizational strategy (Burgelman, 1996).

Pattern B: inertial activity

The inertial pattern involves activity that is shaped by ongoing procedural strategizing. Such activity has structural legitimacy and is embedded in a routinized set of administrative practices. However, as explained in the section on procedural strategizing above, embedding in administrative practices can lead to a focus on the practices themselves and not the goal-directedness of activity. This is particularly likely where the sunk costs of both behaviour and resources within the existing practices cannot be overcome without significant effort (Miller and Friesen, 1984). The goals–means displacement that eventuates progressively leads to an inertial pattern of activity (Cyert and March, 1963). While no activity traced in this study was following an inertial pattern, it may be inferred from the difficulties with changing procedurally embedded activity in the cases, such as research at Collegiate (Exhibit 5.4) and teaching at Modern (Exhibit 5.2). Taking these empirical examples in conjunction with an understanding of how procedural strategizing shapes phases of activity, the inertial pattern over time is hypothesized as ongoing procedural strategizing. This theorizing is supported by the substantial body of strategy and organization research into inertia (for example, Burgelman, 1994; Greenwood and Hinings, 1988; Miller, 1993). Essentially, all activities require some active reconstruction if they are to avoid lapsing into inertial patterns over time. Therefore, ongoing and unalleviated procedural strategizing produces a pattern of inertia.

Pattern C: shaping change in activity

Changing activity involves shaping change in an existing pattern of activity, rather than substituting an old activity with a new activity. Substitution necessitates strategic exit from an activity, which did not occur in the empirical data and therefore does not form part of these patterns. This section deals with activities that are already part of mainstream strategy but are undergoing some form of change. Three sub-patterns for shaping change, each involving two strategizing moves, are discussed:

- reframing;
- re-embedding; and
- chronic reconstructing.

The reframing pattern was exemplified in the size and scope strategy at Collegiate (Exhibit 5.1). It first involves a shift from procedural strategizing, where the activity has high structural legitimacy but has also suffered the inertial effects associated with it, to interactive strategizing. Interactive strategizing is important for reframing the meaning surrounding the activity in order to shift it from its inertial pattern and better align it with intended changes in the activity. This is followed by integrative strategizing in order to develop new formal practices that will structurally embed the changes, but with ongoing reinforcement of the interpretative legitimacy of the change. The move to integrative strategizing supports change by preventing the activity from sliding back into its inertial patterns. This pattern of shaping change in strategy is robust and well grounded within the literature on interpretative models of change, where interpretation mobilizes support for and then helps to sustain a change process (for example, Balogun and Johnson, 2004; Bartunek, 1984; Gioia and Chittipedi, 1991).

The re-embedding pattern was exemplified in the teaching pattern at both Modern (Exhibit 5.2) and Collegiate (Chapter 5, p. 118). As with the sub-pattern described above, the initial shift is from procedural strategizing to interactive strategizing for the same reason of counteracting inertia through reframing. However, the second move is back to procedural strategizing, re-embedding the changed interpretations in modified formal administrative practices. This may be more or less effective at shaping change, depending on the scope of change and some of the situated contingencies identified above (see Table 7.1). For example, at Modern it was less effective because teaching was a historically embedded activity and the change was perceived as radical. Thus, changes were likely to be a source of divergent interests and raise professional resistance. A contained period of interactive strategizing was not enough to reframe teaching activity. Teaching lapsed into its original patterns of activity highlighting the low durability of interpretative legitimacy, particularly where activity is a source of divergent interests between top managers and professionals. However, at Collegiate it was more effective because teaching was not core to the professional identity, so there was less resistance or professional divergence of interests. The changes to service and quality were not radical and, once reframed, were generally straightforward to monitor through formal administrative practices without requiring ongoing attention. The re-embedding pattern follows a punctuated model of changing activity: moving from an existing pattern through a period of reframing followed by re-embedding of the change (Gersick, 1991; Tushman and Romanelli, 1985). In terms of shaping strategy, the re-embedding pattern appears more applicable for changes that are not radical and those that do not incur high professional resistance (Lant and Mezias, 1992; Wilson, 1992).

The final sub-pattern, chronic reconstructing, arises from ongoing integrative strategizing. This pattern is termed 'chronic' because it is recurrent. It involves incremental change through ongoing reinterpretation of the frameworks of meaning and re-embedding of them in the administrative practices. Tightly recursive links between face-to-face interaction and administrative practices ensure that activity is chronically reconstructed in alignment with subtle shifts in the organization and the environment. It is perhaps best exemplified in the research strategy at Entrepreneurial, which was continuously being reconstructed through the two types of strategizing and faced a significant change towards the end of the period of study, when it branched out into dual goals of commercial income and research excellence (Exhibit 5.3). This pattern involves incremental shaping of changes in strategy, which might, over the long-term, constitute quite fundamental changes to activity. Indeed, the adoption of a commercial goal into a professional activity, such as research, is typically seen as a fundamental change (Oakes et al., 1998). Despite the potential for fundamental change over the long-term, the pattern of continuous adjustment in the configuration of interpretative and structural legitimacy is most consistent with incremental or evolutionary approaches that enable managerial learning during a change process (for example, Doz, 1996; Quinn, 1980). It is doubtful whether this pattern of shaping activity, due to its internal coherence, would either enable or necessitate sudden radical change, except in the situation of an external shock to the system.

Pattern D: stabilizing activity

The stabilizing pattern involves activity that is shaped by ongoing integrative strategizing. It was exemplified in the commercial and size and scope strategies at Entrepreneurial, as well as the earlier period of the research strategy (Exhibit 5.3). If activity persists over the long-term but is to avoid the trap of inertia, it needs to be continuously reconstructed. Ongoing reconstruction enables the administrative practices to be continuously aligned to the goals of activity and ensures that the meanings surrounding these practices and goals continue to be relevant to other actors. Integrative strategizing picks up divergence in goals and lapses in the performance of activity through the information provided by administrative practices, and uses that information to actively reinforce the interpretative legitimacy of both the activity and the practices, potentially further modifying the administrative practices. This pattern is similar to the chronic reconstruction sub-pattern of changing activity, but does not involve actively changing the activity. It is concerned with realizing the existing strategy, rather than allowing it to lapse into inertia. Stabilizing activity, while a core practice theme, tends to be less dealt with in the management literature, particularly that on strategy. It involves the effortful accomplishment of ongoing activity (Pentland and Rueter, 1994; Tsoukas and Chia, 2002).

Pattern E: unresolved activity

Finally, the unresolved pattern involves activity that is the subject of ongoing interactive strategizing. This activity is continuously trying to establish interpretative legitimacy in order to move on to a more structurally legitimate status in the organization. If an activity is continuously the subject of interactive strategizing but cannot gain sufficient interpretative legitimacy to enable procedures to be established that will give it structural legitimacy, it is always on tentative ground. Such activity remains unresolved. The latter phases of change in the research activity at Collegiate remained in an ongoing state of interactive strategizing, which had not been resolved in any new formal administrative practices (Exhibit 5.4). This pattern can also be used to interpret Maitlis and Lawrence' (2003) example of an orchestra that was unable to arrive at goal-directed activity. In the orchestra case, extensive strategizing exercises took place over two and half years without an artistic strategy attaining sufficient interpretative legitimacy to progress towards any collective activity. It provides a very clear example of unresolved activity. This pattern is also less examined in the literature, with some exceptions (for example, Greenwood and Hinings, 1988). It is typically recast either as a failure in strategizing (for example, Maitlis and Lawrence, 2003) or tracked through to some form of resolution.

PATTERNS OF ACTIVITY ARE CONCEPTUALLY ROBUST

These five patterns and their associated sub-patterns are empirically supported and also have wider conceptual application. Their potential for wider application derives from the empirically-grounded conceptual framework developed in this study. First, the empirical evidence of top managers' use of formal administrative practices and face-to-face interaction were analysed as conferring structural and interpretative legitimacy. These core concepts were then used to derive four empirically supported types of strategizing that explained phases in the shaping of strategy. Longitudinally, movement between these strategizing types explained variation in five main patterns and associated sub-patterns of activity that were found in the data. These patterns form the basis of Figure 7.2, the activity typology. Each pattern can also be theoretically located within the strategy and change literatures pertaining to that style of pattern. Therefore, individually these patterns are robust. Each pattern makes a contribution by showing the strategizing types involved in its construction, strengthening our understanding of how strategizing types shape strategy over time. Furthermore, as the unresolved and stabilizing patterns are under-explored empirically or theoretically, these two patterns extend knowledge on the construction of stability and of unresolved activity. However, the main contribution is derived from taking the patterns as a whole. Variation in these patterns can be explained according to the sequence of strategizing types that they move through over time, indicating the explanatory power of these strategizing types.

The use of strategizing types to explain variations in patterns of activity is also conceptually robust. The projection of patterns based on the configurations of different strategizing types is consistent with the theoretical principles of archetypes and organizational tracks (Greenwood and Hinings, 1988, 1993; Miller and Friesen, 1980, 1984). Archetype deals with the interdependent configuration of structural and interpretative elements in the organization as a whole. Different configurations indicate different archetypes. For example, Greenwood and Hinings (1993) posit the corporate bureaucracy and the professional bureaucracy as different archetypes because of their different configurations of structure, system and interpretative scheme. Shifts in archetype occur when an organization no longer fits with its environment or moves to another stage of development (Miller and Friesen, 1984). These shifts are termed an 'organization's track', with different tracks possible according to the nature of the shifts in archetype (Greenwood and Hinings, 1988).

The principles underpinning theoretical relationships between archetypes and organizational tracks help theoretically to validate the relationship found in this book between strategizing types and the typology of activity patterns. It is not possible to claim that the patterns here are generalizable. Nonetheless, the careful development of the conceptual framework that underpins the patterns and the theoretical precedent found in the work on organizational archetypes and tracks indicates that they are robust. These patterns are therefore likely to have wider application, particularly in professional and knowledge-intensive contexts, such as the universities in this book, where top-down management control over the pattern of activity cannot be assumed (see Chapter 3 for specific examples of organizations where these patterns are potentially applicable). However, before proposing these concepts as a strategizing framework, it is necessary to examine those contingencies that have implications for the patterns found. The next section, therefore, turns to the third research question on the association between multiple streams of activity.

RELATIONSHIPS BETWEEN MULTIPLE STREAMS OF ACTIVITY

While most strategy literature deals with strategy as a single construct, in this study multiple strategies were found. Each case was pursuing four streams of goal-directed activity – teaching, research, commercial income and size and scope – which had to coexist, since sacrificing one or more to concentrate on the others was not an option in terms of the policy and funding environment. Multiple activities posed a problem because they represented divergent interests and tensions. Their coexistence had different implications for the type of strategizing used and the pattern that any individual activity took. These problems with multiple strategies lie in the conflict between managerial and professional interests (Denis et al., 1996, 2001; Hinings and Leblebici, 2003). Chapter 6 dealt with the problem of multiple streams of goal-directed activity, furnishing five points that have implications for how different types of strategizing are associated with the coexistence of activities.

First, the study found that there is a core activity. This activity is core because it is historically associated with the professional identity and prestige of the organization (Gioia and Thomas, 1996). In the Collegiate and Entrepreneurial cases, the core activity was research, while at Modern it was teaching. Because the core activity is associated with the professional identity, its legitimacy is taken for granted. Additionally, it is a source of professional autonomy and resistance to managerial intervention. Due to these three factors, core activities are likely to be shaped by procedural strategizing, where the activity is structurally embedded and persists with low managerial attention.

Second, the core activity, because it is structurally embedded, is prone to inertia, as found in the core activities at Collegiate and Modern. This indicates that core activities are generally prone to pattern B above, inertial activity. Due to their strong inertial tendencies, core activities are resistant to change. When changing such activities (pattern C), a short phase of interactive strategizing will not be sufficient to account for the divergent goals and interests of a professional workforce. Prolonged interactive strategizing will be important in reframing meaning. Therefore, as the example at Modern showed (Exhibit 5.2), the re-embedding sub-pattern of changing activity is less likely to be successful with the core activity. For changing the core activity, the reframing sub-patterns as at Collegiate (Exhibit 5.1), or chronic reconstructing as at Entrepreneurial (Exhibit 5.3), are indicated.

Third, the community will perceive other activities as a threat to the core activity because they divert attention and resources. Other activities will therefore need to establish a relationship with the core activity, either showing that they support it or, at least, do not threaten it. This is most likely to be generated through high levels of interactive strategizing. Interactive strategizing can confer interpretative legitimacy on the other activities, whilst preserving the integrity of the core activity in the minds of the community. This was skilfully managed at Collegiate, where extensive interactive strategizing was used to frame commercial activity as financially supportive of the research strategy, rather than threatening it by diverting intellectual resources. However, eventually the interpretative links between activities will need to develop some structural substance, such as the tangible commercial resources put into research at Collegiate and, particularly, Entrepreneurial. This indicates a shift towards integrative strategizing to create interpretative and structural links between activities.

Fourth, procedural strategizing may embed relationships between the core activity and other activities but, in the process, is likely to result in conflict with other activities. This is because it is difficult to develop administrative practices that account for the tensions between activities, without ongoing managerial attention and modification of the practices. This was evidenced in the procedural embedding of teaching, research and commercial activity at Modern. While commercial activity could be procedurally aligned with the core teaching activity because similar metrics and targets could be used, research could not. As the structural relationship between commercial and teaching activity became more embedded, unintended conflict with research activity increased. Procedural strategizing on its own thus tends to exacerbate conflict between activities.

Finally, multiple strategies increase the contested and distributed nature of an activity system because different activities represent divergent goals and interests. Tension between activities is an ongoing condition of multiple strategy contexts. Integrative strategizing is therefore indicated to manage the continuous construction of the core activity in ways that accommodate other activities. Integrative strategizing can reinforce the core activity whilst continuously reinterpreting its association with other activities. This both prevents it from squeezing out other activities as well as carefully monitoring the potential for them to unintentionally damage the core activity. Integrative strategizing, as exemplified at Entrepreneurial, is the most accommodating of multiple strategies because it enables mutual adjustment between activities.

This discussion of the way that multiple activities impact upon the types of strategizing used and potential patterns in activity helps to contextualize the strategizing framework being developed in this book. It shows those contingencies of professional, multiple activity contexts that might have implications for strategizing types and the way they shape strategy over time. These points are drawn together in Table 7.3. They provide important boundaries to the conceptual framework, furnishing a more complete understanding of how it applies to the shaping of activity.

Table 7.3: Implications of multiple activities for strategizing and activity patterns

Activity	Implications for strategizing type and pattern of activity
Core activity	• Tends towards procedural strategizing because of historical duration, professional autonomy, and low managerial attention. It is prone to activity pattern B: inertial activity • Tends to be resistant to change. Therefore, in pattern C, changing activity, the reframing or chronic reconstructing subpatterns are indicated as most appropriate for changing the core activity
Other activities	• Interactive strategizing is indicated to frame interpretative links between activities that can counteract perceptions of threat to the core activity • Structural links eventually need to be established, indicating a shift to integrative strategizing when sufficient interpretative legitimacy between activities is established • Procedural strategizing can generate alignment between the core activity and other activities. However, it is also prone to embedding unintended increases in conflict with other activities
Multiple activities	• Integrative strategizing is indicated as a means of continuously constructing and adjusting alignment between multiple activities to accommodate the divergent goals and interests that they represent

CONCLUSION: A STRATEGIZING FRAMEWORK TO TAKE FORWARD

This chapter concludes by proposing a strategizing framework to take forward from this book. The components of this strategizing framework are derived from the empirical chapters. They have been built throughout this chapter in three stages, beginning with the empirically and theoretically grounded concepts of structural and interpretative legitimacy. At each stage, care has been taken to show how the concepts developed shape strategy, and to outline those situational contingences that might affect the application of these concepts. The three interrelated sets of concepts derived and the contingencies under which they apply are now emphasized. Taken together, these concepts and their contingencies comprise a strategizing framework that explains how strategy as a pattern in a stream of goal-directed activity is shaped over time.

1 Structural and interpretative legitimacy are complementary concepts that explain both how an activity attains relevance within an organization and how it gains persistence in that organization. The two confer legitimacy in different ways that serve different purposes and so counteract the

weaknesses in each other. Structural legitimacy gives an activity high persistence, but that activity is also prone to strategic drift from its goals. Interpretative legitimacy frames the relevance of an activity's goals but the legitimacy attained is not durable, needing to be continuously reconstructed. The two forms of legitimacy are thus core to understanding how activity is shaped. Their distinguishing characteristics are summarized in Table 7.1.

2 Different types of strategizing confer different combinations of structural and interpretative legitimacy upon activity and so shape it in different ways. Four types of strategizing have been developed, pre-active, procedural, interactive and integrative, each of which applies to a different phase in the development of strategy. These types are positioned on a strategizing matrix, shown in Figure 7.1, to illustrate the way that they combine structural and interpretative legitimacy. The implications of the strategizing types for different phases of activity are summarized in Table 7.2. This strategizing matrix has explanatory power, indicating those phases of activity in which a particular strategizing type is likely to apply.

3 Movement between the four strategizing types can explain longitudinal patterns in shaping strategy. Variation in five patterns and associated sub-patterns of activity was explained according to the sequences of strategizing types used over time. This led to an activity typology of patterns in shaping strategy, summarized in Figure 7.2:

- introducing localized activity, with two sub-patterns, intended and unintended;
- inertial activity;
- changing activity, with three sub-patterns, reframing, re-embedding and chronic reconstructing;
- stabilizing activity; and
- unresolved activity.

Each of these patterns is conceptually robust and, as a typology, is likely to have broader conceptual application in indicating the likely tracks an activity will take, according to the types of strategizing adopted over time.

4 A framework is only valuable in relation to the conditions under which it applies. These conditions were contextualized according to the coexistence of multiple strategies. Different strategizing types and patterns of activity are likely to apply, depending upon whether an activity is the core activity in an organization or whether it is perceived as threatening to the core activity. These situational contingencies arising from multiple strategy, professional contexts, are summarized in Table 7.3. Most importantly, the discussion of multiple activities points out that tension between activities will be ongoing, giving rise to continuous pressure to adjust strategizing in order to shape activity. Thus, even where some activities are on an inertial track, strategizing is not static.

The primary aim of this book has been to explain how strategy as a stream of goal-directed activity is shaped over time by different strategizing practices. The strategizing framework developed in this chapter meets this aim. It describes and explains how strategizing shapes strategy over time. This framework also makes progress towards a secondary aim of this book: to contribute to the theoretical development of an activity-based view of strategy as practice. Chapter 8 will deal with the other secondary aim of the book, by discussing how the concepts and terminology developed contribute to the empirical and theoretical interpretation of strategy as practice as an emerging field. It will then examine the wider implications and limitations of the theoretical development in this book and its contribution to the field.

8 TAKING THE RESEARCH AGENDA FORWARD

Key points

- Practical implications of the research
- New avenues for research
- Where to next for strategy as practice?

A broad aim of this book has been to define theoretically and interpret empirically the themes and concepts of strategy as practice as a new perspective in strategic management research. More specifically, building on early developments in the field, it set out to develop theoretically and empirically the activity-based view of strategy as practice. This chapter discusses the contributions this book has made and proposes ways to take the strategy as practice research agenda forward. The chapter is in three sections. First, drawing on the findings, it highlights the practical implications of the frameworks in this book. Second, new avenues for research are proposed, both building specifically on the findings from the book and also in terms of further uses of the activity system framework to explore other themes and issues in strategy as practice research. Third, the book dwells on the broader aims of the strategy as practice research agenda and important next steps for taking the field forward.

PRACTICAL IMPLICATIONS OF THE RESEARCH

This book does not set out to be prescriptive about a 'best practice' for shaping strategy. However, the strategizing framework laid out in Chapter 7 certainly has practical implications. First, the four types of strategizing – preactive, procedural, interactive and integrative – are useful ways for top managers to think about the practices they have available to shape strategy. From a practitioner perspective, the strategizing types are based on combinations of face-to-face interaction and administrative practices, which are useful for shaping different phases of strategy, as shown in Table 7.2, and can also be used sequentially to shape the path of a strategy over time, as shown in Figure 7.2. The implications of this strategizing framework are not only theoretical but also can be used by top managers to reflect upon a particular strategy and the ways it might be shaped over time to make it more acceptable to others in the organization. For example, when top managers are introducing a new strategy that they suspect will be contentious or a source of resistance, it would be typical to engage in a pre-active phase of face-to-face interactions with only their closest supporters and avoid launching organization-wide interactive or administrative strategizing practices. The pre-active phase provides time for top managers to marshal their resources and prepare the groundwork for the strategy. This might be followed by a phase of interactive strategizing, during which top managers would engage in extensive face-to-face interaction to generate widespread acceptance of the new strategy. Eventually, the strategy can, and indeed should, be embedded in administrative practices. However, it is advisable that this phase involves integrative strategizing, maintaining ongoing face-to-face interaction to ensure that organizational members acknowledge the necessity of the new strategy and accept the administrative practices associated with it.

Of course, the framework is not only useful for thinking about how to introduce new and potentially contentious strategies. It can be used by top managers to reflect on the progress of any strategy in the organization and the 'phase' that it might be in, such as tending towards inertia, being renewed or becoming a mainstream strategy. They could then use the strategizing matrix and frameworks developed in this book to consider how their current strategizing practices might be influencing the activity and the organizational dynamics, and whether a different combination of strategizing practices might better suit their purposes in shaping strategy. In particular, the frameworks help to increase managerial awareness of strategizing practices, organizational dynamics and their implications for shaping strategy. Managers need to pay attention to the inherent traps in using predominantly one type of strategizing. Rather, they should be aware of the implications of different types of strategizing for introducing new strategies or setting existing strategies on possible paths of stability, change, inertia or unresolved activity. Moving between different strategizing types according to the phase of activity is likely to give top managers more influence over the dynamics of the organization and its consequences for strategic activity and its outcomes.

The main practical value of this research is thus providing top managers with a set of concepts and frameworks with which to reflect upon their own actions and the implications these have for organizational dynamics and the pattern strategy takes over time. While these frameworks may be of particular use in professional and knowledge-intensive contexts that require a more participative rather than top-down approach to strategy making, they are also expected to have wider relevance as post-industrial contexts place increasing emphasis on participative forms of strategy making (Lowendahl and Revang, 1998).

NEW AVENUES FOR RESEARCH

Research in a formative area, such as strategy as practice, will not only answer a series of questions, but also raise new avenues for exploration. This section explains the specific avenues of research where this book has made partial answers and raised further questions. It then examines the contributions of the activity framework developed in this book and discusses how the framework might be applied to future research.

SPECIFIC RESEARCH TOPICS TO TAKE FORWARD

This book has provided a platform for future activity-based research into strategy as practice. It raises three specific research topics to take forward: the issue of multiple strategies; the link between practice and performance; and the study of strategy in university contexts.

Multiple strategies

This study of universities uncovered the issue of multiple, potentially contradictory strategies. Typically, strategic management research considers strategy as a single construct. A firm has a strategy, which it evolves, develops or changes in some way, exiting this strategy if it wishes to introduce a new strategy. Such singular constructs do not reflect the practice of strategy in the university contexts that provide the empirical base of this book. Rather, multiple strategies were found and patterns in these strategies over time were influenced by their association with each other. Particularly, patterns of association between strategies seem to be shaped according to whether professionals identify historically with one strategy as the core strategy, so that other strategies are judged by the way their relationship to this core strategy is legitimated. While the association between multiple strategies was not the main focus of this study, the findings indicate that the strategizing involved with managing multiple strategies merits further research. Universities are not unique, as other professional contexts discussed in Chapter 3 also have multiple, potentially divergent strategies. Neither are multiple strategies unique to professional contexts. Many firms, be they in consumer goods, retail or manufacturing sectors, are multiple-site, multiple-product and multiple-goal organizations that occupy diverse strategic positions. It is thus apparent that the management of multiple, potentially divergent strategies is the norm, rather than the exception. Both theory and practice would be advanced by an analysis of how strategizing practices and dynamics influences the association between multiple strategies, particularly examining whether some practices favour coexistence between strategies while others create tension and conflict.

From practice to performance

Chapter 2 clarified that an organization's realized strategy content is an outcome of its underlying pattern of activity over time. However, this book has not focused on the realized outcomes of activity. While passing reference has been made to the way each of the strategies examined were being realized, the research questions and study examined how strategizing practices shape activity. There is, however, a logical progression from the way an activity is shaped to the outcomes realized. Furthermore, analysis of this link between activity and realized outcome is important to the activity-based view, which is concerned to understand how the micro-practices and actions that comprise activity are associated with strategic outcomes, such as firm performance (Johnson et al., 2003). Of course, the study in this book does have outcomes that are of strategic consequence to the organization – shaping an activity in changing, stabilizing, inertial or unresolved patterns is certainly strategically consequential and constitutes an appropriate 'outcome' for the research question. The book thus makes an important link in the chain from practice to performance. However, further research might take another step in establishing this elusive link by building on the study here to examine the relationship between activity system dynamics and an organization's realized strategy content over time.

Strategizing in university contexts

This book is based on an empirical study of strategy as practice in three UK universities. With some exceptions, universities are not typically used as contexts for strategy research because strategy remains dominated by private sector concepts and notions of free market competition. However, as the empirical material demonstrates, universities do, in fact, do strategy. Indeed, universities are ideal contexts for exposing the complexities of doing strategy when management fiat cannot be assumed. This study provides a considerable body of evidence on the strategies and strategizing practices of universities and addresses a long-standing problem in the literature about universities, namely goal ambiguity. It sheds light on those strategizing practices involved in coping with goal ambiguity that is posed by multiple strategies. The findings on multiple strategies have raised interesting questions for other avenues of research, and are also insightful for the university sector. Two avenues of research are therefore proposed. First, it is hoped that others will conduct more strategy research in the university sector and other non-traditional contexts. Second, the findings from these contexts need to be applied and examined in wider professional and non-professional contexts to provide cross-fertilization between industries and sectors that will broaden our understanding of competition, strategy and practice more generally.

CONTRIBUTIONS AND USES OF THE ACTIVITY SYSTEM FRAMEWORK

The activity system framework developed in Figure 2.1 and used in Part II to model the dynamics of different types of strategizing is helpful in conceptualizing strategy as an organizational activity. It surfaces the socially interdependent dynamics of the organization as an activity system, enabling us to understand how actions in one part of the system will affect actions in other parts of the system; in effect to understand strategy as a distributed activity. Additionally, by defining a relevant activity system, an activity framework provides useful 'boundaries' for an activity-based study of strategy. As an activity, strategy is embedded in many layers of context and sources of influence that help to shape it, such as broad social, political and economic institutions, market forces, industry factors, media, investors, corporate governance, top managers, middle managers, consultants and consumers. By defining an activity system, such as the organization, and isolating the main subject and community involved in the activity, a study is focused upon those influences that are most proximal and relevant to the research question. This book has made only partial use of the activity framework, specifically seeking to understand the activity system dynamics involved with top managers and the strategizing practices that they identified as important in shaping activity. The framework can, however, be taken further in operationalizing different units and levels of analysis that are pertinent to the practice agenda. Two main avenues of future research using the activity framework are proposed.

First, this study has placed top managers at the centre of the dynamics of shaping activity. It is, however, possible to place other actors at the centre and define the community most relevant to them in shaping strategy to their own ends. For example, if a particular group, such as the middle managers from a particular division, were positioned at the centre of the study or, with the universities in this study, a subset of professionals, such as science-based academics, this would provide a different story about the practice of strategy: one of diffuse power, incoherence, resistance and divergence in the shaping of activity. Indeed, the community might identify different strategizing practices as valuable to them in shaping activity. The range of actors that could be placed at the centre of a study is vast; for example, the Chairman, the board of governors, the CEO, the finance director, operational managers, consumers, consultants, regulators, investors, all might be placed as the subject in order to frame the dynamics of strategic activity around their actions and terms of reference. This is not a trivial choice. As the introductory chapter noted, the practice of strategy involves people – lots of people. Studying how these different groups of people attempt to shape strategy as an organizational activity, which actors they define as their relevant community, which practices they identify as enabling or constraining their influence, and the resulting dynamics of the system and its impact upon activity are important research topics. One avenue for future research is, therefore, to repeat the study in this book using a range of different actors to address the question 'How do the strategizing practices of consultants, boards, operational managers and so forth shape strategy as an organizational activity?' In particular, a single within-case comparison of the different activity system dynamics and influences on strategy arising from different actors would provide revealing insights into the distributed nature of strategy and the way that distributed groups understand and contribute to that strategy.

Second, this study examined the mediating role of two types of strategizing practices: formal administrative practices and face-to-face interaction. These were empirically informed, being identified by top managers as practices that were important to them in shaping strategy. However, other practices might comprise the unit of analysis, depending on the theoretical framing and empirical data. For example, interaction might not always be a face-to-face practice. In increasingly virtual forms of organizing, other practices, such as emails, intranet, video and teleconferencing, might be relevant. It would be interesting to investigate how these practices mediate the dynamics of an activity system and what consequences they might have for shaping strategy. Certainly, some outstanding studies in organization theory have shown that different genres of communication are perceived differently, with different implications for action (Orlikowski and Yates, 1994). For example, statements that are permissible in email communication because it is 'transient' are not appropriate in more lasting forms of documentation. Face-to-face interaction as a strategizing practice is both very transient, being conducted in real-time and ceasing at the end of the face-to-face moment, and yet very powerful because of the direct nature of contact (Simons, 1991). In particular, top managers identify face-to-face interaction as influential, but this may be due to their hierarchical advantage in using such a practice. A relevant question, therefore, is whether other practices have different implications for strategizing and, if so, which groups of actors find these strategizing practices more influential in shaping strategy?

Relevant and influential strategizing practices may alter according to the user group. As noted in the introductory chapter, one of the themes in the strategy as practice research agenda is the study of strategizing practices-in-use (Jarzabkowski, 2004a; Whittington, 2002, 2003). The activity system framework could be used to study a range of different practices, from administrative practices to meetings, workshops, PowerPoint presentations, emails and intranet among others, examining how these practices are used to mediate influence over strategy and where within the activity system they confer this influence. In this way we can penetrate not only the innate properties of the practices, but also the skill of actors in using them.

In this vein, it would also be profitable to build on the existing body of research into discourse as a strategic resource, studying how discursive practices mediate influence over strategy (Grant et al., 2003; Hardy et al., 2000). A particular focus of interest that requires empirical investigation is what use practitioners make of the strategy tools and frameworks provided from academic theory. For example, do the strategy frameworks derived from typical strategy courses and strategy textbooks, such as Porter's five forces, value chains and BCG matrices (typical strategic positioning frameworks), provide a 'strategic language' that enables some actors to have a more influential role in shaping strategy than others? Does the lexicon of 'barriers to entry', 'cash cows', 'inimitable resources' and the like, which might have little relationship to any diagnostic use of the corresponding strategy tools and frameworks, give some actors entry into a strategic discourse, while others are excluded by their inability to use this language (see also Astley and Zammuto, 1992; Barry and Elmes, 1997; Jarzabkowski, 2004b)?

These two avenues for further research building on the activity framework enable a more detailed investigation of the relationship between practices, practitioners and practice/activity identified in the introductory chapter. As Figure I.1 illustrated (p. 11), these are three interrelated themes in the strategy as practice agenda. The activity framework maintains the focus on practice as an integrated whole – an activity – whilst permitting the study of practitioners and practices as they are involved in the construction of that activity. The strategy as practice research agenda can only be furthered by studying different groups of practitioners and different practices, and examining their influences on and implications for strategy as an activity, utilising the interdependencies of the activity system framework developed in this book.

NEXT STEPS FOR STRATEGY AS PRACTICE RESEARCH

This book has covered a considerable amount of ground in explaining and establishing strategy as practice as a new perspective in strategic management research. It is, however, still early in the development of a field and there are many exciting directions to take in advancing the research agenda. This book concludes by touching briefly on a few key challenges that are important in taking the next steps for strategy as practice.

Strategy as practice is concerned with going inside the lived experience of strategy as a practice, understanding it from the eyes of those engaged in it. This raises methodological and theoretical issues. First, there is the problem of complexity. Practice is complex because it includes 'everything'. That is, it is hard to exclude some phenomena from examination because they are all components of practice. As noted in the introductory chapter, existing strategy research is characterized by false dichotomies, such as content and process, formulation and implementation, thinking and acting, intent and emergence, strategic and operational. While these concepts divide the world artificially, they have arisen, in part, because they reduce the complexity of practice to some contained and analysable phenomena.

This book has attempted to go beyond such dichotomies, showing how formulation and implementation and strategy and operations 'all get mixed and muddled up together' (Exhibit 2.1, p. 40). In particular, the strategizing types developed – pre-active, procedural, interactive and integrative – offer a radical challenge to concepts of formulation and implementation, showing how the two elide in the strategizing practices of top managers (see Chapter 5). However, there is more work to be done to grasp adequately the complexity of practice methodologically: how do we study and make sense of the interconnectedness between 'everything' without resorting to the existing dichotomies provided in the academic language of strategy? To do this, we need to search more widely for inspiration on how to conduct research. For example, other fields of endeavour, such as anthropology (Geertz, 1973), ethnomethodology (Garfinkel, 1967) and micro-sociology (Goffman, 1959), offer insights that might be adopted in the strategy as practice field. At the very least, the strategy as practice agenda requires broader methodological insights, demanding that we expend effort on developing new or at least non-traditional methods in the strategic management discipline for collecting and interpreting data.

Second, there is the problem of theoretical development of the field. The collection of rich qualitative data on practice lends itself well to description, but is less easy to use in drawing robust theoretical conclusions. However, theory is important in the development of a field. While meta-theories of practice, such as structuration (Giddens, 1984) and habitus (Bourdieu, 1990), are helpful sensitizing frameworks for interpreting practice (Tsoukas, 1994), the development of mid-range theories of practice are important in communicating with a management science and practitioner audience. Mid-range theories explain the relationships between concepts, themes and constructs within a localized setting, enabling others to build upon these relationships in wider contexts. For example, the strategizing framework in this book has made progress towards a mid-range theory of strategizing in professional contexts. In the early stages of a field, however, the development of theory is problematic because of fragmentation. There will be many descriptive pieces that illustrate practice but do not explain it in theoretical terms, and there will be multiple approaches to the problem of practice that have little relationship to each other. Cohesion in the field is thus necessary, requiring willingness to take what others have developed and build upon, elaborate, modify and correct it in order to move towards mid-range theories that establish an identity and a body of explanations that are particular to strategy as practice.

Finally, there is the problem of the relationship between practice and performance. Many discussions within the strategy as practice community have focused on the challenge of outcomes:[1] what constitutes an appropriate 'outcome' for a piece of practice research? The simple answer is that an outcome is an explanation of something proximal to the phenomena under investigation (Wilson and Jarzabkowski, 2004). For example, if a study examines the practice of talk-in-interaction during a strategic decision-making episode (Samra-Fredericks, 2003), the outcome is the effect of the practice upon the decision. This is a logical and appropriate outcome for research, and further work may be done simply on identifying the types of outcomes appropriate to strategy as practice research. However, strategic management as a discipline is focused upon firm performance as an outcome. While the validity of many measures of firm performance may be questionable, the need to speak to this audience is still vital in legitimating practice as a field within strategy research. This study has made some progress towards this end by showing empirically how strategizing practices shape strategy as an activity and building a conceptual link between activity and the realized outcomes of an organization. More work is needed to build the links both empirically and conceptually. Chains of evidence need to show how the details of strategy as a practice, what people do, how they do it and what they use to do it, are implicated in the outcomes firms achieve.

Generally, a strategy as practice perspective offers many interesting and challenging opportunities for research. Innovative and rigorous research in this area can respond to current concerns about the relevance of much strategic management research, as well as advance the broader management science agenda of conducting research that engages both practitioner and academic audiences.

NOTES

1 Thanks to the strategy as practice community www.strategy-as-practice.com and the regular participants at their workshops and conferences for the discussions on theory and on outcomes that have fuelled these last two points.

APPENDIX: RESEARCH METHOD

A longitudinal case-based method was adopted in three UK universities, for the time period 1992–98 inclusive. In 1992 the UK government classified former polytechnics as universities, ranking and funding all universities according to the same criteria. Thus, the policy environment for all three institutions was the same throughout the study, increasing their comparability. However, within that similarity, cases were chosen on the basis of contextual difference in origin and purpose. Variation in cases is helpful in a theory-building study because it provides polar or critical examples of the phenomena under investigation (Pettigrew, 1990). Drawing upon existing typologies of UK universities (O'Leary, 1997), three cases were chosen on the basis of different historical emphases in teaching and research activity. These different emphases provided critical contexts for studying the construction of activity within a common policy and resource environment. However, the three cases were each a good example of their institutional type, being high in the league table rankings and so heightening process comparability (Pettigrew and Whipp, 1991).

Specific details of the three cases are disguised to preserve anonymity. The first case, Collegiate, is from those institutions developed around the turn of the twentieth century for the purpose of furthering the sciences and, therefore, is strongly research oriented. The second case, Entrepreneurial, was established under a government agenda to widen higher education, thus having a founding orientation towards both teaching and research. The third case, Modern, is a former polytechnic, thus having primarily a teaching orientation. The three types chosen are consistent with the types found in other countries, such as the United States (Brewer et al., 2002), Canada and Australia (Slaughter and Leslie, 1999). All three operate within the same policy environment and have relatively similar resource constraints, being without significant endowments, which is typical of the UK university sector (Shattock, 1994). Despite their different historical orientations, the common policy environment meant that the three cases were all dealing with four strategies: research, teaching, commercial income and size and scope.

As top managers were the centre of this study, data were collected from top managers and the committees and other artefacts of strategizing that they were involved with. Top managers comprise an aggregate unit of analysis, since this study did not examine intra-team dynamics but the aggregate team experience of strategizing (Denis et al., 2001; Pettigrew and Whipp, 1991). Top managers were identified initially through hierarchical level (Finkelstein and Hambrick, 1996), which were then validated through interviews. Each case involved essentially similar participants, who have been given the following standardized titles and abbreviations: Vice-Chancellor (VC), Deputy Vice-Chancellor (DVC), Registrar, Deputy Registrar, Senior Academic and Governor. The list of participants is provided in Table A.1.

Table A.1: List of interview participants

Entrepreneurial	Collegiate	Modern
E1: VC x 2	C1: VC	M1: VC
E2: Senior DVC x 2	C2: DVC (Internal Affairs)	M2: Senior DVC x 2
E3: DVC (Research)	C3: DVC (External Affairs) x 2	M3: DVC (Finance and
E4: DVC (Academic)	C4: Registrar x 2	Marketing)
E5: Former Senior DVC x 2	C5: Deputy Registrar	M4: DVC (Corporate Services)
E6: Former DVC (Academic)	(Planning)	M5: DVC (Academic Affairs) x 2
E7: Registrar x 2	C6: Deputy Registrar	M6: DVC (Research and
E8: Deputy Registrar	(Finance)	Consultancy)
(Academic)	C7: Deputy Registrar	M7: Former VC
E9: Deputy Registrar	(Academic)	M8: Former Senior DVC
(Finance) x 2	C8: Deputy Registrar	M9: Deputy Registrar (Planning)
E10: Deputy Registrar	C9: Executive Assistant to VC	
(Commerce)	C10: Senior Academic (1)	
E11: Deputy Registrar	C11: Senior Academic (2)	
(Quality)	C12: Senior Academic (3)	
E12: Deputy Registrar	C13: Senior Academic (4)	
(Research)	C14: Senior Academic (5)	
E13: Governor (1)	C15: Senior Academic (6)	
E15: Governor (2)	C16: Senior Academic (7)	
E16: Senior Academic		

Longitudinal qualitative data were collected for a seven-year period, six years of which (1992–97 inclusive) were retrospective and one year of which (1998) was real-time. Data were triangulated, incorporating multiple interview participants, non-participant observation and documentary searches, to counteract potential investigator, participant and source bias (Eisenhardt, 1989; Jick, 1979). A total of 49 open-ended interviews, 51 strategic meeting observations, two weeks of shadowing, other incidental observational data, and seven years of archival data from strategic meetings in each case were collected. A full list of data sources, collection techniques and purposes is provided in the Table A.2.

Table A.2: Data sources (Precise names and committee descriptions avoided to preserve anonymity)

Data Source	Entrepreneurial	Collegiate	Modern
Interviews: open-ended, audio taped, transcribed	20 interviews of 90 minutes each.	18 interviews of minutes each.	11 interviews of 90 minutes each.
Non-participant meeting observations: detailed field notes taken and written up in 24 hours	• Main strategy committee: 7 • Main income generation group: 6 • Main academic resourcing committee: 5 • Other working party for actioning a strategic issue: 1	• Main academic resourcing committee: 7 • Delegated governing committee: 2 • Academic governance committee: 1 • Strategic meetings with heads of departments: 1 • Other administrative and collegial committees: 6	• Main top managers meeting forum: 3 • Governing committee: 2 • Strategic meetings with heads of departments: 2 • Academic governance committee: 1 • Other meetings used by TMT for consultative purposes: 6 • Strategy day between TMT and Board: 1
Other non-participant observation: detailed field notes as above	• 1 week shadowing TMT 1 • Pre- and post-meeting observation • General on-site data, particularly informal discussion whenever the opportunity arose	• Pre- and post-meeting observation • General on-site data where I sat in the Planning Office, next to the general coffee machine; handy for informal discussion	• 1 week shadowing TMT 1 • Pre- and post-meeting observation • General on-site data, mostly informal chats pre- and post-meetings
Documents: searched twice, with field notes taken for coding. First search to construct strategic activity profile and inform interview questions. Second used to validate interviews and antecedents of current observations	• Minutes of main strategy committee, 1992 to 1997 • Minutes of all 1998 meetings attended • Annual reports; audit documents; strategic plans; academic databases; university calendars; briefing papers; memoranda and minutes of major 1994 strategic initiative; sectoral documents	• Minutes of academic resourcing committee and academic governance committee, 1992 to 1997 • Minutes of delegated governing committee and planning meetings, 1997 to 1998 • Minutes of all 1998 meetings attended • Audit documents; strategic plans; university calendars; briefing papers; handbook for department heads; sectoral documents	• Planning cycle documentation since inception in 1995/96 through to 1998/99 • Major strategic issue reports and summaries from 1993 • Coopers & Lybrand strategy consultation report, 1988 • Minutes of all 1998 meetings attended and minutes of 1998 strategic planning TMT meetings, not attended • Supporting planning documentation; annual reports and accounts; sectoral documents

CODING AND ANALYSIS

Data analysis involved generating themes through interrogation of the data (Eisenhardt, 1989; Langley, 1999; Miles and Huberman, 1994) and examining them in relation to existing literature (Pettigrew, 1990), which progressively helped to shape the definitions of and relationships between themes. Nud*ist, a software package for indexing, searching and theorizing from qualitative data that permits cross-coding of any single data item, was used to support this process, enabling the fragmentation, reassembly and recoding of data in order to generate progressive findings and expose dissonances in preliminary coding (Strauss, 1987). Each coded item of data was read a minimum of five times, and most many more. Through this process the 4521 data items, ranging in length from one line to an A4 page, were developed into an analytic framework built from the patterns in the data but using existing terminology and definitions where possible. All data were also coded by source (that is, interview, document, observation), permitting thorough sifting for anomalies or data biases. As analysis was ongoing throughout data collection, any small anomalies that arose were checked on site.

Cross-coding also helped to confirm consistency between informants about the way they contribute to strategic activity, generating a picture that could confidently be said to represent the top manager experience of strategizing. For example, if one person said something but this could not be confirmed through other participants and other data sources, it could not be assumed representative of the top manager experience. In order to ensure that the resultant top management experience was valid, the findings were presented to the top team in each case, who validated them as an accurate representation. Through this combination of triangulated data, prolonged engagement in the field, thorough coding and recoding, and confirming validity with participants, the trustworthiness of the data and interpretations was enhanced (Lincoln and Guba, 1985; Miles and Hubermann, 1994). The analytic process and themes are explained below.

I began with the broad question: How does strategizing, what managers do, shape strategy as an activity? This question was progressively refined as I interrogated the data, eventually arriving at the three research questions addressed in this book. Data were first coded by the activities identified by participants. Each case was pursuing four activities: research, teaching, commercial income and size and scope. Drawing upon minute books, retrospective and real-time data, a chronological narrative of each activity was developed (Langley, 1999; Pentland, 1999). These narratives were then subjected to fine-grained analysis of how top managers went about influencing strategy. This analysis surfaced two main types of practices that could be consistently identified as key for top managers in shaping activity: formal administrative practices and face-to-face interaction. These were their main strategizing resources.

Following this, I coded all data on key administrative procedures, such as committees and systems for strategic planning, resource allocation and monitoring and control. I also coded how the top team spoke about the purpose of these administrative procedures and evidence from minute books and documents on how they used them to construct activity. For example, 'Penalize departments if they don't recruit to target' (Modern), 'Control and monitor the cumulative impact of expenditure decisions' (Collegiate) and 'Allocate growth of 10 per cent/annum to the sciences and 3.5 per cent to the non-sciences' (Entrepreneurial) are typical evidence of the way administrative practices were used to shape strategy.

I then analysed in depth the relationship between these data and activities, iterating the partial findings with the literature to externally validate the concepts being developed. Through this analytic process, top managers' use of formal administrative practices to shape strategy was labelled 'procedural strategizing'. Top managers used procedural strategizing to emphasize the exchange value of contributing to activity, such as rewards and sanctions (Ferrary, 2002). Procedural strategizing both gave top managers power over the resources used to construct activity (Child, 1972; Hardy, 1996; Lukes, 1974) and embedded contributions to activity within an established set of administrative procedures that could easily be perpetuated with little active top management attention (Cohen and Bacdayan, 1994). While embedding enabled some phases of activity construction by legitimating it (Weber, 1978), it also had limitations in phases of constructing new activity or changing existing activity.

I conducted the same analytic process with the practice of face-to-face interaction between top managers and other actors. This face-to-face interaction was purposive, meaning that top managers used it deliberately to influence others' contributions to strategy. For example, the following quotes are typical of the reasons that top managers used face-to-face interaction: 'It makes people self-conscious about their activity' (Entrepreneurial); 'Bringing people around' (Modern); and 'Getting others to think that they want what we want' (Collegiate). I coded the way that the top team spoke about the purpose of face-to-face interactions as well as evidence from the minute books and documents about face-to-face interactions that had occurred and their inputs to the construction of activity.

Through iterations with the literature to validate my findings on the purposes of face-to-face interaction, I developed the term 'interactive strategizing' (Achtenhagen et al., 2003). The face-to-face nature of these interactions enabled top managers powerfully to communicate their own interpretations of strategy (Simons, 1991, 1994). It is thus an interpretative practice (Gioia and Chittipedi, 1991), but cannot ensure a shared interpretative response (Donellon et al., 1986). However, power asymmetries indicate that, even if others do not share top managers' interpretations, such communications will influence the contributions that they make to activity (Child, 1997; Ranson et al., 1980; Weick, 1979). Through these iterations with the literature, top manager use of interactive strategizing was theoretically grounded in the interpretation and reinterpretation of strategy to others (Achtenhagen et al., 2003; Giddens, 1984; Ranson et al., 1980; Weick, 1979).

Armed with these two concepts, procedural and interactive strategizing, I returned to the chronologies and applied the activity system framework to analysing how these two types of strategizing mediated streams of activity. Extensive activity system mapping of the dynamics of each activity in each case were constructed. These maps helped to capture how influence shifted around the activity system as activities developed. These maps were then clustered into broad shifts in influence, according to whether there was high interactive strategizing, high procedural strategizing or some combination of the two, in which top managers used both face-to-face interactions and formal administrative procedures in a reciprocal link. Alternately, with very new activities I found an absence of either type of strategizing. I was able to isolate different maps of activity dynamics to different phases of activity construction, as well as to explain the chronology of each activity through a sequence of the activity system maps. The maps thus contributed, eventually, towards the broader shifts of influence displayed in mapping the patterns of activity in Chapter 5.

Second order analysis of the strategizing types and the activity system dynamics then took place. As procedural and interactive strategizing were used reciprocally in some situations, separately in others and not at all in still other situations, I delved deeper into what specific purposes these forms of strategizing served. Drawing on social theories of practice, the concepts of structural and interpretative legitimacy were developed. In this I was heavily influenced by Giddens' (1979, 1984) theory of structuration in the initial categorization, but then sought to validate the concepts more widely with other social theories of practice (for example, Bourdieu, 1990; Sztompka, 1991; Turner, 1994). As always, I iterated between theoretical concepts and the data to ensure that these broader social theory concepts were still reflective of the concepts found in the empirical data. Eventually, structural and interpretative legitimacy were confirmed as separate but complementary concepts, whereupon I developed the strategizing matrix in order to separate out the types of strategizing identified according to the combinations of structural and interpretative legitimacy that they conferred on activity. The quadrants were named pre-active, procedural, interactive and integrative strategizing.[1] The activity system dynamics associated with each of these strategizing types then became the basis for the strategizing matrix, the activity typology and, ultimately, the strategizing framework developed in this book.

Finally, the strategizing types were examined against the context of the cases, to ensure that the findings were not particular to context. While different cases were prone to different types of strategizing, and this was historically based, the strategizing-activity relationship remained consistent across cases. For example, when top managers at Collegiate use interactive or procedural strategizing, it has the same purposes and the same implications for shaping activity as at Modern.

NOTE

1 I thank Ann Langley and Richard Whittington for suggesting these names for the quadrants.

REFERENCES

Academy of Management Review (2004) 'Special Topic Forum on Language and Organization', D.M. Boje, C. Oswick and J.D. Ford (eds), *Academy of Management Review*, 29, 4: 571–686.

Achtenhagen, L., Melin, L., Mullern, T. and Ericson, T. (2003) 'Leadership: The role of interactive strategizing', in A.M. Pettigrew, R. Whittington, L. Melin, C. Sanchez-Runde, F.A.J. van den Bosch, W. Ruigrok and T. Numagami (eds), *Innovative Forms of Organizing: International Perspectives*. London/Thousand Oaks: Sage. pp. 49–71.

Albert, S. and Whetten, D. (1985) 'Organizational identity', in L.L. Cumming and B.M. Staw (eds), *Research in Organizational Behavior*. Greenwich, CT: JAI Press.

Alvesson, M. (2001) 'Knowledge work: Ambiguity, image and identity', *Human Relations*, 54, 7: 863–87.

Alvesson, M. and Sveningsson, S. (2003) 'Good visions, bad micro-management and ugly ambiguity: Contradictions of (non-)leadership in a knowledge-intensive organization', *Organization Studies*, 24, 6: 961–88.

Ansoff, H.I. (1965) *Corporate Strategy*. New York: McGraw-Hill.

Ansoff, H.I. (1991) 'Critique of Henry Mintzberg's "The Design School: Reconsidering the Basic Premises of Strategic Management"', *Strategic Management Journal*, 12: 449–61.

Archer, M. (1995) *Realist Social Theory: The Morphogenetic Approach*. Cambridge: Cambridge University Press.

Astley, W.G. and Zammuto, R.F. (1992) 'Organization science, managers, and language games', *Organization Science*, 3: 443–60.

Balogun, J., Huff, A.S. and Johnson, P. (2003) 'Three responses to the methodological challenges of studying strategizing', *Journal of Management Studies*, 40: 197–224.

Balogun, J. and Johnson, G. (2004) 'Organizational restructuring and middle manager sensemaking', *Academy of Management Journal*, 47, 5: 523–49.

Barley, S. and Tolbert, P. (1997) 'Institutionalization and structuration: Studying the links between action and institution'. *Organization Studies*, 18, 1: 93–117.

Barnard, C. (1938) *The Functions of the Executive*. Cambridge, MA: Harvard University Press.

Barnes, B. (2001) 'Practice as collective action', in T.R. Schatzki, K.K. Cetina and E. von Savigny (eds), *The Practice Turn in Contemporary Theory*. London: Routledge, pp. 17–28.

Barney, J. (1991) 'Firm resources and sustained competitive advantage', *Journal of Management*, 17, 1: 99–120.

Barr, P., Stimpert, J.L. and Huff, A. (1992) 'Cognitive change, strategic action, and organizational renewal', *Strategic Management Journal*, 13: 15–36.

Barry, D. and Elmes, M. (1997) 'Strategy retold: Toward a narrative view of strategic discourse', *Academy of Management Review*, 22, 2: 429–52.

Bartlett, C. and Goshal, S. (1994) 'The changing role of top management: From strategy to purpose', *Harvard Business Review*, Nov.–Dec.: 81.

Bartunek, J. (1984) 'Changing interpretive schemes and organisational restructuring: The example of a religious order', *Administrative Science Quarterly*, 29, 3: 355–72.

Bechky, B. (2003) 'Object lessons: Workplace artefacts as representations of occupational jurisdiction', *American Journal of Sociology*, 109, 3: 720–52.

Bettenhausen, K. and Murnighan, K. (1985) 'The emergence of norms in competitive decision-making groups', *Administrative Science Quarterly*, 30: 350–72.

Bettis, R. (1991) 'Strategic management and the straightjacket: An editorial essay', *Organization Science*, 2, 3: 315–20.

Birnbaum, R. (2000) *Management Fads in Higher Education*. San Francisco, CA: Jossey-Bass.

Blackler, F. (1993) 'Knowledge and the theory of organizations: Organizations as activity systems and the reframing of management', *Journal of Management Studies*, 30, 6: 863–84.

Blackler, F. (1995) 'Knowledge, knowledge work and organizations: An overview and interpretation', *Organization Studies*, 16: 1021–46.

Blackler, F., Crump, N. and McDonald, S. (2000) 'Organizing processes in complex activity networks', *Organization*, 7: 277–300.

Boland, R.J. and Tenkasi, R.V. (1995) 'Perspective making and perspective taking in communities of knowing', *Organization Science*, 6, 4: 350–72.

Bourdieu, P. (1977) *Outline of a Theory of Practice*. Cambridge: Cambridge University Press.

Bourdieu, P. (1990) *The Logic of Practice*. Cambridge: Polity Press.

Bower, J.L. (1970) *Managing the Resource Allocation Process: A Study of Corporate Planning and Investment*. Cambridge, MA: Harvard Business School Press.

Brewer, D.J., Gates, S.M. and Goldman, C.A. (2002) *In Pursuit of Prestige: Strategy and Competition in U.S. Higher Education*. Piscataway, NJ: Transaction Publishers.

Brown, J.S. and Duguid, P. (1991) 'Organisational learning and communities-of-practice: Toward a unified view of working, learning and innovation', *Organization Science*, 2, 1: 40–57.

Brown, J.S. and Duguid, P. (2001) 'Knowledge and organization: A social practice perspective', *Organization Science*, 12, 2: 198–213.

Brunsson, N. (1982) 'The irrationality of action and action of rationality: Decisions, ideologies and organizational actions', *Journal of Management Studies*, 19, 1: 29–45.

Burgelman, R.A. (1983) 'A process model of internal corporate venturing in the diversified major firm', *Administrative Science Quarterly*, 28: 223–44.

Burgelman, R.A. (1991) 'Intraorganizational ecology of strategy making and organizational adaptation: Theory and field research', *Organization Science*, 2, 3: 239–62.

Burgelman, R. A. (1994) 'Fading memories: A process theory of strategic business exit in dynamic environments', *Administrative Science Quarterly*, 39, 1: 24–57.

Burgelman, R.A. (1996) 'A process model of strategic business exit: Implications for an evolutionary perspective on strategy', *Strategic Management Journal*, 17: 193–214.

Campbell, A., Goold, M. and Alexander, M. (1995) 'The value of the parent company', *California Management Review*, 38, 1: 79–98.

Chaiklin, S., Hedegaard, M. and Jensen, U.J. (eds) (1999) *Activity Theory and Social Practice*. Aarhus: Aarhus University Press.

Chakravarthy, B. and White, R. (2002) 'Strategy process: Changing and implementing strategies', in A.M. Pettigrew, H. Thomas and R. Whittington (eds), *Handbook of Strategy and Management*. London: Sage.

Chandler, A.D. (1962) *Strategy and Structure, Chapters in the History of the Industrial Enterprise.* Cambridge, MA: MIT Press.

Chaiklin, S., Hedegaard, M. and Jensen, U.J. (eds) (1999) *Activity Theory and Social Practice.* Aarhus: Aarhus University Press.

Chia, R. (1999) 'A "rhizomic" model of organizational change and transformation: Perspective from a metaphysics of change', *British Journal of Management,* 10, 3: 209–27.

Chia, R. (2002) 'Time, duration and simultaneity: Rethinking process and change in organizational analysis', *Organization Studies*, 23, 6: 863–8.

Chia, R. (2004) 'Strategy-as-practice: Reflections on the research agenda', *European Management Review*, 1: 29–34.

Child, J. (1972) 'Organisational structures, environment and performance: The role of strategic choice', *Sociology*, 6: 1–22.

Child, J. (1997) 'Strategic choice in the analysis of action, structure, organizations and environment: Retrospect and prospect', *Organization Studies,* 18, 1: 43–76.

Ciborra, C. and Lanzara, G.F. (1990) 'Designing dynamic artifacts: Computer systems as formative context', in P. Gagliardi (ed.), *Symbols and Artifacts*, Berlin: De Gruyter, pp. 147–65.

Clark, B. (1998) *Creating Entrepreneurial Universities.* Oxford: IAU Press.

Clark, P. (2000) *Organisations in Action: Competition between Contexts.* London: Routledge.

Clegg, C., Carter, C. and Kornberger, M. (2004) 'Get up, I feel like being a strategy machine', *European Management Review*, 1: 21–8.

Clegg, S.R. (1989) *Frameworks of Power.* London: Sage.

Cockburn, I.M., Henderson, R.M. and Stern, S. (2000) 'Untangling the origins of competitive advantage', *Strategic Management Journal*, 21, 10/11: 1123–45.

Cogan, G.W. and Burgelman, R.A. (1990) 'Intel Corporation A: The DRAM Decision', *Stanford Business School* case PS-BP-256.

Cohen, M.D. and Bacdayan, P. (1994) 'Organisational routines are stored as procedural memory: Evidence from a laboratory study', *Organization Science*, 5, 4: 554–68.

Cohen, M.D. and March, J.G. (1974) *Leadership and Ambiguity.* New York: McGraw-Hill.

Cohen, M.D., March, J.G. and Olsen, J.P. (1972) 'A garbage can model of organizational choice', *Administrative Science Quarterly*, 17, 1: 1–25.

Cook, S. and Brown, J. (1999) 'Bridging epistemologies: The generative dance between organizational knowledge and organizational knowing', *Organization Science*, 10: 381–400.

Conner, K.R. (1991) 'A historical comparison of resource-based theory and five schools of thought within industrial organization economics: Do we have a new theory of the firm?', *Journal of Management*, 17, 1: 121–54.

Contu, A. and Willmott, H. (2003) 'Re-embedding situatedness: The importance of power relations in learning theory', *Organization Science*, 14, 3: 283–97.

Cummings, S. (2002) *Re-creating Strategy.* London: Sage.

Cyert, R. and March, J. (1963) *A Behavioural Theory of the Firm.* Englewood Cliffs, NJ: Prentice-Hall.

Czarniawska, B. (1997) *Narrating the Organization: Dramas of Institutional Identity.* Chicago: University of Chicago Press.

Daft, R.L. and Weick, K.E. (1984) 'Toward a model of organizations as interpretation systems', *Academy of Management Review*, 9, 2: 284–95.

Denis, J.-L., Lamothe, L. and Langley, A. (2001) 'The dynamics of collective leadership and organizational change in pluralist organizations', *Academy of Management Journal*, 44, 4: 809–38.

Denis, J.-L., Langley, A. and Cazale, L. (1996) 'Leadership and strategic change under ambiguity', *Organization Studies*, 17, 4: 673–97.

DiMaggio, P. and Powell, W.W. (1983) 'The iron cage revisited: Institutional isomorphism and collective rationality in organizational fields', *American Sociological Review*, 48: 147–80.

Donnellon, A., Gray, B. and Bougon, M.G. (1986) 'Communication, meaning, and organizational action', *Administrative Science Quarterly*, 31: 43–55.

Doz, Y. (1996) 'The evolution of cooperation in strategic alliances: Initial conditions or learning processes?', *Strategic Management Journal*, 17: 55–84.

Dutton J.E., Ashford S.J., O'Neill R.M. and Lawrence K.A. (2001) 'Moves that matter: Issue selling and organizational change', *Academy of Management Journal*, 44, 4: 716–47.

Eden, C. and Ackerman, F. (1998) *Making Strategy: The Journey of Strategic Management*. London: Sage.

Eisenhardt, K.M. (1989) 'Building theories from case study research', *The Academy of Management Review,* 14, 4: 532–50.

Eisenhardt, K.M. and Zbaracki, M.J. (1992) 'Strategic decision making', *Strategic Management Journal*, 13, Winter Special Issue: 17–37.

Eisenhardt, K.M. and Sull, D. (2001) 'Strategy as simple rules', *Harvard Business Review*, 79: 106–119.

Emirbayer, M. and Mische, A. (1998) 'What is agency?', *American Journal of Sociology*, 103, 4: 962–1023.

Engeström, Y. (1987) *Learning by Expanding: An Activity-theoretical Approach to Developmental Research*. Helsinki: Orienta-Konsultit.

Engeström, Y. (1993) 'Developmental studies of work as a testbench of activity theory: The case of primary care medical practice', in S. Chaiklin and J. Lave (eds), *Understanding Practice: Perspectives on Activity and Context.* Cambridge: Cambridge University Press. pp. 64–103.

Engeström, Y., Miettinin, R. and Punamaki, R-L. (eds) (1999) *Perspectives on Activity Theory*. Cambridge: Cambridge University Press.

Engeström, Y., Engeström, R. and Suntio, A. (2002) 'Can a school community learn to master its own future? An activity-theoretical study of expansive learning among middle school teachers', in G. Wells and G. Claxton (eds), *Learning for Life in the 21st Century: Sociocultural Perspectives on the Future of Education.* London: Blackwell.

Ezzammel, M. and Willmott, H. (2004) 'Rethinking strategy: Contemporary perspectives and debates', *European Management Review*, 1: 43–8.

Feldman, M.S. (2000) 'Organizational routines as a source of continuous change', *Organization Science*, 11: 611.

Feldman, M.S. and Rafaeli, A. (2002) 'Organizational routines as sources of connections and understandings', *Journal of Management Studies*, 39, 3: 309–32.

Fenton, E. and Pettigrew, A.M. (2005) 'Leading change in the new professional service organization: Characterizing strategic leadership in a global context', in R. Greenwood and R. Suddaby (eds), *Research in the Sociology of Organizations 24: Professional Service Firms*. JAI/Elsevier.

Ferlie, E., Ashburner, L., Fitzgerald, L. and Pettigrew, A.M. (1996) *The New Public Management in Action*. Oxford: Oxford University Press.

Ferrary, M. (2002) 'Conflicts of interest and games of power concerning the standardization of the workforce', *Journal of Socio-Economics*, 31, 4: 391–403.

Finkelstein, S. and Hambrick, D. (1996) *Strategic Leadership: Top Executives and Their Effects on Organizations*. St. Paul, MN: West Publishing Company.

Floyd, S.W. and Lane, P. (2000) 'Strategizing throughout the organization: Management role conflict in strategic renewal', *Academy of Management Review*, 25, 1: 154–77.

Garfinkel, H. (1967) *Studies in Ethnomethodology*. Englewood Cliffs, NJ: Prentice-Hall.

Garud, R. and Van de Ven, A. (2002) 'Strategic change processes', in A.M. Pettigrew, H. Thomas and R. Whittington (eds), *Handbook of Strategy and Management*. London: Sage.

Garvin, D.A. (1998) 'The processes of organization and management', *Sloan Management Review*, Summer, 33–50.

Geertz, C. (1973) *The Interpretation of Cultures*. New York: Basic Books.

Gersick, C.J. (1991) 'Revolutionary change theories: A multilevel exploration of the punctuated equilibrium paradigm', *Academy of Management Review*, 16, 1: 10–36.

Gherardi, S. (2000) 'Practice-based theorizing on learning and knowing in organizations', *Organization*, 7, 2: 329–49.

Ghoshal, S. and Moran, P. (1996) 'Bad for practice: A critique of the transaction cost theory', *Academy of Management Review*, 21, 1: 13–47.

Giddens, A. (1979) *Central Problems in Social Theory*. London: Macmillan.

Giddens, A. (1984) *The Constitution of Society*. Cambridge: Polity Press.

Giddens, A. (1991) *Modernity and Self-Identity*. Cambridge: Polity Press.

Gioia, D.A. and Chittipedi, K. (1991) 'Sensemaking and sensegiving in strategic change initiation', *Strategic Management Journal*, 12: 433–48.

Gioia, D., Thomas, J., Clark, S., and Chittipeddi, K. (1994) 'Symbolism and strategic change in academia: The dynamics of sensemaking and influence', *Organization Science*, 5: 363–83.

Gioia, D.A. and Thomas, J. (1996) 'Identity, image and issue interpretation: Sensemaking during strategic change in academia', *Administrative Science Quarterly*, 41, 3: 370–403.

Goffman, E. (1959) *The Presentation of Self in Everyday Life*. New York: Doubleday Books.

Grant, D., Hardy, C., Oswick, C. and Putnam, L. (eds) (2003) *The Sage Handbook of Organizational Discourse*. London: Sage.

Grant, R.M. (2003) 'Strategic Planning in a turbulent environment: Evidence from the oil majors', *Strategic Management Journal*, 24, 6: 491–518.

Greenwood, R. and Hinings, C.R. (1988) 'Organizational design types: Tracks and the dynamics of strategic change', *Organization Studies*, 9, 3: 293–316.

Greenwood, R. and Hinings, C.R. (1993) 'Understanding strategic change: The contribution of archetypes', *Academy of Management Journal*, 36: 1052–81.

Hamel, G. (2001) 'Strategy innovation and the quest for value', in M. Cusumano and C. Markides (eds), *Strategic Thinking for the Next Economy*. San Francisco, CA: Jossey Bass. Chapter 8.

Hardy, C. (1996) 'Understanding power: Bringing about strategic change', *British Journal of Management*, 7, Special Issue: 3–16.

Hardy, C., Langley, A., Mintzberg, J. and Rose, J. (1983) 'Strategy formation in the university setting', in J. Bess (ed.), *College and University Organization: Insights from the Behavioural Sciences*. New York: New York University Press. pp. 169–210.

Hardy, C., Palmer, I. and Phillips, N. (2000) 'Discourse as a strategic resource', *Human Relations*, 53: 1227–48.

Helfat, C. (2000) 'Guest editor's introduction to the special issue: The evolution of firm capabilities', *Strategic Management Journal*, 21, 10/11: 955–60.

Hendry, J. (2000) 'Strategic decision-making, discourse, and strategy as social practice', *Journal of Management Studies*, 37: 955–77.

Hendry, J. and Seidl, D. (2003) 'The structure and significance of strategic episodes: Social systems theory and the routine practices of strategic change', *Journal of Management Studies*, 40, 1: 175–96.

Heracleous, L. and Barrett, M. (2001) 'Organizational change as discourse: Communicative actions and deep structures in the context of information technology implementation', *Academy of Management Journal*, 44: 755–78.

Hickson, D.J., Butler, R.J., Cray, D., Mallory, G.R. and Wilson, D.C. (1986) *Top Decisions: Strategic Decision-Making in Organizations.* San Francisco, CA: Jossey-Bass.

Hinings, C.R. and Leblebici, H. (2003) 'Editorial introduction to the special issue: Knowledge and professional organizations', *Organization Studies*, 24, 6: 827–30.

Hodgkinson, G. and Wright, G. (2002) 'Confronting strategic inertia in a top management team: Learning from failure', *Organization Studies*, 23, 6: 949–78.

Hopwood, A. and Miller, P. (eds) (1994) *Accounting as Social and Institutional Practice.* Cambridge: Cambridge University Press.

Hutchins, E. (1995) *Cognition in the Wild.* Cambridge, MA: MIT Press.

Jarzabkowski, P. (2003) 'Strategic practices: An activity theory perspective on continuity and change', *Journal of Management Studies*, 40, 1: 23–55.

Jarzabkowski, P. (2004a) 'Strategy as practice: Recursiveness, adaptation and practices-in-use', *Organization Studies*, 25, 4: 529–60.

Jarzabkowski, P. (2004b) 'Actionable strategy knowledge: A practice perspective', Best Paper Proceedings, Academy of Management Conference, New Orleans.

Jarzabkowski, P. and Wilson, D.C. (2002) 'Top teams and strategy in a UK university', *Journal of Management Studies*, 39, 3: 357–83.

Jick, T.D. (1979) 'Mixing qualitative and quantitative methods: Triangulation in action', *Administrative Science Quarterly*, 24, 4: 602–11.

Johnson, G. (1987) *Strategic Change and the Management Process.* Oxford: Blackwell.

Johnson, G. and Huff, A. (1998) 'Everyday innovation/everyday strategy', in G. Hamel, C.K. Prahalad, H. Thomas and D. O'Neal (eds), *Strategic Flexibility: Managing in a Turbulent Environment.* Chichester: Wiley. pp. 13–27.

Johnson, G., Melin, L. and Whittington, R. (2003) 'Micro strategy and strategizing: Towards an activity-based view?', *Journal of Management Studies,* 40, 1: 3–22.

Knights, D. and Mueller, F. (2004) 'Strategy as a "Project": Overcoming dualisms in the strategy debate', *European Management Review*, 1: 55–61.

Kozulin, A. (1990) *Vygotsky's Psychology: A Biography of Ideas.* Cambridge, MA: Harvard University Press.

Langley, A. (1999) 'Strategies for theorizing from process data', *Academy of Management Review*, 24, 4: 691–710.

Lant, T.K. and Mezias, S.J. (1992) 'An organizational learning model of convergence and reorientation', *Organization Science*, 3: 47–71.

Lave, J. and Wenger, E. (1991) *Situated Learning: Legitimate Peripheral Participation.* Cambridge: Cambridge University Press.

Lawrence, T.B., Hardy, C. and Phillips, N. (2002) 'Institutional effects of inter-organizational collaboration: The emergence of proto-institutions', *Academy of Management Journal*, 45, 1: 281–90.

Leontiev, A.N. (1978) *Activity, Consciousness, and Personality.* Englewood Cliffs, NJ: Prentice-Hall.

Lengnick-Hall, C. and Wolff, J.A. (1999) 'Similarities and contradictions in the core logic of three strategy research streams', *Strategic Management Journal*, 20, 12: 1109–32.

Lincoln, Y.S. and Guba, E.G. (1985) *Naturalistic Inquiry*. London: Sage.

Lockwood, D. (1964) 'Social integration and system integration', in G. K. Zollschan and H.W. Hirsch (eds), *Explorations in Social Change*. Boston, MA: Houghton Mifflin. pp. 244–57.

Lovas, B. and Ghoshal, S. (2000) 'Strategy as guided evolution', *Strategic Management Journal*, 21, 9: 875.

Lowe, A. and Jones, A. (2004) 'Emergent strategy and the measurement of performance: The formulation of performance indicators at the microlevel', *Organization Studies*, 25, 8: 1313–37.

Lowendahl, B. (1997) *Strategic Management of Professional Service Firms.* Copenhagen: Handelshojskolens Forlag.

Lowendahl, B. and Revang, O. (1998) 'Challenges to existing strategy theory in a post-industrial society', *Strategic Management Journal*, 19, 8: 755–74.

Lowendahl, B. and Revang, O. (2004) 'Achieving results in an after modern context: thoughts on the role of strategizing and organizing', *European Management Review*, 1: 49–54.

Lukes, S. (1974) *Power: A Radical View*. London: Macmillan.

Maitlis, S. and Lawrence, B. (2003) 'Orchestral manoeuvres in the dark: Understanding failure in organizational strategizing', *Journal of Management Studies*, 40,1: 109–40.

Mantere, S. (2005) 'Strategic practices as enablers and disablers of championing activity', *Strategic Organization*, 3, 2: 157–84.

March, J. and Simon, H.A. (1958) *Organizations*. NY: John Wiley.

March, J.G. (1991) 'Exploration and exploitation in organizational learning', *Organization Science*, 2: 71–87.

Marginson, D. (2002) 'Management control systems and their effects on strategy formation at middle-management levels', *Strategic Management Journal*, 23, 11: 1019–37.

Marsh, H.W. and Hattie, J. (2002) 'The relation between research productivity and teaching effectiveness: Complementary, antagonistic or independent constructs?', *The Journal of Higher Education,* 73, 5: 603–641

McKiernan, P. and Carter, C. (2004) 'The millennium nexus: Strategic management at the cross-roads', *European Management Review*, 1, 1: 3–13.

Miles, M. and Hubermann, A. (1994) *An Expanded Sourcebook; Qualitative Data Analysis*. London: Sage.

Miller, D. (1991) 'What happens after success: The perils of excellence', *Journal of Management Studies*, 31, 3: 325–58.

Miller, D. (1993) 'The architecture of simplicity', *Academy of Management Review*, 18, 1: 116–38.

Miller, D. and Friesen, P. (1980) 'Momentum and revolution in organizational adaptation', *Academy of Management Journal*, 23, 4: 591–615.

Miller, D. and Friesen, P. (1984) *Organizations: A Quantum View*. Englewood Cliffs, NJ: Prentice-Hall.

Mintzberg, H. (1978) 'Patterns in strategy formation', *Management Science*, 24, 9: 934–48.

Mintzberg, H. (1979) *The Structuring of Organizations*. Englewood Cliffs, NJ: Prentice-Hall.

Mintzberg, H. (1990) 'The design school: Reconsidering the basic premises of strategic management', *Strategic Management Journal,* 11: 171–95.

Mintzberg, H. (1994) *The Rise and Fall of Strategic Planning.* NY: Free Press and Prentice-Hall.

Mintzberg, H., Ahlstrand, B. and Lampel, J. (1998) *Strategy Safari*. New York: Free Press.

Mintzberg, H. and McHugh, A. (1985) 'Strategy formation in an adhocracy', *Administrative Science Quarterly*, 24, 4: 580–89.

Mintzberg, H. and Waters, J. (1985) 'Of strategy, deliberate and emergent', *Strategic Management Journal*, 6: 257–72.

Mohr, L.B. (1982) *Explaining Organizational Behaviour*. San Francisco: Jossey-Bass.

Nardi, B.A. (1996) 'Studying context: A comparison of activity theory, situated action models, and distributed cognition', in B.A. Nardi (ed.), *Context and Consciousness: Activity Theory and Human-computer Interaction*, Cambridge: MIT Press, 69–102.

Neilsen, E.H. and Rao, M.V. (1987) 'The strategy-legitimacy nexus: A thick description', *Academy of Management Review*, 12: 532–3.

Nelson, R. and Winter, S. (1982) *An Evolutionary Theory of Economic Change*. Cambridge, MA: Harvard University Press.

Neumann, R. (1992) 'Perceptions of the teaching-research nexus: A framework for analysis', *Higher Education*, 23: 159–71.

Noda, T. and Bower, J. (1996) 'Strategy making as iterated processes of resource allocation', *Strategic Management Journal*, 17: 159–92.

O'Leary, J. (ed.) (1997) *The Times Good University Guide: 1997*. London: Times.

Oakes, L.S., Townley, B. and Cooper, J.D. (1998) 'Business planning as pedagogy: Language and control in a changing institutional field', *Administrative Science Quarterly*, 43: 257–92.

Orlikowski, W. (1992) 'The duality of technology: Rethinking the concept of technology in organizations', *Organization Science*, 3, 3: 398–427.

Orlikowski, W. (1996) 'Improvising organizational transformation over time: A situated change perspective', *Information Systems Research*, 7, 1: 63–92.

Orlikowski, W. (2000) 'Using technology and constituting structure: A practice lens for studying technology in organizations', *Organization Science*, 12: 404–428.

Orlikowski, W. (2002) 'Knowing in practice: Enacting a collective capability in distributive organizing', *Organization Science*, 13, 3: 249–73.

Orlikowski, W. and Yates, J. (1994) 'Genre repertoire: The structuring of communicative practices in organizations', *Administrative Science Quarterly*, 39, 4: 541–75.

Ortner, S. (1984) 'Theory in anthropology since the sixties', *Comparative Studies in Society and History*, 26: 126–66.

Ouchi, W. (1979) 'A conceptual framework for design of organizational control mechanisms', *Management Science*, 25: 833–48.

Pentland, B.T. (1999) 'Building process theory with narrative: From description to explanation', *Academy of Management Review*, 24: 711–24.

Pentland, B.T. and Rueter, H.H. (1994) 'Organizational Routines as Grammars of Action', *Administrative Science Quarterly*, 39, 484–510.

Pettigrew, A.M. (1973) *The Politics of Organisational Decision-Making*. London: Tavistock.

Pettigrew, A.M. (1985) *The Awakening Giant: Continuity and Change in ICI*. Oxford: Blackwell.

Pettigrew, A.M. (1987) 'Context and action in the transformation of the firm', *Journal of Management Studies*, 24, 6: 649–70.

Pettigrew, A.M. (1990) 'Longitudinal field research on change theory and practice', *Organization Science*, 1, 3: 267–92.

Pettigrew, A.M. (1992) 'On studying managerial elites', *Strategic Management Journal*, 13: 163–82.

Pettigrew, A.M. (2001) 'Management research after modernism', *British Journal of Management*, 12, Special Issue: 61–70.

Pettigrew, A.M., Ferlie, E. and McKee, L. (1992) *Shaping Strategic Change*. London: Sage.

Pettigrew, A.M. and Whipp, R. (1991) *Managing Change for Competitive Success*. Oxford: Blackwell.

Podsakoff, P., Williams, L. and Todor, W. (1986) 'Effects of organizational formalization on alienation among professionals and non-professionals', *Administrative Science Quarterly*, 29, 4: 820–31.

Porac, J. and Thomas, H. (1990) 'Taxonomic mental models in competitor definition', *Academy of Management Review*, 15, 2: 224–41.

Prahalad, C.K. and Hamel. G. (1994) 'Strategy as a field of study: Why search for a new paradigm?', *Strategic Management Journal*, 15, Special Issue: 5–16.

Pratt, M.G. and Foreman, P.O. (2000) 'Classifying managerial responses to multiple organisational identities', *Academy of Management Review*, 25, 1: 18–42.

Priem, R.L. and Butler, J.E. (2001) 'Is the resource-based 'view' a useful perspective for strategic management research?', *Academy of Management Review*, 26, 1: 22–40.

Quinn, J. (1980) *Strategies for Change: Logical Incrementalism*. Homewood, IL: Richard D. Irwin.

Ranson, S., Hinings, B. and Greenwood, R. (1980) 'The structuring of organizational structures', *Administrative Science Quarterly,* 25: 1–14.

Reckwitz, A. (2002) 'Towards a theory of social practice: A development in cultural theorizing', *European Journal of Social Theory*, 5, 2: 243–63.

Regnér, P. (2003) 'Strategy creation in practice: Adaptive and creative learning dynamics', *Journal of Management Studies*, 40, 1: 57–82.

Regnér, P. (2005) 'Managerial activities and social interactions in evolution: Towards a more dynamic strategy view', Working Paper 05/01, Institute of International Business, Stockholm School of Economics: Stockholm.

Robertson, M., Scarbrough, H. and Swan, J. (2003) 'Knowledge creation in professional service firms: Institutional effects', *Organization Studies*, 24, 6: 831–57.

Rouleau, L. (2005) 'Micro-practices of strategic sensemaking and sensegiving: How middle managers interpret and sell strategic change every day', *Journal of Management Studies*, 42, 7: forthcoming.

Rouse, M. and Daellenbach, U.S. (1999) 'Rethinking research methods for the resource-based perspective', *Strategic Management Journal*, 20, 5: 487–94.

Salvato, C. (2003) 'The role of micro-strategies in the engineering of firm evolution', *Journal of Management Studies*, 40, 1: 83–108.

Samra-Fredericks, D. (2003) 'Strategizing as lived experience and strategists' everyday efforts to shape strategic direction', *Journal of Management Studies*, 40: 141–74.

Sapsed, J. and Salter, A. (2004) 'Postcards from the edge: Local communities, global programs and boundary objects', *Organization Studies*, 25, 9: 1515–35.

Satow, R.L. (1975) 'Value-rational authority and professional organizations: Weber's missing type', *Administrative Science Quarterly*, 20, 4: 526–31.

Scarbrough, H. (1998) 'Path(ological) dependency? Core competences from an organisational perspective', *British Journal of Management*, 9, 3: 219–32.

Schatzki, T.R., Cetina, K.K. and von Savigny, E. (2001) *The Practice Turn in Contemporary Theory*. London: Routledge.

Schuler, R.S. and Jackson, S.E. (1987) 'Linking competitive strategies with human resource management practices', *Academy of Management Executive*, 1, 3: 207–19.

Schwartz, M. (2004) 'Strategy workshops for strategic reviews: Components, practices and roles of actors', paper presented at European Group for Organization Studies, Ljubljana.

Scott, R. (1965) 'Reactions of supervision in a heteronomous professional organization', *Administrative Science Quarterly*, 10: 51–81.

Shattock, M. (1994) *The UGC and the Management of British Universities*. Oxford: Society for Research in Higher Education and Oxford University Press.

Shattock, M. (2003) *Managing Successful Universities*. Oxford: Society for Research in Higher Education and Oxford University Press.

Simons, R. (1991) 'Strategic orientation and top management attention to control systems. *Strategic Management Journal*, 12: 49–62.

Simons, R. (1994) 'How new top managers use control systems as levers of strategic renewal', *Strategic Management Journal*, 15, 169–89.

Slaughter, S. and Leslie, L. (1999) *Academic Capitalism, Politics, Policies, and the Entrepreneurial University*. Baltimore, MD: Johns Hopkins University Press.

Spender, J.-C. (1995) 'Organizations are activity systems, not merely systems of thought', *Advances in Strategic Management*, 11: 151–72.

Spender, J.-C. (1996) 'Making knowledge the basis of a dynamic theory of the firm', *Strategic Management Journal*, 17: 45–62.

Spender, J.-C. and Grinyer, P.H. (1996) 'Organisational renewal: Deinstitutionalization and loosely coupled systems', *International Studies of Management and Organization*, 26, 17–40.

Stone, M.M. and Brush, C.G. (1996) 'Planning in ambiguous contexts: The dilemma of meeting needs for commitment and demands for legitimacy', *Strategic Management Journal*, 17: 633–52.

Strauss, A. (1978) *Negotiations: Varieties, Contexts, Processes and Social Order*. California, US: Jossey-Bass.

Strauss, A. (1987) *Qualitative Analysis for Social Scientists*. Cambridge: Cambridge University Press.

Suchman, L. (1987) *Plans and Situated Actions*. Cambridge: Cambridge University Press.

Sztompka, P. (1991) *Society in Action: The Theory of Social Becoming*. Cambridge: Polity Press.

Teece, D.J., Pisano, G. and Shuen, A. (1997) 'Dynamic capabilities and strategic management', *Strategic Management Journal*, 18, 7: 509–33.

Townley, B. (2002) 'The role of competing rationalities in institutional change', *Academy of Management Journal*, 45: 163–79.

Tsoukas, H. (1994) 'What is management? An outline of a metatheory', *British Journal of Management*, 5, 4: 289–312.

Tsoukas, H. (1996) 'The firm as a distributed knowledge system: A constructionist approach', *Strategic Management Journal*, 17: 11–25.

Tsoukas, H. and Chia, R. (2002) 'On organizational becoming: Rethinking organizational change', *Organization Science*, 13, 5: 567–82.

Tsoukas, H. and Cummings, S. (1997) 'Marginalization and recovery: The emergence of Aristotelian themes in organization studies', *Organization Studies*, 18: 655–74.

Turner, S. (1994) *The Social Theory of Practices*. Cambridge: Polity Press.

Tushman, M.L. and Romanelli, E. (1985) 'Organisational evolution: A metamorphosis model of convergence and reorientation', in L.L. Cummings and B. M. Stawe (eds), *Research in Organisational Behaviour*. Greenwich, CT: JAI Press. pp. 171–222.

Van de Ven, A. (1992) 'Suggestions for studying strategy process: A research note', *Strategic Management Journal*, 13: 169–88.

Van de Ven, A. and Poole, M. (1990) 'Methods for studying innovation development in the Minnesota innovation research program', *Organization Science*, 1, 3: 313–36.

Vygotsky, L. (1978) *Mind in Society: The Development of Higher Psychological Processes.* Cambridge, MA: Harvard University Press.

Weber, M. (1978) *Economy and Society: An Outline of Interpretive Sociology.* 2 vols. (Eds: G. Roth and C. Wittich). Berkeley, CA: University of California Press.

Weick, K.E. (1976) 'Educational organizations as loosely coupled systems', *Administrative Science Quarterly*, 21: 1–19.

Weick, K.E. (1979) *The Social Psychology of Organising.* New York: McGraw-Hill.

Weick, K.E. (1995) *Sensemaking in Organizations.* Thousand Oaks, CA: Sage.

Weick, K.E. and Roberts, K.H. (1993) 'Collective mind in organizations: Heedful interrelating on flight decks', *Administrative Science Quarterly*, 38: 357–81.

Welsh, J. and Metcalf, J. (2003) 'Faculty and administrative support for institutional effectiveness activities: A bridge across the chasm?' *Journal of Higher Education*, 74: 445–68.

Wenger, E. (1998) *Communities of Practice: Learning, Meaning and Identity.* Cambridge: Cambridge University Press.

Wertsch, J. (1985) *Vygotsky and the Social Formation of the Mind.* Cambridge, MA: Harvard University Press.

Whittington, R. (1988) 'Environmental structure and theories of strategic choice', *Journal of Management Studies*, 25, 6: 521–36.

Whittington, R. (1989) *Corporate Strategies in Recession and Recovery.* London: Unwin Hyman.

Whittington, R. (1992) 'Putting Giddens into action: Social systems and managerial Agency', *Journal of Management Studies*, 29, 6: 693–712.

Whittington, R. (1996) 'Strategy As Practice', *Long Range Planning,* 29, 5: 731–5.

Whittington, R. (2002) 'Practice perspectives on strategy: Unifying and developing a field', *Academy of Management Conference Proceedings*, Denver, August.

Whittington, R. (2003) 'The work of strategizing and organizing: For a practice perspective', *Strategic Organization,* 1, 1: 119–27.

Whittington, R. (2004) 'Strategy after modernism: Recovering practice', *European Management Review*, 1: 62–8.

Whittington, R., Jarzabkowski, P., Mayer, M., Mounoud, E., Nahapiet, J. and Rouleau, L. (2003) 'Taking strategy seriously: Responsibility and reform for an important social practice', *Journal of Management Inquiry*, 12: 396–409.

Whittington, R., Johnson, G., Melin, L. (2004) 'The emerging field of strategy practice: Some links, a trap, a choice and a confusion', paper presented at European Group for Organization Studies, Ljubljana.

Whittington, R., Pettigrew, A.M., and Thomas, H. (2003) 'Conclusion: Doing more in strategy research', in A.M. Pettigrew, H. Thomas and R. Whittington (eds), *Handbook of Strategy and Management.* London: Sage, pp. 447–90.

Williamson, O.E. (1996) 'Economic organization: The case for candour', *Academy of Management Review*, 21, 1: 48–57.

Wilson, D. (1992) *A Strategy of Change.* London: Routledge.

Wilson, D.C. and Jarzabkowski, P. (2004) 'Thinking and acting strategically: New challenges for interrogating strategy', *European Management Review*, 1: 14–20.

INDEX